# Bent World

THIS BOOK BELONGS TO:
REV. R. E. MORTON
AIRDRIE, SCOTLAND
DATE...................

**Ron Elsdon**

# Bent World
## Science, the Bible, and the environment

And for all this, nature is never spent;
    There lives the dearest freshness deep down things;
And though the last lights off the black West went
    Oh, morning, at the brown brink eastward, springs —
Because the Holy Ghost over the bent
    World broods with warm breast and with ah! bright wings.
                            Gerard Manley Hopkins, *God's Grandeur*

Inter-Varsity Press

**Inter-Varsity Press**
*38 De Montfort Street, Leicester LE1 7GP, England*

© Ronald Elsdon 1981

All rights reserved. No part of this publication may be reproduced, stored in a retrieval system, or transmitted, in any form or by any means, electronic, mechanical, photocopying, recording or otherwise, without the prior permission of Inter-Varsity Press.

Unless otherwise stated, quotations from the Bible are from the Revised Standard Version, copyrighted 1946, 1952, © 1971, 1973, by the Division of Christian Education, National Council of the Churches of Christ in the USA, and used by permission.

First published 1981

British Library Cataloguing in Publication Data

Elsdon, Ronald
  Bent world.
  1. Human ecology – Moral and religious aspects
  2. Conservation of natural resources – Moral and religious aspects
  I. Title
  261.8′362        GF80

ISBN 0–85111–318–4

Phototypeset by Input Typesetting Ltd., London SW19 8DR.
Printed in Great Britain by J. W. Arrowsmith Ltd.,
Bristol BS3 2NT.

*Inter-Varsity Press is the publishing division of the Universities and Colleges Christian Fellowship (formerly the Inter-Varsity Fellowship), a student movement linking Christian Unions in universities and colleges throughout the British Isles, and a member movement of the International Fellowship of Evangelical Students. For information about local and national activities in Great Britain write to UCCF, 38 De Montfort Street, Leicester LE1 7GP.*

# Contents

|   | | |
|---|---|---|
|   | Preface | 7 |
| 1 | Getting Involved – Christianity in the Environmental Debate | 9 |
| 2 | Getting the Picture – The World's Metals | 17 |
| 3 | Getting the Picture – The World's Energy | 37 |
| 4 | Getting the Picture – The World's Cities | 60 |
| 5 | Getting the Picture – The World's Food | 78 |
| 6 | Getting it Wrong – The Effect of Sin on the Environment | 96 |
| 7 | Getting it Right – The Implications of Salvation | 115 |
| 8 | Getting on with the Job – A Christian Contribution to the Solution | 137 |
|   | Index | 163 |

# Preface

Some years ago I was the Honorary Secretary of the Irish Geological Association and one of the events I organized was a seminar on world resources. It was during that seminar that I first realized that environmental problems demand a Christian response and a biblical analysis. This book is an attempt to provide them.

It falls into four sections. The introductory chapter is a justification for Christian involvement in ecological issues; some readers of this book may need no persuading, but I am convinced that there are many Christians who do. Chapters 2 to 5 set out briefly some of the serious issues facing us; these chapters are deliberately written without any biblical analysis or references, in order to let the issues speak for themselves. Chapters 6 and 7 give a biblical perspective in terms of creation, fall, salvation and redemption. The witness of both Old and New Testaments demand this framework within which Christian thinking on the environment must take place; stewardship is then just *one* of the perspectives which help us towards a practical Christian response to the problems caused by man's mismanagement of the world's resources.

Chapter 8 then puts the biblical analysis and the major problems together and suggests, rather than a list of do's and don'ts, some directions to which further thinking and action need to be applied. The reader looking for instant solutions will be disappointed, because the nature and causes of environmental problems are much too complex for that. Without the biblical contribution of Christians it is difficult to see substantial progress; but this must be integrated with the specialist contributions of disciplines such as science, technology, sociology and economics.

The writing of this book has taken a long time and I am deeply grateful to the encouragement and advice of many friends upon whose expert knowledge and co-operation I have presumed. They include Sam Berry, Phillip Budd, Richard Farnell, Mike Fox, Bob Hansford, Peter Openshaw, John Quinn, Mark Shepherd, Andy

*Bent World*

Sleeman, Adrian Smith, Gordon Wenham, David Williams and Arthur Williamson. They must, however be absolved from all responsibility for errors, inaccuracies or misapprehensions contained in this book. These are entirely due to the author who has, in any case, not always followed the advice they have offered! Mrs Rose McCormick typed the final manuscript with cheerfulness, speed and patience. Above all, my wife Janice gave me great encouragement and provided the sort of domestic atmosphere without which the book would probably never have seen the light of day.

*Dublin* *Ron Elsdon*

# 1
# Getting Involved – Christianity in the Environmental Debate

Man has constantly lived in an uneasy relationship with his environment. Wild animals, storms, floods, volcanic eruptions and earthquakes have always constituted threats to life, but man has coped with them with varying degrees of success. As nature has been gradually subdued through advances in science and technology, visions of the future have become more optimistic. Complete mastery of the environment seemed assured; man would have dominion over all the earth.

In the 1960s, however, came the first rumblings of an impending storm which will probably continue to increase in intensity in years to come. This is the 'environmental crisis' – the subject of this book. The 'crisis' is upon us because we have mistreated the earth, which is responding through pollution, upset ecological balances, and the impending exhaustion of some vital physical resources. There exists a complete spectrum of opinion about the future amongst the experts, from those who forecast impending doom to those who contend that all will be well.

Undoubtedly, though, there are serious problems to be faced, and they will not be removed easily. For this reason, it is wrong to refer to an environmental *crisis*, since this word implies the existence in time of a sudden and decisive change, either for better or worse; future changes are more likely to be gradual.[1]

In the heyday of scientific humanism many of the foremost scientists and philosophers would have pronounced the present subject as one which science alone could take care of. In spite of much popular opinion, there is now an increasing realization that science alone does *not* have all the answers. This conclusion has been reached by scientists as well as others. Thus the final report of the 1968 UNESCO Biosphere Conference contains the following statement:

[1] J. S. Black, *The Dominion of Man* (Edinburgh University Press, 1970), pp. 129ff.

> Natural science and technology alone are inadequate for modern solutions to resource management problems.[2]

It is widely recognized that political, social and economic factors are important, and some of the questions which have been posed are directed to theologians. The Committee on Resources and Man of the US National Academy of Sciences and the National Research Council have referred to 'the complex of nonmaterial factors that affect man's use of and demand for resources', and urge 'the formation of another group to study the various social, psychological, legal, medical, religious and political aspects of the problems of resources and man'. One question asked by the Committee is of special relevance here:

> What is the effect of religion and religious differences on the nature of and demand for resources?[3]

A number of more recent conferences have brought scientists and theologians together to discuss this, as well as other areas of mutual concern.

Christians are forced into the debate in a second way, namely because a number of writers have laid the blame for environmental abuse at the door of Judeo-Christian teaching on creation. It is alleged that Genesis 1:28, in which man is given dominion over the earth and is charged to subdue it, encourages a ruthless and selfish exploitation of nature. This is what has actually happened (it is further alleged), with the support of Christian teaching over the centuries. Thus, Professor Lynn White, in a now-famous address to the American Association for the Advancement of Science in 1966, stated:

> We are superior to nature, contemptuous of it, willing to use it for our slightest whim . . . We shall continue to have a worsening ecological crisis until we reject the Christian axiom that nature has no reason for existence but to serve man . . . Both our present science and our present technology are so tinctured

---

[2] H. Montefiore, *Can Man Survive?* (Collins, 1970), p. 47.

[3] Study and Recommendations of the Committee on Resources and Man of the United States National Academy of Sciences and National Research Council, *Resources and Man* (Freeman, 1969), p. 16.

with orthodox Christian arrogance towards nature that no solution for our ecologic crisis can be expected from them alone. Since the roots of our trouble are so largely religious, the remedy must also be essentially religious, whether we call it that or not.[4]

Professor White is not a lone voice; Ian McHarg, the well-known environmentalist, has this to say:

In the history of human development, man has long been puny in the face of overwhelmingly powerful nature. His religions, philosophies, ethics and acts have tended to reflect a slave mentality, alternately submissive or arrogant towards nature. Judaism, Christianity, Humanism tend to assert outrageously the separateness and dominance of man over nature . . . these same attitudes become of first importance when man holds the power to cause evolutionary regressions of unimaginable effect or even to destroy all life.[5]

There are many other voices adding volume to the attack on Christianity, and calling for the modification or abandonment of Christian teaching as a viable base for understanding the environment.

These charges have promoted much new thinking about the biblical view of creation. This will be discussed more fully in chapter 6, but here we need to note the danger which Christians face in succumbing to these pressures by watering down what the Bible says on the subject. Professor John Macquarrie has argued, rightly, that the Scriptures contain a balance between two views of God and his creation – a monarchical view and an organic view. But he then goes on to state that 'we need to move away from the

---

[4] L. White, Jr, 'The Historical Roots of Our Ecologic Crisis', *Science*, 155, 1967, pp. 1203–1207. This address has been reprinted in a number of books, including F. Schaeffer, *Pollution and the Death of Man* (Hodder, 1970).

[5] I. L. McHarg, 'Our Role in Nature', in R. Detweiler, J. N. Sutherland, M. S. Werthman (eds.), *Environmental Decay in the Historical Context* (Scott, Foresman & Co., Illinois, 1973). See also F. F. Darling, *Wilderness and Plenty* (BBC, 1970), p. 35; M. Caldwell, 'World Resources and the Limits of Man', in P. H. G. Hettena and G. N. Syer (eds.), *Decade of Decision* (Conservation Society, 1971), p. 16; I. G. Simmons, 'Pressures, Problems and Politics', *ibid.*, p. 74; P. R. Ehrlich, *The Population Bomb* (Pan/Ballantine, 1972), p. 151; A. Toynbee, 'The Religious Background of the Present Environmental Crisis', *International Journal of Environmental Studies*, 3, 1972, pp. 141–146; M. Nicholson, *The Environmental Revolution* (Pelican, 1971), p. 305; T. Passmore, *Man's Responsibility for Nature* (Duckworth, 1974), pp. 10ff.

monarchical model of God toward the organic model', and follows slightly later with '. . . the monarchical model of God has become increasingly less credible to many people today'.[6] Whether Professor Macquarrie intended to imply that Christian theology must accommodate itself to the leanings of others, that meaning seems to be inherent in the words quoted. There are certainly writers who are calling explicitly for such an accommodation, such as Antony Etté and Robert Waller:

> In any conflict between Christian and ecological principles, ecological principles must have precedence. Christianity must re-identify with ecological principles if it wishes to survive.[7]

Similarly, Paul Ehrlich argues that, since Christian teaching has given us such a wrong attitude to the environment, it is to the religious ideas of the 'non-Christian East' that we must turn to make any progress.[8]

It has been argued that Lynn White's view of Christian teaching makes too much of the little evidence which is available.[9] Certainly it is true that it is the western world, with centuries of Christian tradition, which has played such a large part in exacerbating environmental problems, but the precise nature of the link between religious belief and the western view of the physical world is by no means clear. Nor are environmental pressures unique to this tradition, either in history or at the present day. Thus Thomas Sieger Derr reminds us:

> Over-grazing, deforestation, and similar errors, of sufficient magnitude to destroy civilisations, have been committed by Egyptians, Assyrians, Romans, North Africans, Persians, Indians, Aztecs and Buddhists. Centuries before the Christian era, Plato commented in his *Critias* on the deforestation of Attica. Since primitive times, man has been altering his environment dramatically, in ways that upset ecological balances. Early hunt-

---

[6] J. S. Macquarrie, 'Creation and Environment', *Expository Times*, 83, 1971, pp. 4–9.
[7] A. Etté and R. Waller, 'The Anomaly of a Christian Ecology', *Ecologist Quarterly*, 2, 1978, pp. 144–148.
[8] P. R. Ehrlich, *op. cit.*, p. 165.
[9] L. W. Moncrief, 'The Cultural Basis for our Environmental Crisis', *Science*, 170, 1970, pp. 508–512.

ers used fire to drive out their game. Agricultural people everywhere clear fields and dam streams and wipe out stock predators and kill plants that get in the way of their chosen crops. In the modern industrial era, western technology is widely copied elsewhere in the world, including areas where Christianity has had little effect. Japan has a pollution problem worse than any in the world.[10]

Christianity's accusers have, nevertheless, provided a welcome impetus to think out seriously the teaching of the Bible on man's relationship with the world in which he lives. Where Christian tradition has contributed towards abuses, repentance is needed and a new example required as a matter of urgency.

The church has come under attack for another reason and this time, perhaps, with more justification. We have been seen as slow to realize our social responsibilities, and in this context those of evangelical persuasion are singled out sometimes as the worst offenders.

Extreme other-worldliness, where it does exist, is often a reaction against the secularization of theology. Professor Sir Norman Anderson has succinctly commented that 'fear of secular theology has prevented a theology of the secular'.[11] Pietism is no substitute for a balanced biblical outlook. Its practice is based on the belief that the *only* issue which matters is the individual's experience of Jesus Christ. Thus there is no sense of responsibility towards the physical dimension of man's life, only towards saving his soul. This deviation has, sadly, been taken as normative by Etté and Waller:

> At one time religion and the land were inseparable, but when people become separated from the land, religious abstractions take the place of day-to-day practical guidance and religion thus loses its anchor in reality. Practical and moral guidance in the everyday physical world were exchanged for the salvation of the individual soul . . . The Doctrine of the Second Coming has also militated against ecological living as it teaches that this world is ephemeral and hence unimportant.[12]

[10] T. S. Derr, *Ecology and Liberation: A Theological Critique of the Use and Abuse of our Birthright* (WSCF Books, 1973), p. 19.
[11] J. N. D. Anderson, 'Christian Worldliness', in J. I. Packer (ed.), *Guidelines* (Falcon, 1967).
[12] A. Etté and R. Waller, *op. cit.*, pp. 145–146, 148.

*Bent World*

Although the problems of the environment began to be appreciated and discussed in the early 1960s, it was a long time before the church realized that it had a role to play. The Second Vatican Council, in its document *De ecclesia in mundo huius temporis*, refers only in general terms to industrial society, urbanization, hunger and the increasing gap between rich and poor. In the section headed *Some Problems of Special Urgency*, the environment receives no mention. Indeed, discussion of the whole document occupied only two days of the Council's time; in one commentary on the Council, John Findlow criticized the document as too long-winded, and asked:

> Will the weight be brought to bear at the point where it is most required to counterbalance the portentous horrors hurriedly heaping up on the other side of the scale?[13]

The Church of England began to appreciate the need for involvement in the environmental debate in 1964, when it convened an ecumenical group to consider and assess the developing situation. The outcome was a report entitled *Man in His Living Environment*. The disappointing feature of the report was the almost total absence of theological discussion and diagnosis.

The first National Evangelical Anglican Congress took place at Keele in 1967. There is no indication in the conference's final statement of awareness of environmental problems; there is a general reference to the role of civil authority to 'create conditions conducive to the material and moral well-being of all',[14] and a recognition of the changes wrought upon our life-style by advances in technology.[15]

Since then, however, awareness of the problems has increased rapidly. In 1972, the UN Conference on Human Environment in Stockholm was addressed in the following words by Dr Elfan Rees, of the World Council of Churches' Commission for Churches in International Affairs:

---

[13] J. Findlow, 'The Church in the Modern World', in B. C. Pawley (ed.), *The Second Vatican Council – Studies by Eight Anglican Observers* (Oxford University Press, 1967), p. 208.

[14] Final statement of the National Evangelical Anglican Congress, P. Crowe (ed.), *Keele '67* (Falcon, 1967), pp. 26–27.

[15] *Ibid.*, pp. 28–29.

I admit, Mr President, that the churches were slower than you were in realizing the terrible implications of this problem. You have awakened us, but in so doing you have lit a fire you cannot extinguish. We will follow you as long as you advance, we will spur you if you halt, and we will take a vociferous lead if you turn back.[16]

Since then, more detailed attention has been given to the environment at many other conferences and consultations.[17]

Given that we are aware of the increasing participation in these matters by theologians and church leaders, we need to be clear as to why this really is a fundamentally Christian matter. Without clarifying this question, the motivation for a sustained contribution will be difficult to maintain. Various perspectives can be suggested, which are helpful and which are largely related to each other.

The first such perspective is the view that, unless Christians are seen to be actively involved in social issues, the gospel becomes an irrelevance in the eyes of others. This was stressed at the Lausanne Congress of 1974, although one theologian commenting on this meeting warned of the dangers of social involvement simply to lend respectability to evangelistic activity.[18] Both must spring from compassion and obedience.[19]

The effects of environmental mismanagement will be felt for many years, and we need now to be showing compassion for the world of our children, and for their children yet unborn. This is an important consideration and the mainspring of J. S. Black's strategy for future environmental management:

It seems to me that almost the only course open to western man is based on a vision of all mankind stretched out along the dimension of time . . . By expanding our view of the general good of mankind, by redefining 'mankind' in terms of the whole of humanity, dead, living or as yet unborn, we may perhaps be able to assess what we do in terms of the good of mankind,

---

[16] *The Churches in International Affairs: Reports 1970–1973.* Commission of the Churches on International Affairs of the World Council of Churches (World Council of Churches 1974), p. 144.

[17] As, for example, at the National Evangelical Anglican Congress at Nottingham in 1977. See P. King, 'Global Stewardship', in I. Cundy (ed.), *Obeying Christ in a Changing World*, 3 (Collins, 1977), pp. 132–156.

[18] B. N. Kaye, 'Theology Comes Tomorrow', *Churchman*, 88, 1974, pp. 277–287.

[19] J. R. W. Stott, *Christian Mission in the Modern World* (Falcon, 1975), pp. 15–34.

regardless of the position of the individual along the time axis of the world.[20]

Although Black's view is an outworking of compassion, a biblical foundation for environmental action will, as we shall see, go much deeper than this. Further, Thomas Sieger Derr has pointed out a number of difficulties in translating this kind of futuristic philosophy into concerted action.[21]

There is another compelling reason for Christian involvement and one which helps us to see in what direction compassion should take us. If the Christian faith contains a true and unique revelation of God to man, and if the environmental problems which face us stem from the fallen character of man (chapter 6), then our participation is essential. This is because Christian insights are vital in trying to find effective solutions to these problems. Chapters 7 and 8 will show how we can begin to look for solutions through a consideration of the meaning of salvation as a righting of wrong relationships.

But first it is necessary to look in some detail at the problems confronting us; only then will it be possible to consider in detail how the teaching of the Bible is relevant in the environmental debate. The next four chapters, therefore, seek to deal with four aspects: the rapid depletion of the world's metal resources and the imminent exhaustion of some; the problems of large-scale energy consumption and the hazards associated with the major fuels, coal, oil and gas, and nuclear power; the physical and social problems which accompany the rapid urbanization of the modern world, and their causes; and the outlook for world food supplies and the physical reasons for widespread malnutrition.

[20] J. S. Black, *op. cit.*, p. 123.
[21] T. S. Derr, *op. cit.*, pp. 61ff.

# 2
# Getting the Picture – The World's Metals

Until quite recently we have taken for granted the continued abundance of the material resources on which our physical well-being depends. The roofs over our heads depend upon supplies of bricks and cement; without wood there would be no furniture of the kind we are used to, nor would we have books and newspapers. Cars, bicycles, TV sets, tape recorders, washing machines and a host of other consumer durables are made from such raw materials as metals, glass, plastic, wood and rubber. Our gadgets work only when there is a source of energy. To maintain our standard of living, therefore, we rely upon our world to supply large quantities of raw materials. The one event which probably most intensified awareness of what the future might hold was the publication in 1972 of a report entitled *The Limits to Growth* which produced computer-simulation models of the prospects for physical resources and pollution.[1] The report forecast impending disaster on the basis of the trends apparent at that time. There had been other such forecasts but the impact of *The Limits to Growth* was due to the mathematical basis of the investigations.

Disaster was forecast because of predictions of exhaustion of physical resources, resulting in economic collapse and starvation on a huge scale; pollution would become intolerable, as would overcrowding due to the rapid increase in the world's population. In one sense the team responsible for the report was not heralding doom, simply proclaiming that current trends could not be allowed to continue indefinitely. Not all agreed, however; the assumptions and simplifications of the study were open to question. As a result, there is now a wide range of opinions on the seriousness of environmental problems ranging between extremes of pessimism and optimism. While the majority of those working on environmental

[1] D. H. Meadows, D. L. Meadows, J. Randers and W. W. Behrens III, *The Limits to Growth* (Universe Books, 1972).

problems would occupy positions close to the middle of the road, even eminent scientists do occasionally take up one or other extreme. One of the most outspoken of the pessimists is Professor Paul Ehrlich, an eminent American biologist; at the other end of the spectrum are John Maddox, and Alvin Weinberg, former director of the Oak Ridge National Laboratory in Tenessee.[2]

It is, of course, difficult for the layman to decide on which position is correct, partly due to the complexity of the scientific issues involved. Also, as we have seen in chapter 1, other issues are equally important.

The present chapter will concentrate on the physical resources, mainly metals, which constitute the raw materials of many consumer durables. Rapidly increasing rates of consumption in some cases threaten to exhaust reserves before the turn of the century. How can this threat be avoided? How far can geologists contribute towards alleviation of the problem? What are the side-effects of mining and how severe are the pollution hazards which accompany industrial activity? Before attempts are made to answer these questions it is necessary to discuss the role of physical resources in the history of nations as a pointer to future trends in consumption.

## Physical resources in international relations

A dominant theme in history is the rise and fall of great nations and the relationships of these nations with others. The stature of super-powers depends in part on the abundance of their natural resources, since this determines their economic power in large measure.

Russia and the USA have not always been at the head of the world power league. The Middle East, Greece and Britain have all been leading economic powers whose influence was connected with mineral wealth. It seems reasonable to suppose that changes will occur in the future as rich nations become poor and vice versa; it is possible, too, that as raw material consumption rises all over the world, such changes could become more frequent and less predictable than in the past.

But the connection between national influence and economic power is today more complicated than in the past. Modern trans-

---

[2] See, for example, J. Maddox, *The Doomsday Syndrome* (McGraw-Hill, 1972); A. Weinberg, 'Raw Materials Unlimited' *Texas Quarterly*, 11, 1968; and P. R. Ehrlich, *The Population Bomb* (Pan/Ballantine, 1972).

port allows nations to export and import raw and manufactured materials on a large scale, whereas in previous times nations were largely independent or else derived raw materials from other countries by conquest and enforced domination.

In 1973, the USA imported $19 billion worth of raw materials for its mineral and energy requirements and was *totally* dependent on imports for its supplies of platinoid metals, mica, chromium, strontium, cobalt, tantalum and columbium.[3] Similarly, in 1973 the EEC imported 63% of its fuel requirements.[4] In such a situation the continued stability and well-being of the importing nation depends in large measure on the continuing availability of the imports and on *the continuing goodwill of the exporting partner(s)*. This goodwill has been under severe strain on more than one occasion in recent years and is especially important when we consider the growing resentment among Third World countries over the economic stranglehold exerted by the rich nations.

The over-dependence of the rich nations on imported materials to maintain and increase their high standards of living has enabled other suppliers to push up their prices. Thus the USA has to pay inflated prices for its aluminium ore from Jamaica, while North African fertilizer is much more expensive than a few years ago. One of the major factors in the increasing charges made for petroleum by the OPEC nations in the late 1970s has been the huge and apparently unlimitable demand of the USA for imported oil. One of the tragic sequences of this process is that many of the poorer countries which most need raw materials find their purchasing power rapidly eroded.

We can see from these examples how natural resources have in the past played an important role in shaping international relations and continue to do so. In the past few years prices of key commodities such as oil have played a very large part in politics. As demands increase around the world, this aspect of the international scene will doubtless become even more important. The dependence of one country upon another for raw materials could lead to greater co-operation and partnership in the future; it could on the other

---

[3] E. F. Osborn, *Our Mineral Resource Problem and What We Can Do About It*, Edward H. Kraus Memorial Lecture, The University of Michigan, Ann Arbor, Michigan, September 12, 1974, pp. 1–4. Throughout the present work, 'billion' refers to the USA billion, *i.e.* a thousand million.

[4] See chapter 3.

hand lead to greater tensions and threats of war. Thus Sir Eric Ashby has written:

> Competition for scarce resources will undoubtedly exacerbate the natural hostility between nations with different ideologies. It will create tensions that – if we have anything to learn from history – tempt nations into war or international blackmail.[5]

## Pollution

Pollution is inextricably linked with economic growth. This is because industrial processes inevitably produce a certain amount of waste that must be disposed of. Depending on the process and the nature of the waste product, air, water or land may be polluted. Atmospheric pollution can lead to pollution of land and water when the pollutant is brought down by rain or fog.

In times past the obvious way to dispose of industrial waste was into rivers, which transported the materials into the seemingly infinite volume of the seas and oceans. This practice is now leading to severe dangers because of the huge amounts of waste involved. The extent of the pollution problem is now quite staggering. Rivers with little or no life in them are all too common. Some waters are dangerous for bathing.

The Adriatic Sea receives every day some 64% of Italy's industrial effluent (as well as nearly one-half of its sewage). The Italian authorities have, in the past, been forced to seize large quantities of tuna fish containing dangerously high amounts of mercury and to keep fishermen away from one area where a local factory is discharging into the sea large quantities of a toxic arsenic compound.

Probably the most notorious of polluted rivers is the Rhine. The *daily* chemical discharge by German industry into the river in 1973 was as follows:

> 31,800 tons of chloride
> 14,000 tons of sulphate
> 9,700 tons of calcium

---

[5] E. Ashby, *Reconciling Man with the Environment* (Oxford University Press, 1978), p. 86. See also D. Cupitt, 'God and the Futures of Man', in H. Montefiore, *Man and Nature* (Collins, 1975), p. 184.

3,440 tons of magnesium
3,000 tons of nitrate.

High levels of the toxic metals lead, cadmium and mercury are also reported, the content of the third metal being 45% above the maximum level recommended by the World Health Organization. At that time the pollution level was still rising by 6–8% per year and the river could be depolluted only by the most modern and expensive treatment plants, with storage basins for toxic pollutants thus extracted.[6]

It would be hypocritical to criticize industry, which exists to supply our demands at the minimum price. It would also be hypocritical since the consumer society of the rich countries produces astronomic amounts of rubbish. In 1974, the 3 million inhabitants of the Irish Republic generated half a million tons of rubbish. Each Irish home produced 30lb of waste per week, while in the city of Dublin the figure was 50lb.

Rubbish consists mainly of paper, glass, rubber, plastic and metal. Most of these materials are 'non-biodegradable', that is, they do not rot, and the rubbish tips which ensue form an ugly tribute to the consumer society. So do the litter which gathers on the pavements of every street, the spoiled picnic sites and the countryside dotted with abandoned cars.

## The future of the world's metal resources

Metals such as iron, aluminium, tin, silver and mercury are obtained from *ores*, the technical name given to rocks containing one or more such metals in economic quantities. As affluence increases, the demand for these metals rises *exponentially*; that is, the rate of increase itself increases, except during periods of recession. It is this rapid rise in consumption which, if continued for many more years, threatens exhaustion of vital and non-renewable metal resources.

Some of our metals are abundant on a world-wide basis; others are found in relatively small amounts and may be geographically very restricted. Mercury, for example, is comparatively scarce and is found in large quantities only in Spain and Italy (the once vast

---

[6] For a general review, see W. T. Edmondson, 'Fresh Water Pollution', in W. Murdoch (ed.), *Environment* (Sinauer Associates, 1975), pp. 251–271.

amounts found in California and Nevada are now almost completely worked out). Similarly, much of our tin and tungsten comes from south-east Asia, while much of the world's antimony is located in China.[7]

There are two schools of thought concerning the future of metal and other resources. One school is represented by the following statement from a 1974 report of the US National Academy of Sciences Committee on Mineral Resources and the Environment:

> Man faces the prospect of a series of shocks of varying severity as shortages occur in one material after another . . . the first real shortages (are) perhaps only a few years away.[8]

The other is represented by these two statements which are based on optimism over man's scientific and technological potential:

> (Limits to physical resources) are beyond any sensible planning horizon. More important, it has been established that most of the pollution effects of man's increasing consumption can be physically controlled with a relatively small switch in expenditure.[9]

Fortunately the real situation is not all that gloomy, for a variety of reasons. First, the indicated 'life-time' for known reserves should not be taken too seriously; accurate information on many reserves is not available and these figures are more indicators of short-term scarcities than results of exhaustive global studies. Secondly, in the mineral field, spectacular new discoveries are being made which completely change the outlook . . . While all wastages of mineral resources should certainly be avoided and relative shortages will be encountered for specific minerals, it appears that major difficulties in this field can be avoided for the coming decades.[10]

---

[7] C. F. Park and R. A. MacDiarmid, *Ore Deposits* (Freeman and Co., 1975).
[8] C. Norman, 'Material Shortage Shocks Ahead?', *Nature*, 253, 1974, p. 674.
[9] *Irish Times*, January 20, 1975, reporting a Thomas Davis lecture broadcast by Radio Eireann by D. J. O'Hagan, Lecturer in Economics, Trinity College, Dublin.
[10] M. Batisse, 'Global Prospects for Natural Resources', *Nature and Resources*, 10, 1974, pp. 2–7.

In the presence of such conflicting expert opinions, it is difficult for the layman to come to any settled conclusions, especially when the conclusions are so often quoted without the arguments on which they are based. The ensuing section examines the data relating to five common metals which illustrate the anxieties of the 'pessimists'; there will follow a consideration of the arguments of the 'optimists' and criticisms thereof, followed by some general conclusions.

*Some common metals*

Figures currently available for *tin, tungsten, zinc, lead* and *copper* indicate that these metals, amongst others, are in danger of exhaustion within decades. The method of prediction is simple; from reliable figures for *reserves* (the amount available for economic extraction), for the quantity used by industry every year and for the rate of increase of consumption, it is possible to calculate the number of years for which reserves will last.

The figures used in a typical prediction exercise[11] are set out in table 1. The results of the calculations are quite alarming, indicating exhaustion, in all cases, within a few decades.

*Table 1. Reserves expectations of five important metals*

|  | Tin | Tungsten | Lead | Zinc | Copper |
|---|---|---|---|---|---|
| Reserves (millions of tons) | 4.4 | 1.3 | 123.7 | 91.0 | 393.4 |
| 1968 consumption (millions of tons) | 0.3 | 0.03 | 5.8 | 4.0 | 8.6 |
| 2000 consumption (high estimate) | 0.5 | 0.1 | 15.4 | 8.1 | 38.8 |
| 2000 consumption (low estimate) | 0.3 | 0.1 | 11.3 | 5.6 | 24.7 |
| Estimated year of exhaustion (low estimate) | 1998 | 2002 | 1992 | 2000 | 1997 |
| Estimated year of exhaustion (high estimate) | 1988 | 1996 | 1988 | 1993 | 1993 |

There are similar situations with other metals, including molybdenum, tantalum, titanium, nickel, mercury, silver and van-

---

[11] G. J. S. Govett and M. H. Govett, 'Mineral Resource Supplies and the Limits of Economic Growth', *Earth-Science Reviews*, 8, 1972, pp. 275–290.

dium,[12] as well as the much-used gas helium. This, briefly, is the concern of many environmental scientists; those who do not share these concerns accept the figures but point optimistically to a number of realized and potential scientific and technological developments which will totally alter the supply situation in the future. We now look at the basis for optimism in some detail.

## *The optimistic school of thought*

The first of several lines of reasoning is that the world's reserves of mineral supplies are continually rising as new deposits are discovered and that this trend can be expected to continue. Thus in 1962 V. E. McKelvey wrote:

> This dark supply picture from which one could easily forecast thundering collapse of our society within a decade or two, is misleading . . . It overlooks the fact that we have literally only scratched the surface in our search for usable materials.[13]

McKelvey is right in that modern geological exploration is uncovering large new reserves of important minerals. This is due to the continuing advance in modern technology which contributes at several different levels. Thus modern forms of transport are helping to open up previously inaccessible tracts of the earth's surface. At another level, there are now available a range of sensitive monitoring instruments which can detect small variations in certain physical properties of rocks; these variations may indicate the existence of subsurface ore deposits which might otherwise have remained undiscovered. At a third level, scientific research and development have done much to increase our understanding of the processes by which these deposits come into being; this often leads to predictions of the type of geological environment in which other deposits might occur. Further progress is anticipated in this field as a result of high-level photo-reconnaissance carried out by US Skylab astronauts and by the unmanned Earth Resource Technology Satellites.

---

[12] For an account of the wide range of industrial uses of metals, see W. Alexander and A. Street, *Metals in the Service of Man* (Penguin, 1964).

[13] V. E. McKelvey, 'National Coal and Mineral Resources: Efficient Development and Field Use', in 'Minerals and Energy – Problems, Practices and Goals. Western Resources Conference, 1962'. *Colorado School of Mines Quarterly*, 57, 1962, pp. 143–152.

A second line of argument proposed by the optimists is the 'technological argument'. As man's technological capabilities increase, so he will be able to utilize materials from which extraction of metals is, at the moment, totally uneconomic. In particular, it is foreseen that ores of steadily decreasing *grade* will be worked, with a gradually falling *cut-off grade*.[14]

Bernado F. Grossling, an economic geologist from Washington, has written:

> The historic record shows a consistent and substantial decrease in cut-off grade. If the cut-off grade can be decreased then there is a substantial increase in the supply that can be obtained. Thereby the potential supply from the presently mined shallow layers of the crust could be substantially increased.[15]

What Grossling is saying is that low-grade ores are more abundant than high-grade ones, so that once we have the know-how to use the low-grade deposits at an economic price, abundant new metal reserves come into being. He is in fact quoting a much-used law of economic geology known as Lasky's Law, which can be used to calculate the approximate quantities of various metals present on a world-wide basis in ores of different grades.

Further, as lower grade ores become economic propositions, not only can new mines be opened but old ones can be reworked. At present, for example, there is renewed interest in Cornish tin deposits, some of which were abandoned long ago after removal of the richest ore. Possible, though far yet from practical realization, is the forecast that mining will in future be able to go to far greater depths below the surface than is possible today; figures of 20–30 miles have been mentioned.[16]

An offshoot of the technological argument concerns mining the sea and ocean floors which cover two-thirds of the earth's surface. Only in recent years has there been the technology to explore the

---

[14] Grade is a measure of the concentration of the metal in its ore; *high-grade* ores are relatively rich in the metal, *low-grade* ores relatively poor. *Cut-off grade* is the grade below which, at any point in time, economic extraction of the metal from the ore is not possible. In the past, technological advances have pushed cut-off grades gradually lower.
[15] B. F. Grossling, 'Future Mineral Supply', *Economic Geology*, 65, 1970, pp. 348–350.
[16] *Ibid.*, p. 348.

seabed properly, let alone mine it. In 1967 the American geologist Willard Bascom wrote:

> Undersea prospecting for minerals is plainly a complicated, expensive business where the risk is great and the rewards are unknown.[17]

In the years which have elapsed since Bascom wrote, the situation has changed so radically that even in 1970 Grossling could write:

> The manganese oxide nodules contain enormous quantities of copper, nickel and cobalt that probably could be recovered at costs less than 2–3 times those we are paying now and some believe at costs that eventually might be lower.[18]

The nodules to which he refers occur only in the deep parts of the oceans, far from land.[19] Others not so optimistic believe that economic mineral extraction can still be carried out in the shallower waters close to the continents.

A fourth line of argument used by the optimists is concerned with *substitution*. If certain metals do run short, other materials can be found to substitute for them – that is, materials with similar physical properties capable of doing the same job. Among the metals the best-known example of substitution is aluminium for copper. The former is very plentiful, its properties are very similar to those of copper, with which also it easily forms alloys. Technology is now available for growing fine silica fibres, which, it is hoped, will one day replace copper in certain types of telecommunications cables. Other substitutions possible are nickel for cobalt and molybdenum, vanadium and niobium for chromium, and plastics and aluminium for tin.

A final argument used by the optimists concerns the recycling of scrap metal. It is undoubtedly true that this obvious source of material has in the past been neglected, but attention is turning back to it. Mention has already been made of the large amounts

---

[17] W. F. Bascom, 'Mining the Ocean Depths', *Geoscience News*, 1, 1967, pp. 10–11, 26–28.
[18] B. F. Grossling, *op. cit.*, pp. 348–349.
[19] A. Granville, 'The Recovery of Deep-Sea Minerals: Problems and Prospects', *Minerals Science and Engineering*, 7, 1975, pp. 170–188.

of rubbish generated by the consumer society. Once more it is Grossling who sums up the position well:

> The argument has often been used that the mineral deposits of the earth are finite, and hence, exhaustible. With the same kind of logic we ought to add that the earth is a closed system and that, with minor exceptions, no mineral substance that is mined ever leaves the earth. If anything, because of man's activities, it is brought to the surface, to be buried in junk piles or in recent sediments, or washed away to the sea. Some mineral elements can be used over and over again. Eventually the 'garbage piles' resulting from the accumulation of increasing effluents of debris may come to be considered as ore deposits.[20]

It has been pointed out that recycling performs two useful functions: first, it cuts the amount of waste to be disposed of; and secondly, it cuts the amount of new material to be obtained by mining. This can lead in some cases to substantial savings in energy. It has been estimated, for example, that it takes 30 times more energy to extract aluminium for its ore than to recover it from scrap;[21] it should be stated, however, that the savings are not always so great, and for some other materials the recycling process consumes *more* energy.

A prototype recycling unit has been developed which can process 50 tons of rubbish every day (equivalent to that produced by a town of 50,000 people). The rubbish goes through a bag burster on to a rotating drum which contains seives for sorting the material into a group of size categories. The different types of material are next separated within each size category by means of magnets, low-powered fans, a water bath and a series of high-speed spin-off drums. The result is a separation of three grades of paper, tin cans for remelting, vegetable matter for compost or animal feed, coarse rags for the manufacture of floor-covering material and fine particulate matter for soil conditioning.[22]

Another refuse recycling experiment is being conducted in west Sussex in which refuse is used in the fuel in the Blue Circle Group cement kilns at Beeding. The area produces 280,000 tons of rubbish

---

[20] B. F. Grossling, *op. cit.*, p. 349.
[21] C. Thomas, untitled article in *Nature*, 253, 1975, p. 148.
[22] J. Newell, untitled article, *ibid.*, p. 149.

annually and Blue Circle hope to be able to use nearly one quarter of it.

The optimists thus base their views on four factors: the discovery of new deposits as exploration becomes more efficient; the utilization of advancing technology; substitution of materials; and recycling of waste. The potential for increasing world metal reserves is such as to render forecasts of impending exhaustion quite irrelevant. The picture painted is a rosy one; the years ahead promise increasing affluence for all. But is this really so? In fact the future is much less certain than the optimists would believe, because the grounds for optimism are themselves open to criticism.

## *The pessimists' reply to the optimists*

Each of the four major arguments used is open to doubt on grounds which will now be explained.

There is, *first*, the 'historical' argument which looks at the history of exploration and concludes that the past trend of increasing reserves will extend indefinitely into the future. Qualification of this argument takes three forms.

(1) It is dangerous to argue into the future simply in terms of the past. On the one hand, environmental pressures have never been so intense as now, and on the other, the earth is *finite*: that is, there is only so much land on the face of the earth, and no more. It is therefore reasonable to suppose that there is a limit to the amount of ore still to be found. Of course, the trends in exploration are such that it is impossible to know when such a limit might be reached; at the same time it would be foolish to carry on as if those limits did not exist.

(2) The revolution in transport over the past century is such that few areas of the earth's land surface remain inaccessible. There is therefore a limit to be placed on the ore-bearing capacity of areas not yet explored, especially because of the likely cost of the ore.

(3) The very nature of exponential growth is such that it is impossible to make a close comparison of the past and the future. As resource consumption gradually increases, impending exhaustion (assuming this to be a real possibility) is approached much more quickly in later years of growth than in earlier years. Small changes in resource availability are not then enough; they would need to be enormous.

The *second* argument used by the optimists, the 'technological' one, can be criticized on two accounts.

## Getting the Picture – The World's Metals

(1) The assumption that Lasky's Law will be valid to very low grades may be challenged. It is the use of this law which leads to forecasts of huge quantities of low grade ore. Modern research on ore genesis is beginning to show, however, that ore deposits form by processes which actively concentrate the metal in question by several or many orders of magnitude relative to an 'average' rock. This 'enrichment factor' varies from 25,000 for mercury through 4,000 (gold and lead) to 100 (nickel and copper) and down to 5 (iron and aluminium).[23]

The concept of enrichment implies a minimum enrichment factor for each metal and a certain grade below which there is little ore to be found. Thus the vast quantities of low-grade ore forecast by the optimists may not exist. Caution needs to be applied until there is a much fuller understanding of the genesis of metal ores.

(2) A further criticism concerns the consequences of mining such huge quantities of low-grade ore. To extract 1 ton of copper entails at 1% grade the mining of 100 tons of rock, which has somehow to be disposed of afterwards. By today's standards 1% grade is a very rich copper ore and we must next suppose that the day will come when mining of 0.1% ores will be necessary. To produce 1 ton of copper will then involve 1,000 tons of waste rock, ten times as much as for a 1% ore.

Concerns over the environmental effects of mining are exactly the same as those expressed by Agricola in 1556:

> Yields are devastated by mining operations, for which reason formerly Italians were warned by law that no one should dig the earth for metals and so injure their very fertile fields, their vineyards, and their olive groves . . . The woods and groves are cut down, for there is need of an endless amount of wood for timbers, machines, and the smelting of metals. And then the woods and groves are felled, then are exterminated the beasts and birds, very many of which furnish a pleasant and agreeable food for man. Further, when the ores are washed, the water which has been used poisons the brooks and streams, and either destroys the fish or drives them away.[24]

---

[23] L. F. Laporte *et al.*, *The Earth and Human Affairs* (Canfield Press, 1972), p. 80.
[24] G. Agricola, *De Re Metallica*, translated by H. C. and L. H. Hoover (Dover, 1912), p. 8.

There are also increasing pressures on the land from other directions. In densely populated areas agricultural land is at a premium; in California 90,000 acres of some of the world's richest agricultural land are gobbled up every year for suburban expansion, roads, airports and industry. Similar problems arise every time a mine is envisaged in a land-hungry area.

Other problems are subsidence and erosion. The former is especially serious in heavily populated areas and where there is low-lying agricultural land which then becomes liable to flooding. Erosion can cause ecological imbalance in a mining area, as can many other human activities which result in the removal of large amounts of soil – agricultural over-production (chapter 5), urban development and the building of roads, bridges and factories. It was for this reason that the Council of Europe in 1972 issued a Soil Charter, urging all concerned with the land to do everything possible to protect it. Some mining companies have done valuable development work in the area of environmental protection. How successful this is can be assessed only in the long term but it is an expensive operation which may, in the future, contribute towards greater costs of extracting raw materials from the ground.[25]

A further problem connected with mining operations is that of the inevitable change in the character of an area – social and aesthetic – where large-scale mining development takes place. Around the mine there must be new housing, new amenities and services, the total effect of which may be out of keeping with the prior character of the area. This can be a source of friction and it has been claimed that it is an impetus to moral decay (as exemplified by Peterhead since the beginning of the North Sea oil boom).

There is therefore little wonder that strenuous opposition arose when it transpired that there was a plan to mine for gold in the Snowdonia National Park. Another scheme in the same area was to mine copper.[26] A similar issue was the now-abandoned proposal to build the third London Airport in Bedfordshire, in the midst of a rich agricultural area.

It has been suggested that landscaping and reclamation of abandoned mining land can provide housing in ground previously useless. This is an attractive proposition, but before it can be

---

[25] E. F. Osborn, *op. cit.*, pp. 6–7.
[26] G. Searle, 'Copper in Snowdonia National Park', in P. J. Smith (ed.), *The Politics of Physical Resources* (Penguin, 1975).

properly assessed pertinent questions must be asked, as John Wright has done:

> Will it then be inhabited by people displaced from another area, newly opened up for mining? And what happens when decreasing cut-off grades turn reclaimed areas into economic propositions once more?[27]

The consequences of large-scale mining of low-grade ores, then, are far-reaching and serious. There are enormous problems in the long term. The pessimist does not say that they are insoluble; rather that they exist and must be faced.

The optimists also look to vast potential reserves of metals *beneath* the land surface and to the metallic nodules and other deposits of the ocean floors. With regard to ore deposits underground, the main problem is finding them. Increasing numbers of underground deposits have been located by indirect techniques but the difficulties multiply rapidly as the depth increases. The depths of 20–30 miles mentioned by some commentators may turn out to be unrealistic for another reason: namely, that the chemical nature of the earth's crust changes with depth. The change is such that we might expect platinum, nickel and cobalt to be more plentiful deep down, but exactly the reverse is true for most other metals. Techniques are being developed, however, which give rise to hopes of finding more deeply buried deposits, such as satellite imagery[28] and the detection of 'geochemical haloes'.[29] Exploration and development of deep mines will undoubtedly prove enormously expensive. These problems have been underlined by G. J. S. and M. H. Govett:

> Notwithstanding the promise of fully automated mining within the next decade, geophysical exploration techniques below 90 metres, drilling to depths below 4500 metres and remote sensing of characteristics with drill holes . . . it is not obvious how large

---

[27] J. B. Wright, 'Affluence and Future Mineral Supplies', *Economic Geology*, 66, 1971, pp. 576–579.

[28] R. P. Viljoen *et al.*, 'ERTS Imagery-applications in Geology and Mineral Exploration', *Minerals Science and Engineering*, 7, 1975, pp. 132–168.

[29] G. J. S. Govett, 'The Development of Geochemical Exploration Methods and Techniques', in G. J. S. and M. H. Govett (eds.), *World Mineral Supplies* (Elsevier, 1976), pp. 343–376.

numbers of deep deposits will be found – considering the present difficulties of locating ore deposits only 10 metres below the surface. Also, the additional energy required and the effects on the environment of mining deep deposits may be limiting factors.[30]

When we consider the potential of the ocean floor we must differentiate between the resources of the shallow continental shelf and the deep ocean floor thousands of miles out to sea. The former sounds a more feasible proposition, but even here there are all the problems of finding land-based ore plus those peculiar to the marine environment – the overlying layer of sea water (which may be deep and/or rough) and the burial of submarine rocks under a layer of sand, silt and other loose rock material.[31] The continental shelf, though, yields rich supplies of certain other types of material, mainly phosphates for fertilizer, gravel for the construction industry, and oil and gas. All of these are technically much easier to locate than metallic ore deposits, mainly because of scale.

Much research is being carried out on economic extraction of manganese, copper, nickel and cobalt from nodules on the deep ocean floor. The prospects look good but these resources will not completely solve the supply situation: also, there must first be international legislation on ownership of the sea floor.[32] Law of the Sea conferences have not yet solved the problem, though there are hopes that agreement will eventually be reached. At the same time a US company called Deepsea Ventures has declared itself ready to commence mining operations in the Pacific Ocean and stated that it is legally entitled to do so. Clearly such unilateral action cannot be permitted and should perhaps be seen as a sign of mounting pressure within a heavily industrialized country with steadily increasing demands for raw materials to override all interests beyond its own economic prospect.

The metals dissolved in sea water have also been considered as a potential reserve. Yet in spite of the huge quantities actually present in the vast expanse of the world's oceans, there seems little

---

[30] G. J. S. and M. H. Govett, 'Mineral Resource Supplies and the Limits of Economic Growth', *Earth-Science Reviews*, 8, 1972, pp. 275–290.

[31] P. Cloud, 'Mineral Resources from the Sea', in *Resources and Man* (Freeman, 1969).

[32] F. F. H. Wang and V. E. McKelvey, 'Marine Mineral Resources', in G. J. S. and M. H. Govett (eds.) *op. cit.*, pp. 221–286.

## Getting the Picture — The World's Metals

prospect of economic recovery of these metals. The average concentration of zinc, for example, is 0.09 lbs per million gallons of water; on 1968 zinc prices, this weight was worth ½p! To make sales totalling £50,000 would require the complete extraction of the metal from 9 billion gallons of sea water. The 400 tons thus obtained is an insignificant amount compared with world annual demand. Even in the Red Sea, where there are abnormal concentrations of some metals, the economic potential seems rather low except for sodium, potassium and magnesium.

Almost nothing is known about the possible effects of large-scale extraction of metals from the oceans or the ocean floors. The thermal properties of seawater are closely linked with its chemical composition; change this, and what might happen to world climatic patterns? There is no answer yet to this vital question. Changes in chemistry and temperature would certainly affect the delicate ecological balance of marine life. As before, there are many serious questions which must be answered before we can even consider the possibility of deep ore deposits and the mineral wealth of the oceans.

The *third* argument used by the optimists is concerned with substitution of a scarce metal by a more plentiful material. This is an important safety valve to pressure on mineral supplies but substitution can lead to increased demand for energy (as, for example, when aluminium substitutes for copper). As demand for mineral resources increases, the 'lead times' for finding and developing suitable substitutes will become more critical.

Finally, we come to the question of recycling waste. Current development work is promising, as already mentioned, and it is certain that the scale of recycling will increase in the years ahead. Lead, tin, copper and aluminium can be recovered in large part (100% recovery is economically impossible); recycling of other raw materials is more difficult. Into this category go zinc, tungsten, manganese, chromium and molybdenum. Recycling may also become expensive, since it is an energy-intensive operation and transport is a major factor in this industry.

There are other barriers to successful resolution of resource problems by recycling; the effect of the economic depression of the 1970s was to retard the development of the recycling industry[33], while economic models have indicated that so long as we live in

---

[33] C. Thomas, *op. cit.*, p. 148.

a growth situation the gap between what we demand and what recycling can provide is bound to widen.[34]

There are, however, immense benefits to recycling, some of which have been mentioned already. The process would, on a large scale, obviate the need for large amounts of land for waste disposal, especially around urban areas where disposal is already a severe problem.[35]

In spite of all the arguments of the pessimists, there is no doubt that metal reserves will grow considerably in years to come. On the other hand, economic planning for the future predicts continuing increases in consumption and industrial activity. Let us suppose that reserves of metals will soon be at *five times* their present level. Because of the continued growth previously mentioned, it cannot be assumed that projected metal reserve lifetimes will grow fivefold. The mathematics of the exercise lead to the surprising but grim conclusion that there is *still* an acute resources problem, as table 2 shows:[36]

*Table 2. Projected date of exhaustion*

|  | present reserves | 5 × present reserves |
|---|---|---|
| Tin | 1998–1988 | 2093–2027 |
| Tungsten | 2002–1996 | 2042–2028 |
| Lead | 2000–1993 | 2066–2038 |
| Zinc | 1992–1988 | 2038–2023 |
| Copper | 1998–1993 | 2042–2028 |

The resources problem refuses to go away and is simply postponed if current consumption trends are continued. The pessimists must be heeded when they say that optimism about the future of metal resources is unrealistic; the consequences in economic and environmental terms are still extremely serious in spite of scientific advances. There is in some quarters a reluctance to face up to this. It is argued, for example, that the crisis exists only 'within the present system of exploration and exploitation',[37] but it is not specified what alternative systems might exist. It is also argued

[34] M. Radetzki and L. E. O. Svensson, 'Can Scrap Save Us from Depletion?', *Natural Resources Forum*, 3, 1979, pp. 365–378.

[35] L. F. Laporte *et al.*, *op. cit.*, pp. 82ff.

[36] G. J. S. and M. H. Govett, *op. cit.*, p. 282.

[37] *Ibid.*, p. 288.

## Getting the Picture – The World's Metals

that if only enough money can be poured into research and development, then sufficient materials remain until entirely new resource-use processes are developed. This may, in years to come, prove to be a correct argument but at the moment only vague hopes are being expressed here.

The imbalance between the West and the rest of the world is being forced to our notice. Our affluence is the ideal for everyone else and we are having to pay for it with ever-increasing commodity prices. The causes of inflation are various, but one is the joint action taken by the OPEC countries in raising the price of oil. The same could happen in the future with other commodities such as metals.

The OPEC initiative showed just how effective joint action can be. The poor countries want more for their raw materials so that they can begin to catch up their rich brothers. The Govetts see this as one of the factors which will accentuate the resources problem in the future:

> The crisis arises now because for the first time in the history of man there is a possibility – in fact, a declared aim – of all people reaching a level of affluence hitherto restricted to a very small group in a few areas of the world.[38]

They go on to point out that growth in the developed nations cannot be sustained at the present rate and that there are simply not enough resources for the poor countries to be able to catch up. Yet these same countries have declared their aim to do so and they view with considerable suspicion western-inspired plans for conservation as a ploy to keep them poor and powerless. It is our wealth which contributes towards their continued poverty.

The world's resources will inevitably come under increasing pressure unless there are drastic changes of some sort. Metals will never run out *in practice*; what will happen is that, as supplies dwindle and demands increase, the prices will go very high. The consequences will be economic in the first place but with repercussions in every aspect of human life. Yet the philosophy of continued growth is maintained, for various reasons, by politicians, economists, industrialists, advertisers and trade-unionists. Our well-being is seen purely in economic terms and is therefore

---

[38] *Ibid.*, pp. 287–288.

equated with producing more and more goods. In ecological terms this is a disastrous way to proceed, leading ultimately to ruin, national and international, social, economic, political and human. The strains we are placing on our environment and on our societal framework are too great to be absorbed indefinitely. It is likely that the chill wind of consequence will be felt before long.

# 3
# Getting the Picture – The World's Energy

Three momentous advances in the field of energy utilization have totally changed man's lifestyle. The first was the use of coal; the second was the harnessing of energy from natural gas and petroleum; the third was the development of nuclear power. At present, nuclear power is being used on a relatively small scale, the majority of the world's energy coming from coal, petroleum and natural gas – the 'fossil' fuels. This distribution is expected to change substantially in years to come.

Other sources of energy are tapped locally. Hydroelectric power can be obtained in mountainous areas such as in the Scottish Highlands and Scandinavia. In some parts of the world much use can be made of tidal power, solar energy and geothermal energy, where steam rises to the surface in the vicinity of active volcanoes. These miscellaneous sources make only a small contribution, however, to total energy consumption.

Just as world demands for raw materials are rising rapidly (chapter 2), so are demands for energy, bringing dangers of two kinds: those associated with impending shortages of certain types of fuel and those which are side-effects of large-scale energy production.

A moment's thought will reveal how greatly we rely on instant energy to maintain our lifestyle – electricity at the press of a switch and the car outside the front door. Blackouts bring inconvenience to all and hardship to many. Our reliance on energy was also strikingly brought home when the OPEC countries quadrupled the price of oil in 1974. Since then, the 1978 revolution in Iran has led to a cutback in the availability of petroleum, bringing the prospect of shortages of petrol, home-heating oil and other commodities, with rapidly increasing prices. Sheik Yamani of Saudi Arabia has warned that shortages in the 1980s could be severe enough to make previous ones look trifling. In the meantime, economies in consumption seem difficult to implement, as in the USA, where President Carter's Energy Bill was rejected by the Senate in 1979.

*Bent World*

One trend which will change little in Europe and North America during the next decade is the dependence on imported fuel. The world's supplies of fossil fuels are very unevenly distributed so that 50% of the petroleum is situated in the Middle East.[1] In 1973 the EEC imported no less than 63% of its fuel requirements, and while an OECD report has predicted that this figure will fall to 42% by 1985, trends prior to the 1978 Iranian revolution indicated a slight rise. At the same time, 1985 energy consumption will probably be 50% higher than 1973 levels.[2]

These uncertainties over the future abundance of oil supplies have accelerated the swing towards nuclear power. The above-mentioned OECD report projects a rise from 3.4% of total EEC energy output in 1973 to 12–13% in 1985. This figure could go even higher if the oil situation deteriorates further. Spain expects to commission 15 nuclear reactors by 1980.

The demand for petroleum and the hunt for alternative energy supplies are major factors in politics. In 1979 Chancellor Schmidt of West Germany warned of the possibility of future war as a result of fierce competition over limited supplies of fossil fuels. Oil has also, in the past, strained relations between Britain and her EEC partners by the former's insistence on an independent seat at a big energy conference in 1975. The discovery of North Sea oil has changed Britain's stance on oil prices; the cost of utilizing North Sea reserves is so high that any substantial fall in oil prices would be disastrous for her national oil and gas industry.

These and other factors combine to ensure that the days of cheap and limitless energy are past. At the same time, the consequences of being deprived of something as vital as energy are almost unthinkable. This chapter, therefore, looks at the expectations of continuing supplies of energy from coal, oil and gas and from nuclear reactors. The side-effects of large-scale energy production will be outlined and possible alternative sources will be mentioned.

## Energy from coal

In Europe coal was first used extensively in the twelfth century, as a substitute for wood. Shortly afterwards it was introduced to

---

[1] Open University Course Team, *The Earth's Physical Resources. Block 2: Energy Resources* (Open University Press, 1973), p. 74.
[2] Organization for Economic Co-operation and Development, *Energy Prospects to 1985* (OECD, 1974).

## Getting the Picture – The World's Energy

London, where the inhabitants complained about the pollution it caused. More extensive use began with the Industrial Revolution. In 1971, some 68% of Britain's energy needs came from coal, compared with 21% from oil and gas and the remainder from other sources, mainly nuclear and hydroelectric.

Many other countries rely heavily on coal, and it is therefore important to know the extent of world reserves. The most generally accepted estimated is 8,616 billion tons.[3] In fact there is much more coal than this but many seams are too thin to be economically viable and up to 50% of what is extracted is lost in various ways. Other deposits are too deep to be a paying proposition, the economic limit being about 6,000 ft.

There are two ways of estimating coal demands in the future. One is to assume continuation of the present growth rate of world demand (approximately 3.8% per year); under these conditions reserves would be exhausted by 2050. The other is to construct a mathematical model in which demand would level off and then gradually fall as reserves dwindled. On this model, production would reach a peak at 2140 and 90% of reserves would be used up by 2380. Obviously both models use approximations but the indications are instructive.

In 1970 the National Coal Board estimated British coal reserves at 7,200 million tons, with an annual consumption of 145 million tons, which ensures supplies for only another fifty years. Since then, however, three 'new' coalfields have been discovered – one beneath Oxfordshire, one in the Vale of Belvoir, Leicestershire, and the other in the Selby area of Yorkshire. So there is no short-term crisis in coal supplies but the long-term prospect must be for alternative sources of energy.

As supplies of coal become depleted, it may be an important factor in international politics. This is because of the uneven distribution of world resources. 65% of known reserves are in Asia (mainly the USSR), and 27% in North America, so that many countries have to rely on large volumes of imported coal. Dwindling resources and increasing demand in the future could increase its strategic importance to the level of that of oil and gas in the 1970s.

---

[3] P. Averitt, 'Coal', in D. A. Brobst and W. P. Pratt (eds.), 'United States Mineral Resources', *US Geological Survey Professional Paper* No. 820, 1973, pp. 133–142.

## Side-effects of the use of coal

These can be considered in two categories: first, the effects of extracting coal from the ground; and secondly, the effects of burning coal.

(1) Coal is obtained either by mining or by open-pit methods (as in parts of the USA), when the seams are relatively close to ground level. Mining causes subsidence, which may occur without warning and cause extensive damage. A survey of US coal mining showed that for every 1,000 tons of coal removed, one-fifth of an acre of land subsides by up to 4 ft.[4] The danger is not only in built-up areas but in agricultural regions, which become more prone to flooding as land level falls.

Slag heaps are a common sight in coal-mining areas. The land they occupy is useless unless attempts at reclamation are made; they are generally steep-sided and become unstable after heavy rain. It was such a situation which led to the tragedy of Aberfan in South Wales in 1966, when 144 children were killed in a school in the path of the landslide which resulted. Concern was subsequently expressed over the state of other tip-heaps in that region; some were then moved to safer positions. It has been stated that similar accidents occur frequently in the USA,[5] but this statement refers to landslides rather than to any loss of life.

Open-pit extraction of coal has environmental effects of a rather different nature. By the very nature of the operation, extraction of the coal is much faster than from mines and land is gobbled up at such huge rates (up to 5,000 acres per week) that efforts at reclamation are necessary. Two problems arise: one is the trouble sometimes encountered in enforcing reclamation laws; the other is that even the best attempts may be far from successful.[6] In addition, adjacent land is affected by soil erosion, landslides and 'dirty' water. It has been estimated that the total area affected is three to five times that actually used for coal extraction.[7]

(2) The energy stored in coal is released by burning, in power stations, furnaces and domestic fires. There are always impurities

---

[4] R. Wilson and W. J. Jones, *Energy, Ecology and the Environment* (Academic Press, 1974), p. 192.

[5] *Ibid.*, p. 192.

[6] E. F. Osborn, *Our Mineral Resource Problem and What We Can Do About It*, Edward H. Kraus Memorial Lecture, University of Michigan, Ann Arbor, Michigan. September 12, 1974.

[7] J. B. Marion, *Energy in Perspective* (Academic Press, 1974), p. 177.

## Getting the Picture – The World's Energy

present which, using conventional burning techniques, are released into the atmosphere. The gaseous impurities will be considered with petroleum and natural gas but the burning of coal also releases fine-grained solid matter known as 'fly-ash'. Because of its fine grain size it remains suspended in the atmosphere and the main danger is its long-term effect on lung tissue.

It is claimed that 99% of the fly-ash can be removed from the exhaust gases before release into the atmosphere, but this figure must be treated with caution. The figure for the finest (and most dangerous) particles may be only 50%. It has been calculated that the average coal-fired power station releases 1,500 tons of fly-ash into the atmosphere every year, even after a 99%-efficient removal process.[8]

A major breakthrough seems imminent, however, in the development of the process known as *gasification*. Coal is converted at the mine into coal-gas, and sulphur dioxide and fly-ash can be almost completely removed. The price could soon be commercially competitive, especially if the prices of alternative energy sources continue to rise rapidly.

## Petroleum and natural gas

One-half of the earth's land surface is underlain by potential *reservoirs*[9] at various depths. The presence of a reservoir, however, is no guarantee that petroleum and/or natural gas are present. Prospecting companies have to undertake much preliminary geological and geophysical work before the sinking of an exploratory well can be even considered, because of the cost of drilling. This cost is related to the depth of oil and gas reservoirs; the average is 5,000 ft. below the surface and a few are at more than twice this depth.

Offshore exploration is a much more costly operation. The preliminary work and the drilling programme need specialized equipment on land but even more so at sea, so that oil from the North Sea is five times as expensive as from the Middle East. A high rate of return on investment is therefore sought and the figure

---

[8] *Ibid.*, p. 183.

[9] *Reservoirs* consist of rocks with interstices in which the petroleum and gas are stored. Fissured limestone and porous sandstone are the most common types of reservoir.

of 25% has been mentioned. It has been suggested that high rates of inflation could push that figure up to 40%.[10]

Such are current world requirements and exploration costs that James Adamson of Chase Manhattan Bank has calculated that the cost of developing the world's needs for the next ten years works out at $1,345,000,000,000, a staggering sum which, whatever the *immediate* source of this funding, will ultimately come from the consumer.[11]

Given a reasonable knowledge of the world's reservoir capacity, it is possible to make an estimate of reserves of oil and gas. In one sense this exercise is easier than for metal ores, because the geological structures are on a larger scale and therefore easier to identify. But two assumptions have to be made: one is that the proportion of potential reservoirs which actually contain petroleum and gas is the same in those areas which have still be be fully explored as in those which are already completely known; the other concerns the average *recovery rate*, the proportion of fuel actually present which can be economically extracted (usually less than 50%).[12]

Estimates of reserves for petroleum range from 1,500 billion to 3,500 billion barrels.[13,14] Our knowledge of reserves has improved over the years and reserves figures have been gradually revised upwards. An upper limit may be reached very soon, however, since consumption has continued to rise rapidly, while relatively few areas of the world remain to be explored.

Over-estimation of reserves may have taken place in the past. In 1975 the US Department of the Interior published a report compiled by the US Geological Survey in which the previous year's estimates of the nation's oil and gas reserves were slashed by more than 65%. Estimates of offshore oil were cut by 80%. The report concluded that

> US independence from external sources is essentially impossible

---

[10] Dr David Fleming, oil consultant to the Bank of Scotland, addressing the Offshore Europe '75 conference in Aberdeen in September, 1975. Report in *Irish Times*, 19 September, 1974.

[11] B. Andrews, 'Wanted: $1,345,000,000,000 for World Oil Bill', *Irish Times*, January, 1978. Bruce Andrews is the Editor of the *Financial Times* North Sea Letter.

[12] B. J. Skinner, *Earth Resources* (Prentice-Hall, 1968), p. 118.

[13] *Ibid.*, p. 119 gives the range.

[14] See J. B. Marion, *op. cit.*, p. 65 for a typical intermediate prediction.

on the basis of increased production of petroleum during the next decade.[15]

Another conclusion was that alternative sources of energy had to be developed since reserves were calculated as sufficient for only 37–62 years.

Similar calculations for world oil and gas reserves, based on recent trends in consumption, suggest that reserves will be dwindling by the end of the century, with almost complete exhaustion by 2030. Yet the experience of the 1970s has made nations increasingly aware of the problems of over-dependence on oil and gas and consumption rates could level off or even begin to fall if alternative energy sources can be harnessed. The lifetime of the world's reserves of oil and gas could then be extended but it still seems certain that their future as large-scale energy sources is limited.

Caution is needed in assessing the benefits to Britain of North Sea oil and gas. Already, reserves are apparently at a peak, because the rate of consumption has started to outstrip the rate at which new fields are being discovered.

The truth is therefore that the future of energy supplies is seriously compromised by over-dependence on dwindling stocks of oil and gas. Yet the oil and gas still to be discovered are mainly underneath the continental shelf in water deep enough to ensure that its extraction will be increasingly expensive.

## Side-effects of oil and gas production

All stages in production of oil and gas – extraction of oil and gas from reservoirs; refining the 'crude' material; transportation of crude and refined materials; and burning the final product – have environmental side-effects which we shall now consider.

(1) The tapping of oil and gas reservoirs causes little environmental disturbance, except for occasional cases of subsidence. In the Wilmington oilfield, California, the ground sank by up to 26 ft. in a 25-year period; horizontal ground movement also occurred, causing extensive damage to wharves, pipelines, buildings, roads and bridges. Eventually the movement was arrested by

---

[15] The 1975 report of the US Geological Survey to the Department of the Interior. See *Nature*, 255, 1975, p. 184.

*Bent World*

pumping water into the reservoir at a rate of 700,000 barrels a day.[16]

Offshore oil production is a more hazardous process; leaks can occur, with potential damage to marine life, beaches and other amenities. The Californian Santa Barbara field is instructive because of the background to the spillage and the sequel to it. The local residents had long objected to offshore rigs because of the potential threat to the tourist industry. It has been suggested that the establishment of oil production against the wishes of at least a section of the local community was the result of collusion between the oil company concerned and the US government. The residents found themselves powerless, although it was they who were affected by the catastrophic leakage which went on for a long time.[17]

In 1976 oil experts predicted that two holes drilled into the North Sea fields would eventually 'blow', and Norway complained that Britain had not done enough to prepare for the resulting pollution such an event could cause.[18] Then in April 1977 the Bravo rig in the Ekofisk field blew out, resulting in a 1,100 square mile oil slick. Fortunately for the fishing industry, the event occurred between the spawning seasons of cod and mackerel. But every such event brings severe danger to marine life, not only from the oil itself but also from the chemicals used to disperse it. The dangers would have been especially severe if attempts to cap the 'blown' well had been unsuccessful.

(2) Oil refining is carried out at large refineries such as those in Britain at Milford Haven, Canvey Island and Fawley. The first reaction of many to a new refinery is to welcome the increasing local prosperity and new job opportunities it brings. It is illuminating, therefore, to record the conclusions of the planning inspector who advised the Irish Minister for Local Government to refuse planning permission for an oil refinery to be constructed at Bantry Bay, County Cork, a famous scenic area:

---

[16] M. N. Mayuga and D. R. Allen, 'Long Beach Subsidence' in R. Lung and R. Proctor (eds.), *Engineering Geology in Southern California* (Association of Engineering Geologists, 1966), pp. 281–285.

[17] H. Molotch, 'Santa Barbara – Oil in the Velvet Playground' in R. W. Tank (ed.), *Focus on Environmental Geology* (Oxford University Press, 1973), pp. 352–373.

[18] R. Cocking, 'Norway Prepared Now for Potential Disaster with North Sea Oil', *Irish Times*, 21 September, 1976.

An oil refinery is not a clean industry and I consider that even with the inclusion of all modern expertise in design, monitoring and supervision, very serious damage to the environment would be caused in the Bantry area:
a) to visual amenity, because it is practically impossible to landscape and screen from view the major elements of the refinery such as the high stack, which would need to be substantially larger if, as I anticipate, expansion would be inevitable;
b) by oil pollution, which would have serious adverse effects on the marine life and ecology of the bay – the fishing industry would at best be limited;
c) by air pollution and noise which would be significant in an area which is eminently free from such pollutions.[19]

The inspector even considered that the refinery would hinder the over-all development of the area because of the effect on tourism. It is instructive to note that the Minister subsequently granted permission for the refinery to be constructed.

The air pollution mentioned by the inspector is due to sulphur dioxide (sulphur-bearing compounds are major impurities in many types of crude oil). It is pungent and, in the air, it can constitute a threat to health (see chapter 4, where this is considered further). When washed down with rain it is absorbed by the soil and can constitute a threat to plants and animals. This problem is shared by coal- and oil-fired power stations and by brickworks which use clay as a starting material. The local effects can be minimized by building a high 'stack' from which the pollutants are emitted and dispersed over a wider area. Sulphur dioxide from British power stations is now well documented in the atmosphere over Scandinavia.

It is claimed that building refineries creates jobs and brings increased prosperity, especially in regions of high unemployment. In the short-term, theory and practice agree well; longer-term experience shows that the problem of unemployment in such areas can become more acute, since the labour necessary for construction usually has to be 'imported' and many workers settle down during the two to three years of the building operation. This has hap-

---

[19] *Life and Environment*, September, 1974. This is the journal of An Taisce, the Irish Conservation Society.

pened, for example, on Anglesey, during the construction of an offshore oil terminal and an aluminium smelter.[20]

Another hazard associated with refineries is that of fire and explosion, accidental or deliberate; textbooks on energy and ecology devote whole chapters to the subject.[21] Stricter safety measures have led to a decrease in refinery fires but risks are still being taken. In 1979 a catastrophic explosion occurred on board a tanker being unloaded at the Bantry oil refinery terminal previously referred to; nearly fifty people, including the entire crew of the ship, were killed. Some of the evidence presented at the inquiry suggests that routine precautions, such as the maintenance of fire-fighting equipment, had been unattended to for a period of months.

Many refineries are situated close to major petrochemical complexes which are often themselves near major centres of population. There are further risks here in that, should a large explosion occur, the huge clouds of black smoke which would be given off by the combustion of the oil and its refined products could be potentially toxic.

The modern refinery is safer than its older counterpart but the dangers of human error and lack of safety measures continue. On 19 January 1975, there was a major petrol spillage in Dublin Docks; a petrol fire had started in the same locality on 6 November 1974. The subsequent investigation blamed operator error for both accidents and criticized the undue delay in taking precautionary measures. The inquiry also found that there was no co-ordinated plan to protect lives and property in the event of a serious hazard arising. The conclusions were challenged by the local Residents Association, whose insistent pressure had led to the summoning of the inquiry:

> The Association is not satisfied with this report for the following reasons: it had asked for a public inquiry and all they got was the report of an interdepartmental committee; it asked for outside experts to report on the safety precautions in the port area but this was not acted upon; it asked for the association to be given representation on the committee, or at least, observer status. This was refused.

---

[20] R. West and P. Foot, 'Anglesey: Aluminium and Oil', in P. J. Smith (ed.), *The Politics of Physical Resources* (Penguin, 1975).

[21] *E.g.* R. Wilson and W. J. Jones, *op. cit.*, chapter 10.

Here the Residents Association ran into a common problem — the machinery used for inquiries prevented them from obtaining access to the information they needed to present their case properly and to which they felt entitled.[22]

(3) Almost invariably, crude oil has to be transported from the production rig to the refinery. Sometimes the journeys are short but even long journeys can sometimes be achieved by pipeline. In other cases a long sea voyage is necessary and to satisfy modern demands a new fleet of giant oil tankers has been built.

Oil spillages from tankers first became headline news with the shipwreck of the *Torrey Canyon* in 1967, which released 50,000 tons of crude oil (29 million gallons) into the sea; the disastrous effect upon marine life in the area was compounded by the then rudimentary techniques used to deal with the oil which had escaped; the chemicals used were as injurious to marine life as the oil itself (see also chapter 5). Since then, there have been a number of gigantic spillages associated with naval accidents, notably the running aground on the French coast of the *Amoco Cadiz* in 1978. The cost of removing the oil from the shores in the area ran into many millions of francs.

Deliberate spillages result from ships cleaning out their bunkers at sea (contrary to international marine law). Culprits could be identified by adding radioactive tracers to the oil of each international trading company; there are sufficiently few of these to give each one a unique tracer. Unfortunately, the practicalities of the operation are difficult and the impression gained is one of unwillingness to act, coupled with the difficulty of tracking down culprits by methods currently available.

(4) Burning oil and gas releases into the atmosphere mixtures of nitrogen oxides, sulphur dioxide, carbon monoxide and carbon dioxide. On a global scale there is no problem in the immediate future, although the long-term climatic effects are not understood. On the local scale, however, the problem of air pollution by these gases is already serious. Many cities suffer from photochemical smog due to chemical reactions which take place in polluted air; Tokyo and San Francisco are notable, if extreme, examples. The effects are especially acute in urban areas, simply because of high population density (see also chapter 4).

---

[22] *Cf.* R. West and P. Foot, *art. cit.*

## Nuclear fission

The basis of nuclear fission, either natural or artificially induced, is the disintegration of an atom into two smaller ones, invariably with the emission of a large amount of energy. Uranium and thorium are by far the most important fissionable elements. The natural decay rate of uranium is too slow to be able to utilize the emitted energy, with the added problem that uranium-235 (the unstable isotope) accounts for only 0.7% of natural uranium, the remainder being mainly the stable isotope uranium-238. It is therefore necessary to concentrate the former in special processing plants and to speed up the fission process in a nuclear reactor by irradiating the uranium with sub-atomic particles called neutrons.[23]

Uranium occurs naturally in rocks but in small amounts. The total world uranium reserves which could be extracted at an economic price were 3.4 million tons in 1973.[24] On the other hand, a 1,000-megawatt nuclear power station consumes only 3,900 tons of natural uranium during a 25-year period and a rough calculation shows that the estimated uranium reserves will be exhausted in that time if they feed 750 stations of 1,000-megawatt capacity. In fact, there are fewer than this working at present and consumption trends for uranium reserves will last into the next century.

In the meantime, intensive exploration is uncovering further reserves; equally important, however, is the possibility of superseding the present generation of *burner* reactors with a new type called a *breeder reactor*. In the former, the energy comes solely from the neutron-induced fission of uranium-235. During this process a phenomenon called *breeding* occurs, in which a small amount of the uranium-238 is converted into the fissionable plutonium isotope 239. Breeder reactors can utilize this plutonium while burner reactors cannot. The real advantage of breeder reactors is that the initial fuel requirement is drastically cut. A breeder reactor can produce the same amount of energy from 100 tons of uranium and 2,300 kilograms of plutonium as a burner reactor can produce from 3,900 tons of uranium. A breeder reactor construction programme could then lead to a slackening of the increasing demand for uranium, especially since uranium-238 and plutonium have been stockpiled for a number of years in anticipation of the breeder reactor becoming technologically feasible.

---

[23] R. Wilson and W. J. Jones, *op. cit.*, chapter 5.
[24] Open University Course Team, *op. cit.*, p. 94.

## Side-effects of nuclear power

There is a wide spectrum of opinion on the safety of the nuclear industry. At the same time, as already stated, there are strong pressures for a large expansion of world nuclear power capability. So when the European Nuclear Energy conference ended in April 1975, the official conference spokesman, M. Marcel Boiteux (Director-General of Electricité de France) said:

> We have come to the conclusion that nuclear energy is indispensable to the world's energy requirements. Because of the unrestrained increase in the world's population for some time to come, the world will need to create new energy possibilities and nuclear energy, as we see it, is the only means to supplement such a necessitated increase in energy requirements.
>
> We see no reason why the world should not pass over to nuclear energy as a main source of supply within the next 30 years.[25]

M. Boiteux is not a lone voice. European self-sufficiency in energy production has been predicted on the basis of a more extensive use of nuclear power.[26] It is certainly true that if higher *per capita* energy consumption is to be achieved, this is the only immediate way, except for reliance upon dwindling and ever more expensive stocks of Middle East and other oil.

As we shall see later, there are possibilities of revolutionary new energy sources but these are still a long way short of commercial viability and it is impossible to anticipate what future contribution they might make. Given, therefore, that nuclear-fission energy will become much more important in the immediate future, we must look at the potential hazards involved. They can be grouped as follows: the effects of uranium mining; the effects of transporting uranium and plutonium; problems associated with reactor operation; the transport and storage of radioactive waste; the effects of disposal of coolant; the international sale of nuclear technology.

(1) The hazards associated with uranium mining are similar to those for coal, with two additional ones relating to the particular nature of uranium. The first is the high incidence of lung cancer amongst uranium miners, known long before its use as a nuclear

---

[25] *Irish Times*, 28 April, 1975.
[26] W. Marshall, 'Self-sufficiency in Energy', *Atom*, 223, 1975, pp. 62–66.

fuel, since it is also used in glass-making. Especially at risk are miners who smoke, and it has been suggested that minute quantities of the associated radioactive metal polonium are absorbed by tobacco smoke and inhaled into the lungs.

The second problem is one which was discussed fully in chapter 2; namely, the large-scale extraction of rock containing only small quantities of the ore material being sought. If breeder reactors are brought into production, this will not constitute a major problem.

(2) Transport of nuclear fuel rods is an issue upon which there is much public disquiet. As more nuclear power stations come into use in the USA there will be up to 9,000 annual railway shipments of up to 30 tons each or 30,000 road transfers of up to 10 tons each.[27] If the average journey is 400 miles, 1.5 major railway accidents per year are predicted involving nuclear material, or 15 road accidents.[28] The containers are, of course, extremely strong; they are constructed to withstand being dropped on to concrete from a height of 30 ft. or to withstand temperatures of 1,350°F for three hours. The fuel, being solid, would not be dispersed if the containers were broken, unless they were to fall into a river, in which case there would be the possibility of contamination of drinking water.

More hazardous is the movement of 'spent' rods being taken to reprocessing plants. Not only are they highly radioactive but they also contain extremely toxic plutonium as a result of the breeding process. Safety precautions are being continually improved and accidents involving this kind of material will be few and far between. Accidents will occur, however, and contamination by plutonium and other radioactive materials is a possibility; long-term degradation of the environment will then be avoided only by prompt action and a well-organized system of emergency procedures.

One alternative which will eliminate the need for extensive movement of material is the 'nuclear park', in which it is envisaged that uranium processing plants, reactors and waste storage tanks will be situated in close proximity.

(3) A nuclear reactor is, basically, a very dangerous piece of equipment. The uranium fuel rods at the core of the reactor become

[27] R. Wilson and W. J. Jones, *op. cit.*, p. 302.
[28] *Ibid.*, p. 302.

## Getting the Picture – The World's Energy

highly radioactive due to the reactions which take place when they are irradiated with neutrons. There is the added complication of the extremely high temperatures attained. What would happen if the cooling system were to fail?

> If a plant . . . lost its cooling water supply . . . the uranium core could heat up to 5,000 degrees within minutes and burst its protective covering. Tons of molten steel and uranium would plunge through the container floor and burn into the earth. It wouldn't quite reach China, but it would go a long way down. The reactor itself could easily build up the radioactive equivalent of a Hiroshima bomb, which instead of exploding into the atmosphere, would send a cloud of deadly gas into the countryside.[29]

A number of accidents at nuclear reactors have taken place during the last thirty years,[30] including the one at Three Mile Island on 28 March, 1979. The technical details of the accident are summarized elsewhere,[31] but subsequent events reveal issues of vital concern. One of these was the training given to the control room operators which left them unprepared for coping with the situation which developed, especially since their instruments were conveying data which were either wrong or difficult to interpret. As a result of this, senior officials at the plant were in the dark for some hours as to whether it was advisable to evacuate the local population. A hydrogen explosion within the plant, due to a build-up of the gas after the initial reactor failure, was reported to the US Nuclear Regulatory Commission only ten hours after it had taken place. The accident began with a combination (as yet not fully clarified) of operator error and technical failure. But these other operational shortcomings at Three Mile Island could have contributed to a much more serious incident than actually occurred. As it is, some radiation was released into the atmosphere and there is still considerable debate about the likely physiological damage which will be caused to local people and animals as a result.

Extensive research continues into ways of making nuclear power progressively 'safer'; accidents which have so far occurred have, at

---

[29] *The Observer*, 6 August, 1972.

[30] R. Wilson and W. J. Jones, *op. cit.*, p. 283.

[31] P. Bunyard, 'Living on a Knife-edge – The Aftermath of Harrisburg', *The Ecologist*, 9, 1979, pp. 97–102.

least, afforded valuable experience. Modern reactors contain a whole array of standby and safety facilities designed to ensure, *so far as is feasible*, that when failures do occur, the effects will be contained within the reactor area. Thus the uranium core, contained within an inner metallic vessel, is also surrounded by an outer concrete jacket. It is admitted, however, that to build this jacket sufficiently thick to contain the effects of the worst conceivable accident is just not feasible. There remains, therefore, the possibility of an explosion which would rupture the concrete jacket and emit a cloud of highly radioactive material into the surrounding countryside. It has been estimated that such an accident in a 100–megawatt reactor could produce enough radioactive material to render 100 square miles of land uninhabitable; such a catastrophe could kill over 3,000 people and cause damage costing £700 million (at 1975 prices).[32]

The Rasmussen Report, commissioned by the American Atomic Energy Commission, treated the likelihood of an accident statistically and concluded that the chance of death at a nuclear power plant in one year is 1 in 300 million; the chance of any nuclear accident killing 100 people is 1 in 1 million per year per plant, lengthening to 1 in 100 million for 1,000 deaths.[33] Since the publication of the Rasmussen Report the figures have been subject to continuous debate and it is reported that Professor Rasmussen himself is re-evaluating them after the incident at Three Mile Island.

At present, then, our knowledge indicates that accidents can and do occur, although rarely, but with so little experience there is a great deal of uncertainty about the incidence of accidents and especially about their effects. Rapid advances in nuclear technology, and economic and political pressures, add to the uncertainty. Meanwhile, a large expansion in the world's nuclear power capability seems to provide the only way of supplying the projected rise in energy consumption and of easing international dependence on imported oil.

The hazard of sabotage must also be considered. This is often not taken seriously enough, and one textbook states:

---

[32] R. Wilson and W. J. Jones, *op. cit.*, p. 268.
[33] N. C. Rasmussen, 'Reactor Safety Study', draft of summary report of the Reactor Safety Study, in L. C. Ruedisili and M. W. Firebaugh, *Perspectives on Energy* (Oxford University Press, 1975).

## Getting the Picture – The World's Energy

In fact, saboteurs usually stop short of destroying many other people; there seems to be a mental block here. This is fortunate, because otherwise the human race would probably have been destroyed long ago.[34]

Terrorist activity in recent years throws some doubt on the validity of this conclusion; the cause is often more important than human life. In 1974 Basque Nationalists attacked a nuclear power station in southern France; the attack was a clumsy one and there was never any danger of a serious threat. The incident does show, however, that nuclear power stations are now 'legitimate' targets for offensive action and that the World Council of Churches conference at Nairobi in 1975 was right to draw a distinction between the place of nuclear power in stable and in unstable societies.

Only a small number of terrorists would be capable of carrying out such an attack successfully; those concerned would need to be educated maniacs, with a detailed knowledge of the particular reactor selected, able to evade all the security systems operating at the plant and to sabotage simultaneously the reactor and all its safety mechanisms.

At the same time as the Basque attack, Arthur Palmer MP, the chairman of the Commons Select Committee on Science and Technology, expressed publicly the fear that Britain and America could find their nuclear power stations on lists of terrorist targets, and expressed concern that security was not tight enough. A spokesman for the Central Electricity Generating Board made the following reply which, as careful study will show, did nothing to allay Mr Palmer's fears:

> It would be very difficult for terrorists to get near the radioactive fuel elements unless they knew how to operate the machinery. Even if they did they are only likely to kill themselves before being able to cause further damage.
>
> There are complicated security arrangements at nuclear power stations. They are pretty closely guarded and have electrified fences and other electronic defence mechanisms.[35]

One fellow MP later criticized Mr Palmer for making public 'a

[34] R. Wilson and W. J. Jones, *op. cit.*, p. 284.
[35] *Sunday Telegraph*, 10 August, 1975.

possible weak link in our security network'. The concern is not limited to Britain. Professor Fred Ikle, head of the American Arms Control and Disarmament Agency, has several times warned of the dangers of terrorist attacks. Since Mr Palmer's public utterances, at least one Anglo-American conference on nuclear security has taken place 'behind the scenes', and in May 1976 security at all fifty-eight US reactors was strengthened after a tip-off to the Nuclear Regulatory Commission. Spending on security at US nuclear power stations now runs into hundreds of millions of dollars.

Sabotage could also be the act of a disgruntled employee. At least two such cases are known, in neither of which was any serious damage caused. A more dangerous happening was the 'accident' at the National Reactor Testing Station in Idaho during 1961, when uranium from a fuel rod was spattered around the laboratory building (there was no containment vessel for this reactor), resulting in the death of all three operators. The subsequent inquiry showed that the uranium rod must have been removed *deliberately and by hand*. There is no certainty as to why it was done and the report suggested a suicide motive.

(4) The safe disposal of radioactive waste materials is one of the most intractable problems facing the nuclear industry. The chemical elements involved are by-products of the breakdown of the uranium. Some of them are gaseous, such as krypton-85, hydrogen-3 (tritium) and radon-222; all of these have short half-lives[36] and can be safely released into the atmosphere from tall chimneys, although this practice might have to be curtailed if expansion of nuclear power continues.

The real problem arises with the radioactive isotopes which have to be extracted from the spent uranium as solids or dissolved in water. They range from iodine-131 (half-life 8 days) to zirconium-96 (half-life 100,000,000,000,000,000 years!), and the crude waste product has therefore to be considered radioactive on a permanent basis. They cannot be safely released into natural waterways, especially since some, such as radioactive iodine and strontium, are easily absorbed by the human body.

At present there are two methods of dealing with these wastes:

---

[36] *Half-life* is the time taken for the decay of one-half of a quantity of a given radioactive isotope. It ranges from small fractions of a second to thousands of millions of years.

they can be either stored as liquids in stainless steel tanks, or fused into solid blocks. Britain's nuclear wastes are stored in fifteen 150-gallon stainless steel tanks, but in America, where there are more reactors, the volume is correspondingly larger. Britain also processes wastes from other countries such as Japan. The tanks are buried underground and are enclosed in outer tanks to prevent leakage; the radioactive heat they generate necessitates continuous cooling. This process is unsatisfactory in that both constant surveillance and constant cooling are required.

A number of leaks have been reported. The tanks are large and the volume of liquid which can escape is appreciable before the drop in level triggers the alarm system. There is also the problem of how to stem the flow of dangerous liquid from the tank once it has been located.

Other batches of radioactive waste have been sealed into concrete blocks or stainless steel containers and dumped at the bottom of the Atlantic Ocean. The site used for one consignment in June 1976 was 560 miles south-west of Land's End at a point where the ocean is nearly 3 miles deep. It is envisaged that the material will be completely buried by new sediment before corrosion releases the radioactive elements into the ocean.

Another method of disposal which is more feasible is to fuse the waste into solid glass; this occupies far less space than the tanks needed to store it in liquid form. The volume of solid waste from a large reactor in twenty-five years of operation would fill only two large wardrobes. Yet disposal must now be even more carefully thought out; since the radioactive isotopes are more concentrated in this form, the radiation hazard is more serious and the material becomes very hot. Where can it go? One suggestion has been to dump it on the ocean floor in certain areas where, it is thought, it will eventually be sucked into the earth's interior. This would certainly happen but the time before the waste is effectively removed from all contact with the marine environment is still too long for safety.

A more feasible solution is to use abandoned salt mines as depositories for radioactive waste. Salt conducts heat better than most rocks and it is usually enclosed above and below by shale, an impervious rock which acts as a trap. Furthermore, it flows like a liquid under stress so that, should an earthquake occur, there would be no danger of the solid blocks of radioactive glass being shattered and dispersed.

A further method of disposal which has been considered is to bury the glass blocks in sealed stone vaults under deserts. In such an environment there would probably be little danger of escape of pollutants but in such areas it is difficult to have a clear picture of the small-scale structure and properties of the rocks involved. There would also be the need for a continuous guard to prevent the material falling into undesirable hands.

A more revolutionary suggestion is to dispose of solid waste at the bottom of very deep drill holes which can then be sealed. The radioactive heat will first melt the surrounding rocks, after which cooling will seal the disposal site more or less permanently. A severe problem at the moment is that of being certain enough of the small-scale structures of the rocks so far below ground level; without this knowledge there remains a nagging, though slight, possibility that undesirable chemical elements might find their way back into our immediate environment.

(5) Evidence shows that the cooling system of a nuclear power station situated beside a flowing river will return water to the river at temperatures of up to 100°F (38°C), rather higher than those associated with 'conventional' stations. This has caused some concern since 100°F is the optimum for the development of pathenogenic bacteria such as those which cause typhus. This temperature is also the optimum for the destruction of organisms known as *bacteriophages* ('bacteria-eaters'), a process which contains another health risk. The atomic energy industry has claimed that the temperature does not, in fact, rise above 81°F (28°C) as a result of their activities but this is an *average* which fails to take into account seasonal variations and annual periods when the power stations are switched off for maintenance work.[37]

A further problem when the water temperature rises far above normal is the appearance of blue algae in the water and on the banks. There is, again, a health risk which is all the more a source of concern since these algae are difficult to eradicate once established, and even after purification the water from the river may be unsafe to drink.

(6) The international sale of nuclear technology is a major source of concern to many apart from environmentalists and is a live political issue in a number of industrial nations with established

---

[37] K. Holl, 'Dangers due to the heating of river waters by atomic power stations', *Naturopa*, 20 1974, pp. 21–23.

## Getting the Picture − The World's Energy

nuclear industries. The amount of money involved is enormous. The contract won by France in 1976 to supply South Africa with two stations was worth £550 million.

The plutonium produced by the reactors has now given to a number of countries a supply of plutonium which could be used for making nuclear weapons. In 1976, when President Gerald Ford issued the annual report of the Arms Control and Disarmament Agency, he warned that by 1985 nearly forty countries would have enough plutonium to make bombs. These countries include at least twelve − Argentina, Brazil, Chile, Cuba, Egypt, Indonesia, Israel, Pakistan, South Africa, Spain, Turkey and Switzerland − which have not signed the Non-Proliferation Treaty; thus they have not bound themselves not to acquire the bomb and have not agreed to allow their nuclear installations to be inspected by the International Atomic Energy Agency. The US State Department has apparently conceded that material supplied to India was used in a nuclear test explosion in 1974.

There have been moves to tighten restrictions on the use of exported nuclear technology. Canada has cut back supplies of materials to two Indian nuclear power stations; the USA has attempted to impose severe limitations on the uses of materials to be supplied to other countries. The effectiveness of such moves remains to be seen. Whatever the ethics of the international trade, it seems likely that the pressures of economics will maintain this lucrative business.

## Prospects for the future

The world-wide demand for energy, coupled with real and contrived shortages of fuel and environmental deterioration, has already speeded the search for alternative energy sources. 'Natural' sources, such as solar energy, wind and tidal energy, and geothermal energy (that is, from hot rocks) are under active examination;[38] the other major development is that of nuclear fusion. It is probably accurate to say that the 'natural' sources can make important but relatively local contributions to the energy supply situation. For example, high-grade geothermal energy can be obtained only from areas of contemporary volcanic activity, as in Iceland and New Zealand; lower-grade energy is more widely

[38] See, for example, P. R. Ehrlich, A. H. Ehrlich and J. P. Holdren, *Ecoscience: Population, Resources, Environment* (Freeman, 1977), chapter 8.

available, but its potential contribution is limited.[39] Suitable rocks are found at depth under substantial areas of Britain, but exploration is yet at an early stage. Nuclear fusion, a process in which large amounts of energy are released by the fusing together of two light atoms, is fraught with technical problems and it is not possible to estimate how long it will yet take to harness this form of energy production process and make it economically viable.[40]

Meanwhile, energy demands, which have largely levelled out due to economic recession, will almost certainly start to rise again. This is not just because of the rising world population and our increasing material expectations but also because of industrialization; this process performs three functions. It provides jobs, it supplies our requirements and it enables poorer countries to begin to find their economic feet. Yet we have seen that the environmental hazards are a threat to man's well-being; expansion of energy consumption is being projected and planned for with the inherent assumption that science can take care of all these hazards. This is particularly critical in the case of nuclear fission. The assumption may or may not prove to be correct; the necessary precautionary and preventative measures could turn out to be extremely expensive; there will always be the danger of underestimating the environmental dangers because of economic and social pressures.

Whatever its source, most of the energy produced by human activity finds its way into the atmosphere, raising its temperature. At present this effect (*calcefaction*) is only very small but will increase in magnitude as consumption rises. Meteorologists cannot yet predict in detail the effects of such heating. If, as has been calculated, the temperature rises by up to 2°F in the next 100 years then melting of the polar ice caps and a rise in sea level would follow. It is not possible to state with any confidence what might happen to world climatic patterns. This is a critical question for a consideration of food supplies to a hungry and expanding population (chapter 5).

Thus we are left with a deep-seated paradox. On the one hand material expectations and the need for more jobs demand more

---

[39] J. D. Garnish, 'Geothermal Energy and the UK', *Atom*, 263, 1978, pp. 242–248.

[40] International Fusion Research Council, 'Status Report on Fusion', *Atom*, 260, 1978, pp. 150–158, gives a recent overview of the subject.

*Getting the Picture – The World's Energy*

industrialization and more energy; on the other hand, pressures on the environment will continue to increase, and there are some grounds for postulating strict controls on energy consumption. This is more than a scientific problem. Further development must await the discussion of some biblical perspectives in chapters 6 and 7.

# 4
# Getting the Picture – The World's Cities

The big city is essentially a modern phenomenon, as is the depopulation of the countryside which goes with it. This process of *urbanization* is considered here because of the poor quality of many aspects of urban living which seem to go hand in hand with the very growth of the city. On the one hand there are problems of the physical environment: city centres have growing numbers of poor aliens; housing in these areas suffers from decay due to age and lack of maintenance; jobs are migrating from city centres towards suburban areas; city-centre housing supply is no no way related to need or demand; public and private transport systems are inadequate; some large cities are on the verge of bankruptcy.[1]

There are problems of a social nature also. Professor Colin Buchanan has identified them as follows: the maintenance of law and order; lack of meaningful leisure activities; the extent of organization, control and bureaucracy; loneliness and poverty; the complicating factors of race, religion, ideology or history.[2] Some of these problems Professor Buchanan confessed himself to be unsure of because they are, by their very nature, not so easily open to scientific investigation.

There are two ways of tackling the problem of the urban environment. One is to seek to return to rural life; the other is to improve urban living. This chapter is more concerned with the latter, although in the long term, the former may prove extremely effective and pioneer groups are already experimenting with various kinds of low-technology rural lifestyles.[3] But even in the worst slums in which many of the inhabitants may be newly

---

[1] D. Netzer, *Economic and Urban Problems: Diagnoses and Prescriptions* (Basic Books, 1970).
[2] C. Buchanan, 'Living in Cities', in S. Verney (ed.), *People and Cities* (Collins, 1969), pp. 146–147.
[3] P. Rivers, *The Survivalists* (Eyre Methuen, 1975).

*Getting the Picture – The World's Cities*

arrived from the country, the majority are determined not to return whence they came.[4]

There are many possible definitions of a city, either geographical (dealing with size, population and density) or sociological (concerned with the activities and inter-relationships of the inhabitants) and any accurate definition must convey something of the complexity of its fabric. As a result, no two cities are the same; and in any discussion over-generalizations are inevitable. This chapter is, however, more concerned with the cities of the industrialized world than with those of the Third World. In the latter case, urban growth is often a response to pressures which often force people into the city; in the former it is more a matter of choice.[5]

## The emergence of the city

There have been big cities in the past. At the height of the power of the Roman Empire in about AD 150, Rome accommodated one million people; there were 750,000 in Alexandria, 600,000 in Seleucia and 250,000 each in Antioch and Carthage.

Archaeological investigations show that ancient cities were transient phenomena. Technological limitations meant that they were prone to destruction by fire, flood or famine; their societies were generally of conservative theocratic character which hindered effective responses to changing political and economic conditions.[6]

It was only during the Industrial Revolution that cities began to spring up in any number, and this was because of the transformation of the economic system which it brought about.[7] The factory replaced the cottage industry; the cheap labour force replaced the craftsmen. The cities grew around the factories and the depopulation of the countryside was accelerated by the poverty of rural life. These are the cities of today although their character has long since changed.

It is now necessary for us to examine some of the characteristics of the modern city, bearing in mind its complexity. The first characteristic is the continued growth of the city, due to the social

---

[4] For statistical data on this rather surprising fact see P. Wiltshire and R. Richter, *The Exploding Cities* (André Deutsch, 1975), p. 48.

[5] G. Breese, *Urbanisation in Newly-Developing Countries* (Prentice-Hall, 1966).

[6] See a series of articles under the general heading *The Earliest Cities* in K. Davis (ed.), *Cities: Their Origin, Growth and Human Impact* (Freeman, 1973).

[7] B. Ward, *The Home of Man* (Penguin, 1976).

outlook of the present age, which finds city life attractive for a variety of reasons.

## Motives for migration

The term 'migration' can be used to describe movements of people both *into* and *within* a city. One estimate puts the British suburban growth rate at 100,000 people per year, of whom 90% come from more central areas while only 10% are accounted for by rural depopulation.[8] There seem to be two reasons for migration, termed *social mobility* and *geographical mobility* respectively. The former includes those for whom a bigger and better house and a 'nicer' neighbourhood reflect success in their chosen career. The latter describes employees with a firm, usually large, where a promotional or lateral job change will often involve moving from one city to another. This mobility, which modern industrial strategy demands, is one of the main reasons for the continuing demand for outer-suburban housing estates.[9]

Statistically, movement from the countryside is relatively unimportant, but is important because of its effect on rural life. It may exacerbate the very pressures which cause this kind of migration in the first place.

*Rural life and urban migration*
For some, rural life is a constant battle. A report from the Low Pay Unit in 1975 highlighted the poverty of farm workers, perpetuated by, amongst other factors, the continuing demand for cheap food. The basic weekly wage on the farm was then £30–50 and average net earnings not much higher, at £38–50, 40% lower than the equivalent industrial figure; in the country there are relatively few job opportunities for wives. One-half of the farm workers interviewed by the Unit went without breakfast regularly; two-thirds bought their clothes from jumble sales; the families tended to go to bed early to save fuel; they had no holidays, no winter coats and no 'evenings out'.

The city has certain attractions which rural life cannot offer. In a study of rural-to-urban migration in north-east England, two groups of people were interviewed: of those who had already

---

[8] H. Lindh, *Migration in Britain* (NIESR unpublished manuscript, 1968).
[9] P. Hall et al., *The Containment of Urban England* (Allen & Unwin, 1973).

## Getting the Picture – The World's Cities

moved, nearly three-quarters gave employment as their main motive; exactly one-quarter cited marriage as the reason and the remainder mentioned children's education. Of those intending to move soon, 36% mentioned employment; the remainder were influenced by prospects of a better life in the city – shopping facilities, social amenities, transport, education and housing.[10]

This survey revealed that a disproportionately large number of those involved were young people; some were dissatisfied with income levels while others talked about the lack of promotion prospects and of the 'unfavourable social atmosphere' of country life. Women were migrating in larger numbers than men because of lack of job opportunities. The *general* conclusion of the survey was that the major cause was the low level of real incomes relative to living costs. It considered that the inconveniences of rural life would be more tolerable if higher real incomes and more personal mobility were assured.

The whole life of the rural community suffers because of migration, through a series of inter-related processes. The continuity of life in the community is broken, bringing a feeling of apathy and hopelessness which feeds back into the whole community. Then the vacant houses are bought by city people wanting a second home. Outwardly things may look the same but at the level of communal life the changes may be profound. The houses are occupied at weekends only; the new residents may make little or no contribution to village life or to the local economy. Their children go to school in the city during the week and so the local primary school may be jeopardized. The new source of demand for rural dwellings pushes their price far beyond the means of the farm worker, who may then find it necessary to commute from the nearest urban area. Local amenities may also dwindle and public transport services deteriorate. In the Shropshire village where my wife lived as a child, the railway station was closed during the Beeching era; but there were, at the time, several buses every day into the nearest town. Now the village is fighting to retain the single bus which runs *each week*.

---

[10] J. W. House, *Rural North-East England (Northumberland and Durham) 1951–61*. Report to the Development Commissioners. Papers on Migration and Mobility in North-East England, No. 1, January 1965.

## The way the city grows

Urban migration works only when certain basic amenities are made available, such as houses, shops, transport and schools. In asking how these are provided, the basic question is: How does the necessary land become available? A related question arises. Is this process of growth related to the total *needs* of the people of the city? Harvey Molotch believes that

> American cities are failures: they have not delivered the good life, and the way they continue to operate stops them from providing the amenities that the current state of technology is quite capable of providing . . . American cities do not work as human settlements – as integrated 'means of livelihood and ways of life' – because they were not meant to work.[11]

Molotch has outlined the way the city grows in a totally free-enterprise system and calls the process 'the growth machine'. The person with land to sell will tend to look for the highest price; price is not related so much to *need* as to *demand* and in the context of urban expansion the price levels created are sufficient to ensure that it will always be attractive to sell to urban developers. Some governments operate 'zoning' policies, related to an over-all development programme, but as Molotch has further pointed out, landowners can constitute a pressure group whose interests may conflict with the interests of others.[12] It was this kind of system operating in Britain in the nineteenth-century and the appalling slums which thus arose which gave birth to the concept of urban planning.

'Planning' began as a social movement, but today is a bureaucratic activity and a professional occupation. It can be defined as an intervention in the free-market system where that system is producing undesirable results. The concept of centralized planning or urban development gained acceptance during the first half of the present century, culminating in the publication of the 1940 Barlow Report and the 1947 Town and Country Planning Act. This Act led to the creation of planning authorities and the nationalization of development rights, still allowing private development

---

[11] H. Molotch, 'The Urban Growth Machine' in W. Murdoch (ed.), *Environment* (Sinauer, 1972).
[12] *Ibid.*

but taking away its incentives. The 1947 Act was also concerned about the need for urban containment, the apparently permanent imbalance in the economic development rates in different parts of Britain and the formulation of goals towards which planning should be directed.

This and subsequent legislation have failed to bring about the desired results and the reasons are outlined at great length by Peter Hall and others in their definitive work *The Containment of Urban England*. Just one is a conceptual one; the planners of the time envisaged a slow rate of growth and of change in society, whereas the past thirty years have seen very rapid change, especially in patterns of social mobility.[13]

## Characteristics of city life

The quality of city life is intimately connected with the growth of the city and the economic pressures which influence it. Certain characteristics arise from these influences; we may single out three of these – *geographical*, *transportational* and *philosophical*.

### Geographical

The division of the city outlined above can be viewed as a logical extension of capitalism.[14] Increasing competition for land forces up prices in city centres, where it is most profitable to concentrate shops, offices and entertainments. As a result, the centres become depopulated as people move to the suburbs, where houses are within the price-range of most middle-income families. The outwardly expanding, commerce-oriented city centre grows gradually outwards, encroaching upon the inner suburbs.

The inner areas of the cities then hold three categories of people – day 'visitors' (workers in shops and offices, and shoppers), evening 'visitors' in search of entertainment, and a core of residents. Some of the latter remain because they want to, others may be effectually 'trapped' by poverty. The housing stock tends to be old, with a low proportion of owner-occupiers, and much of it is in poor repair. Some 4 million people are living in poverty in the inner areas of Britain's cities, with the worst situations occurring in London, Birmingham and Liverpool.

[13] P. Hall *et al., op. cit.*
[14] B. Ward and R. Dubos, *Only One Earth* (Penguin, 1972), p. 147.

These inner areas often have disproportionately high immigrant populations and as well as the crime and poverty which seem to thrive here, racial tensions may also be acute. Tom Caulcott, secretary of the Association of Metropolitan Authorities, has said that the problems of inner-city areas are so great that a massive redistribution of the nation's financial resources is needed in order to deal effectively with them.

The outer suburban areas, including the satellite towns, may be at considerable distances from the city centre. Milton Keynes, for example, is 50 miles from the centre of London. Here the population density is lower since they are a product of the car age. The housing tends to be of better quality and younger; much of it is owner-occupied, so that it is in good repair. Suburban living also has its problems, however, and these will be considered later.

### Transportational

The two transportational characteristics of the city are *commuting* and the *weekend exodus*. Commuting refers to travelling between homes and places of work. Travelling times can be long, not only because of the distances involved (the London commuter belt extends outwards some 60 miles to places like Oxford, Cambridge, Northampton, Clacton and Brighton) but also because of congestion near city centres, where road systems may be the product of a previous car-free age.

Transportation is a major item in every city budget, especially where there are capital costs for new roads, motorways or railways. Commuting also raises the cost of public transport; the system has to carry large numbers for two relatively short periods every day, so that large amounts of capital equipment are idle for a large part of each day.

The reasons for the weekend exodus are less obvious but it probably reflects a desire to leave behind the pressures of the city. But this movement brings its own pressures since it may be directed towards a relatively small number of places, such as seaside resorts or local beauty spots. Congestion, crowds and noise can disrupt the very atmosphere being sought, enough often to raise antagonism amongst local residents.

### Philosophical

City life is characterized by high population density, a high level of organization (mainly external, through law enforcement, traffic

## Getting the Picture – The World's Cities

regulation, social welfare and other channels) and a high degree of social mobility. In this sense urban life is a completely new phenomenon. What seems to happen is that human relationships become more impersonal, transitory and utilitarian.

In the past, there have been ages of permissiveness (such as the eighteenth century) and of strict morality (as in Cromwellian and Victorian Britain), each of which was a reaction against the other. The present climate in Britain is undoubtedly highly permissive and it seems likely that urbanization and television have helped to create the conditions under which the permissive society can flourish. Each person, with large numbers of superficial contacts, is freed from outlooks which are closely controlled in a tightly knit community; the individual is precisely that and can believe what he wishes, deriving information, ideas and opinions not so much from personal contact as from the mass media.

Another cause of the lack of meaningful relationships is lack of participation in urban planning.[15] As mentioned earlier, what was firstly a social movement is now a professional and bureaucratic activity. Thus people coming to the city for the first time, while possibly attracted by the very anonymity promised, may find themselves forced into a state of personal withdrawal when so much of city life is beyond their control.

The consequences of this changing philosophical outlook are a source of disagreement among sociologists. Some foresee a complete breakdown of relationships, while others see the emergence of stable new kinds of lifestyle. Thus Wilensky and Lebeaux can write:

> We find not a madly mobile, rootless mass, disintegrating for want of intimate ties, but an almost bucolic contentment with the narrow circle of kin and close friends, with the typical urbanite spending most of his time with the family at home, caring for the children, watching television, maintaining the home, reading. Occasionally, he makes forays into the world outside, mainly to visit relatives, sometimes to demonstrate his attachment to a formal organisation or two.[16]

---

[15] R. Hauser, 'The Invisible Community', in S. Verney (ed.), *op. cit.*, pp. 172–189.
[16] H. L. Wilensky and C. N. Lebeaux, *Industrial Society and Social Welfare* (Free Press, 1965), p. 129.

*Bent World*

While these writers may hold such views it is by no means certain, from the quotation, whether they consider the kind of 'stability' they envisage to be satisfactory.

## The problems of the urban environment

There is, firstly, a set of *physical resource problems* including large-scale waste-disposal, water supply, air and water pollution and the supply of raw materials for construction. Some aspects of these problems have been outlined in chapters 2 and 3, so that references to them here will be minimal.

The second set of problems may be termed *physical overload problems*, under which heading may be included noise, congestion, environmental stress and disease.

*Noise*

> Of all forms of pollution, noise is perhaps the most inescapable for the urban dweller. It pursues him into the privacy of his home, tails him on the street and quite often is an accompaniment of his labour. We do not begin to know the price we pay in impaired hearing, in enervation, in aggravated hostilities and nervous tension. But scientists report that, when animals are made to listen to noise, 'they grow sullen, unresponsive, erratic or violent'. May not the same be true of us?[17]

This statement puts succinctly the possible impact of noise. The city is full of noise. Much of it is 'organizational', generated by traffic, construction, road repairs and industrial activity. The trend is towards bigger and more powerful machines, with gradually increasing noise levels.

Little is known about the long-term effects of noise except on the hearing system. At 90 decibels (slightly louder than a food blender and almost as loud as heavy traffic close by) it is temporarily impaired and takes time to recover; the subject may experience a buzzing noise inside the head. When exposure to 90 decibels is for longer periods, recovery may be incomplete and progressive deafness then sets in. Other changes are more difficult to understand: the heart rhythm is affected and breathing may become

---

[17] B. Ward and R. Dubos, *op. cit.*, p. 148.

## Getting the Picture – The World's Cities

irregular; there are changes in the composition of blood and body fluids; the eyes are affected – the pupils dilate and colour receptivity can be impaired.[18] It has also been suggested that noise might be connected with peptic ulcers and hypertension (high blood pressure) but the evidence is circumstantial only.[19]

### Congestion

Modern man is a creature who enjoys personal independence; for this and other reasons the car is highly desirable. A person can travel to work alone and be independent of the idiosyncrasies of public transport, many of which he has actually helped to make.

In most cities the motorist is travelling through a road system made for the horse and the tram and for a much smaller volume of vehicles than exists now. The main traffic flow is into the city centre in the morning and out in the evening. The road may be choked on one side and virtually empty on the other. This, combined with the long distances travelled by many commuters, cancels the benefits of the shorter working week.

### Disease and environmental stress

The city is not the most healthy of environments in which to live. There are two reasons, which give rise to two sets of medical 'conditions' which are now very characteristic of urban living.

The first reason is *atmospheric pollution*, due to car exhaust, domestic coal and oil heating exhaust and industrial activity. The air becomes charged with minute dust particles, with sulphur dioxide, oxide gases of carbon and other substances. The relationship between dirty air and conditions like lung cancer and bronchitis is well established. The effects of lead from car exhaust are less certain; it has been found, for example, that the lead levels in the blood streams of residents near the Gravelley Hill motorway interchange ('Spaghetti Junction') in Birmingham are significantly higher than normal. These levels are still a long way below those associated with acute lead poisoning; the *long-term* effects are not known but there is a possible link with some types of mental retardation.[20]

Other injurious components of the air include asbestos (used in

---

[18] *Health Hazards in the Human Environment* (World Health Organization, 1972).
[19] P. R. and A. H. Ehrlich, *Population, Resources and Environment* (Freeman, 1972).
[20] H. V. Warren, 'Environmental Lead, a Survey of its Possible Physiological Significance', *Journal of the Biosociological Society*, 6, 1974, pp. 223–238.

construction) whose minute particles are inhaled and lodge in the lungs, resulting in various respiratory conditions including cancer. High levels of carbon monoxide can lead to a deterioration of visual and manual functions and a fall-off of intellectual ability. Persons with heart disease are especially at risk since absorption of carbon monoxide into the blood stream cuts the amount of oxygen the circulatory system can absorb.[21]

The second reason why the city is an unhealthy place is the pressures typical of city life. We will consider some of these pressures more fully in a later section, but there is medical evidence to link physical and mental illness with *stress*. Among various factors related to the incidence of tuberculosis, for example, are migration from rural to urban life and stress during the two-year period before the visible manifestation of the disease. Certain kinds of stomach ulcers are due to stomach acidity promoted by stress,[22] and coronary disease has similarly been linked with stress:

> Although there is a great deal yet to be resolved concerning heart disease . . . there is no question but that social styles of living influence in various ways risks of developing coronary heart disease.[23]

There is also a definite relationship between physical health and the level of affluence within a given area of a city. Paul and Anne Ehrlich, writing of American cities, have summed up the situation in terms which apply elsewhere also:

> The environmental deterioration . . . is most obvious to the poor who live in them . . . their concern is 'ghetto ecology', including the wildlife of their homes – rats, mice and cockroaches. Air pollution reaches its highest levels in city centres; here also there are most likely to be inadequate sewage disposal and solid waste disposal systems. Heat in winter is often insufficient, space is at a premium . . . food often inadequate, medical care poor at best . . . his environmental syndrome is reflected in

---

[21] P. C. Wolf, 'Carbon Monoxide – Measurement and Monitoring in Urban Air', *Environmental Science and Technology*, 5, 1971, pp. 212–215.
[22] D. Mechanic, *Medical Sociology* (Collier-Macmillan, 1968), pp. 274–275.
[23] *Ibid.*, p. 278.

higher mortalities among the poor, especially infant and child mortalities, than for the general population.[24]

So far, nothing has been said about *behavioural problems* in cities, where crime may make it unsafe to venture out alone after dark and even in daylight. In the next section we will explore the relationship between the structure of the city, the attitudes and stresses which are thereby generated and the responses which people make.

## Behavioural problems in the city

### *The administration of the city*

We have already considered city growth and the forces which drive it. Yet little is known about how man's built-up and natural environments interact to meet or frustrate his real needs; beyond bare biological facts there are less well-formulated ideas of what these needs are.[25]

We can identify a number of features of the city which in some way induce responses from its inhabitants. These features can be set out as follows.

(1) There is the sheer size of cities, which are bigger than ever and more numerous. In the USA they become large enough to merge into each other and the term 'megalopolis' has been coined. An increasing proportion of people live in these cities; some people cope relatively well but for others the adjustment is difficult, even impossible. New styles of personal relationships mean that some are inevitably lonely because they do not 'fit in'.

(2) City dwellers, it has been claimed, tend to be pragmatic in outlook.[26] This contributes to the continuing decline in church attendance in industrialized countries.[27] But it is too simple to equate pragmatism with the city environment. It is probably more accurate to see pragmatism as working-class in origin and thus able to flourish in the city. Certainly the type of social relationships encouraged by the very nature of the city is an influential factor;

[24] P. R. and A. H. Ehrlich, *op. cit.*, p. 179.

[25] B. Ward and R. Dubos, *op. cit.*, p. 143.

[26] *On The Other Side*, The Report of the Evangelical Alliance Commission on Evangelism (Scripture Union, 1968), pp. 33–37.

[27] A. McIntyre, *Secularization and Moral Change* (Oxford University Press, 1967).

another is the predominantly materialist intellectual climate. A third suggestion is the new affluence which enables the family unit to be self-dependent.[28]

(3) Cities are increasingly under the control of a remote bureaucracy. As a city grows, efficient adminstration becomes increasingly difficult, involving more organization, more officials, more expense, more rules, more 'interference'. Transport, for example, needs more planning in the large city than in the smaller one. There is a greater volume of traffic, necessitating more parking meters, more traffic wardens, more signs, signals and restrictions. In one sense this is inevitable but at the same time restricts freedom. Bureaucracy is therefore an activity which has acquired a derogatory meaning.

The situation is made worse by the role of the urban planner. It has already been mentioned that the Town and Country Planning Act of 1947 envisaged the right of the planner to shape the physical life of the urban community. Nearly thirty years later W. Harvey Cox wrote of 'insensitivity and self-righteousness on the part of those in power in urban government'.[29]

There are feelings that those in control are not always *competent* to be so. It has been suggested, for example, that they are 'without real education, whose only skills have been in "administrative" manipulation'.[30] Cox quotes the famous American urban sociologist Herbert Gans, who pointed out some forty years ago that 'planning has been typically the approach of the middle-class reformer'.[31] These references to specific situations may be symptomatic of a wider weakness in the regulation of the urban environment.

There are proven cases of corruption of the urban bureaucratic machine; wrongly but predictably we come to look on all bureaucracy in this light. The remoteness of a typical city administration is a wider problem which promotes alienation. It is often experienced in trying to contact the 'right' person. Thus David Ley writes:

> We can understand such responses as the North Philadelphia woman who, served by nine separate city welfare departments

---

[28] R. Sennett, *The Uses of Disorder* (Penguin, 1970).
[29] W. H. Cox, *Cities: The Public Dimension* (Penguin, 1976), p. 9.
[30] L. de Paor, 'An Ignorant Middle Class,' *Irish Times*, December 12, 1975.
[31] W. H. Cox, *op. cit.*, p. 163.

and their rapidly changing staff, threatened to shoot the next social worker who came to her door.[32]

There appear to be various kinds of response to the nature of this bureaucracy. One is apathy (known technically as a *disengagement strategy*[33]), and judging by polling in local elections this would seem to be the dominant response; others may sell out and move (*flight strategy*); only a small minority take up *resistance strategies* which include a wide range of activities from civil disobedience to the setting up of residents' associations.

(4) Because of its structure, the city is a place where stress situations may be most serious. A stress situation has been defined as 'a situation which causes people to react as if they had been threatened'.[34] Some of them are strongly associated with urban living. These include rapid cultural change, intense competition, frustration, failure and isolation. Even promotion or the chance of a move to a better house can be a stress situation. Promotion may encourage a person to doubt his ability to cope with the new job; moving to a new home entails the severance and remaking of secure social networks.[35]

(5) Another factor important here is poverty, particularly close to city centres, which often contain high proportions of ethnic minorities or people of low abilities. Of particular importance is not the *absolute* level of poverty but that *relative to* the general level of prosperity and the difficulty of improving matters. While some may resign themselves to the situation, others, particularly the young, may react against it strongly or even violently.

## *Behaviour breakdown in the city*

Crime is increasing at a rapid rate and there is evidence that crime rates are highest in the largest cities.[36] As well as apparently motiveless violence, petty offences such as burglary and vandalism show the sharpest increases. Newspaper reports claim that in central London 50% of boys have committed a theft by the age of twelve.

---

[32] D. Ley, 'The City and Good and Evil: Reflections on Christian and Marxist Interpretations', *Antipode*, 6, 1974.
[33] *Ibid.*
[34] D. Mechanic, *op. cit.*, p. 279.
[35] *Ibid.*, p. 299.
[36] 'The Ecologist', *Blueprint for Survival* (Penguin, 1972), pp. 111f.

It is often stated that civilization breaks down where there is deprivation. This is true, but certain qualifications are needed. Firstly, massive urban reconstruction has meant that overcrowding is far less common than a few decades ago.[37] Secondly, crime is a hallmark of the city *as a whole* rather than certain areas of it. The overcrowding theory, thirdly, is based on experiments on rats and cannot necessarily be applied directly to human communities; some scientists believe that crowding simply encourages pre-existing tendencies.

Given the existence of poor city centre areas, however, it would be wrong to exaggerate the situation. As already mentioned, some of their residents remain out of choice. They are often characterized by a sense of community which is not found elsewhere.[38]

At the same time, the high price of urban land poses a huge problem for any urban corporation contemplating reconstruction schemes. The high-rise flat complex, once seen as the ultimate answer, is now generally acknowledged to be a failure. It *can* work where people are able to adapt, but the results are sometimes disastrous:

> They give many of their occupants acute uneasiness. Some people arrange their furniture so as to avoid any view of the vertiguous plunge from their thirtieth-floor window. For mothers with small children they present insuperable problems of play and supervision. The elevators become places of dirt and danger. The wholesale bulldozing of little streets and houses to make way for them destroys delicate networks of service and friendship which are simply not recreated between different floors in new apartment houses.[39]

Because of the high price of urban land, there is often little space for amenities. What are the young people to do? These are often the same ones whose backgrounds have already set them at an intellectual and emotional disadvantage. High unemployment exacerbates the problem. Some spend their money on alcohol and many drift into crime, a trend acknowledged in the 1974 report of the Inspector of Constabulary of England:

---

[37] M. Young and P. Willmott, *Family and Kinship in East London* (Penguin, 1957), pp. 23–24.
[38] B. Ward and R. Dubos, *op. cit.*, p. 145.
[39] *Ibid.*, p. 151.

These crimes appear mainly to be the work of groups of children and young persons whose motives are as obscure as their objectives. In the long term the cure for such ills must be to a considerable extent lie in education and constructive use of leisure time . . . this may reflect changing attitudes, lowered standards, the spread of urbanisation, inflation, unemployment and increased opportunities to commit crime.

It is not only crime which can be classed as a symptom of behaviour breakdown. Illegitimacy, alcoholism, mental disorders of various kinds, suicide and violence within the family are all problems which make newspaper headlines although constantly with us. It is suggested here that deprivation is a contributory factor, although the links may be quite complex.

Urban population growth takes place mainly in outer suburban areas. Many of those purchasing the houses made available are young couples, often buying their first home. Why do people buy houses in particular areas in the first place? Motives may vary considerably but the economic factor is very important. People are also concerned with factors such as the quality of the house they buy, the local facilities, distance to work and ease of access. In general, however, the decision to buy is made without reference to the people of the area in question.

As a result, various studies of suburban life have emphasized its problems and Herbert Gans summarizes these studies as pointing to:

. . . too much socializing, useless hyperactivity in voluntary associations, competition and conspicuous consumption. Many of these evils are thought to be the result of boredom produced by the demographic homogeneity of suburban life . . . a matriarchy and child-dominated society, resulting from the lack of job opportunities within the average suburb and the husband's consequent absence from the home during the child's waking hours. . . . The suburban way of life is a product of excessive social mobility and is so full of stress that it increases psychosomatic illness, divorce, alcoholism, suicide attempts, and mental illness generally.[40]

[40] H. J. Gans, 'Effects of the Move from City to Suburb' in L. J. Duhl (ed.), *The Urban Condition: People and Policy in the Metropolis* (Basic Books, 1963), p. 184.

The researches of Gans and others indicate that this is an exaggeration. There is less boredom than in the city centre; people moving out into suburbia say they feel better and more satisfied with life; there is no forced social conformity; the crime and 'problem' rates are lower.

Certain problems do exist, although on a smaller scale than that sometimes predicted.[41] They include:

(1) The social isolation felt by some teenagers and by a minority of adults who do not 'fit in'. This is especially true on a new housing estate, which may lack amenities and entertainment.

(2) The financial problems of those buying their own house, usually in the early years, where even a few extra and unexpected commitments can 'tip the scales'.

(3) A minority complain of feeling cut off from their old friends and surroundings. This is especially true of those who may have no private transport.

Nevertheless, the aspirations to home ownership which help to perpetuate the outward growth of suburbia *do* lead to a kind of homogeneity in suburban society that will actively reject certain kinds of intrusion. The desire for privacy and preservation of the closeness of the family unit noted by Gans and others can show itself in total insensitivity to the needs of others.

Thus there have been protests over council purchases of private houses, over the siting of mental institutions, over itinerant encampments and at efforts to settle itinerants in permanent housing. Fear of falling property values seems to be the commonest motive.

It would be wrong to pick out the inner areas or the suburbs as the breeding grounds for the social malaise of the cities. This malaise seems to be related to the city as a whole and the aim of this chapter has been to explore the phenomenon. Technology can help to improve the physical environment of the city. But the cost involved, especially at a time of financial stringency, is enormous, and the technological problem ceases then to be purely technological. Man has many other dimensions to his existence, however, some of which have been neglected in the development of the urban environment, and the social problems which have arisen can be seen as a response to this. The problems which now have to be faced in the cities are great and encompass a wide variety of factors,

---

[41] R. E. Gordon, K. K. Gordon and M. Gunther, *The Split-Level Trap* (Dell, 1962).

*Getting the Picture – The World's Cities*

all related to the nature of man himself – scientific and technological, economic, sociological, spiritual. Realistic responses and solutions must take all these factors into account.

# 5
# Getting the Picture – The World's Food

The statistics of hunger and the emaciated children of the Oxfam posters have long been with us. Relief agencies and missionary societies do an invaluable job in relieving extreme poverty and hunger and in teaching self-sufficiency techniques to the victims.

Because of the enormous scale of the problem of malnutrition, these efforts only scratch the surface. One estimate is that, of the two thirds of the world's population living in the Third World, 20% are *undernourished* (not enough calories per day) and 60% are *malnourished* (serious dietary deficiencies in one or more essential nutrients, usually protein).[1] To this total can be added the poorer people of many rich countries.

One estimate of deaths due to malnutrition puts the total at 10–20 millions per year.[2] Professor Parpia of the UN Food and Agriculture Organization has warned that *per capita* food supplies are not keeping pace with the rise in population in the Third World.[3] On the basis of past trends, food production in 1985 will be 84% above 1962 levels while the internal demand of Third World countries will have risen by 142%; food imports will need to rise in value from $3,000 million in 1962 to $40,000 million by 1985. Unless there is to be a catastrophic breakdown, food production in the future will have to increase far faster than in the past.[4]

The world food situation constitutes a vast and complicated problem with no easy answers. It threatens the security of food supplies in the western world, so that the response of the rich

---

[1] P. R. and A. H. Ehrlich, *Population, Resources and Environment* (Freeman, 1972), p. 82.

[2] Other estimates are lower. Starvation is the primary cause; there are various *secondary* causes, usually organic or infectious diseases.

[3] Willwood Lecture at the Institute of Food Science and Technology, University College, Dublin on 19 May, 1976. Reported in the *Irish Times*, 20 May 1976.

[4] P. R. and A. H. Ehrlich, *op. cit.*, pp. 109ff.

countries to the plight of the poor contains a measure of 'enlightened self-interest':

> While we share our plenty with them, their plight raises spectres of a possible destiny for us. Both to help them and to protect our own future, we are introspective about our present well-being and look ahead to what the obvious wants of others portend.[5]

We will look first of all at the nature of malnutrition in the Third World, then at the prospects for world food production. Various environmental threats will then be considered and it will become apparent that the well-fed West is involved on a number of levels.

## Food needs and supplies

There are four types of food which supply ingredients necessary for physical and mental well-being. They are as follows:
  (1) Milk and dairy products, which supply proteins, vitamins, calcium and other substances.
  (2) Meat, fish and poultry. These supply proteins, fat and vitamins. In terms of cost, agricultural and environmental demands they are enormously expensive.
  (3) Grains and starchy vegetables. These supply carbohydrate, vitamins and some proteins. Rice, corn and potatoes predominate in the diet of most poorer people, whose protein is derived almost entirely from them.
  (4) Fruit and vegetables. These provide carbohydrates, vitamins and minerals. They are uncommon except in rich countries due to cost and faulty food distribution systems (fruit rots very quickly).

The five kinds of ingredient mentioned, namely carbohydrate, proteins, fat, vitamins and minerals, are essential to good health. *Fat* and *carbohydrates* supply the energy for life processes and activity. If not consumed in sufficient quantity, the body starts to 'burn' its own protein in order to obtain necessary energy. Average calorie requirements are 2,300–2,700 per day, whereas daily consumption in rich countries is equivalent to 3,000–3,200 per day, pointing to over-consumption.

[5] S. B. Hendricks, 'Food from the Land', in *Resources and Man* (Freeman, 1969).

*Fat* is also used by the body as a structural constituent of cell membranes, nerve sheaths and supports for internal organs. *Proteins* are essential for growth and development, healing and recuperation from disease; *vitamins* perform a variety of functions in the regulation of life processes. *Minerals*, required generally in minute amounts, fulfil a wide range of needs; they include calcium, phosphorus, iron, sulphur, salt, potassium, iodine, zinc, magnesium, manganese, chromium, copper, molybdenum and selenium.

To state that people die of starvation is an oversimplification; disease is often the agent which deals the killer blow upon bodies too weak to fight back. Thus it is possible to define a starvation death as:

> Any death that would not have occurred if the individual had been properly nourished . . . regardless of the ultimate agent.[6]

Immediate causes include dysentery, measles and pneumonia but the killers are often diseases which arise as a direct result of dietary deficiency.

### The deficiency diseases

There is a large number of such diseases, of which the following are the main ones.

(1) *Marasmus*, which kills children less than one year old. It results from an over-all dietary deficiency, often combined with early weaning and is especially common in the shanty towns around big cities. The child is deprived of essential milk, and the new staple diet of corn, sago or arrowroot gruel is simply inadequate.

(2) *Kwashiorkor* is the result of protein starvation where children are given starch and sugar as the main diet. In its mildest form it causes retardation of physical growth, loss of appetite and pot belly; when more severe, legs and feet become swollen and the digestive system breaks down. By this stage even the best medical care may be unable to prevent death.

(3) *Vitamin A deficiency* (accompanied by protein deficiency) causes blindness through drying up of the eye membranes and softening of the cornea.

(4) *Beriberi* is a disease especially prevalent in south-east Asia,

---

[6] P. R. and A. H. Ehrlich, *op. cit.*, p. 87.

due to deficiency in a vitamin named *thiamine*, which is found mainly in the husks of rice grains. These husks are removed during the milling process (huskless rice has better keeping quality and the husks can be used as stock feed). The occurrence of beriberi is aggravated by the introduction of community rice mills and by the traditional poverty-induced restricted diets given to pregnant and nursing women. Mothers and babies are thus particularly vulnerable. This attitude to the 'weaker' members of the family is widespread. Professor Cepede of the Institut National Agronomique in Paris, recalls a conversation with an African colleague:

> I realise now, he said, why I am taller and stronger than my brothers and sisters. I was my grandfather's favourite and ate sitting on his lap. The dishes which were offered to him first, as was only proper, contained meat. The other children, who ate with the women, found there was no meat when the food came to them last.[7]

(7) *Iron-deficiency anaemia* is due to lack of protein, vitamin $B_{12}$ or folic acid. In Third World countries anaemia is a particular problem among young women, since during pregnancy the foetus absorbs large amounts of iron from the mother's blood. If this is not replenished, low fertility, premature births and still-births result.

(6) *Rickets and osteomalacia* (bone softening) are due to lack of calcium and vitamin D. Once again, pregnant and nursing women are especially at risk. Vitamin D is synthesized in the skin by sunlight and the rickets outbreaks during the Industrial Revolution were due to the poor living and working conditions of ordinary people which deprived them of sunlight.[8]

## Malnutrition in the Third World

There are also long-term consequences of food shortages in Third World countries. Even short-term under-nourishment makes permanent marks on a human life. It leads to dwarfing and delayed maturity, especially when the victims are children. Protein deficiency is especially critical. In children of three, the brain has

---

[7] M. Cepede, 'Sociology and Nutrition', *Science and Public Policy*, 3, 1976, pp. 114–119.

[8] W. Loomis, 'Rickets', in K. Davis (ed.), *Cities: Their Origin, Growth and Impact* (Freeman, 1973).

reached 80% of its final size if a good supply of dietary protein is available. Otherwise mental development can be seriously and permanently impaired. Adults suffer for long periods after even temporary episodes of deprivation. A study has been made of ex-Nazi prisoners who, even twenty years later, exhibited reduced brain size, and mental and emotional disorders.[9]

Apart from the suffering and waste of human life involved, there are two other consequences of malnutrition which need to be mentioned. One concerns the somewhat colonial but apparently persistent attitude of some towards the 'lazy natives'. It certainly seems to be true that in some areas of Asia and Africa the indigeneous population seems lethargic and incapable of heavy physical work, but this is due to the effects of prolonged undernourishment, which saps physical strength and will alike and impairs mental ability.

The other consequence concerns the ability of Third World countries to help themselves. Ideally, they need drastic national plans involving sustained hard work and sacrifice for the sake of the common good. But is this feasible and does it ask too much of the hungry? Governments cannot make demands upon their subject beyond their capabilities:

> All proposals to increase food production in the undeveloped countries are inevitably attached to elaborate plans for economic development. Can they possibly achieve either with a weakened, malnourished populace and with the prospects of physical and mental impairment in a large portion of the coming generation?[10]

The present age is unique in the apparent permanence and scale involved in famine. Moreover, the situation in the Third World is deteriorating, while *per capita* food consumption is rising in the rich countries as populations level off. The critical factors for the poor countries are, first, the continuing rise in population, and secondly, the economic pressures forcing them to export much needed foodstuffs for the sake of their balance of payments. In 1970 Argentina, Brazil, Uruguay and Paraguay exported 2 billion pounds of beef to Western Europe and Japan, where 'the morbid craving for meat now far exceeds recognised nutritional

---

[9] P. R. and A. H. Ehrlich, *op. cit.*, p. 93. As the authors point out, it is not clear in this case as to the relative importance of starvation and severe emotional stress.
[10] *Ibid.*, p. 93.

## Getting the Picture – The World's Food

requirements'.[11] Some of the protein reserves available in the Third World are fed to livestock, used for fertilizer or sold abroad for foreign exchange.[12] The importing countries often use them for feeding pets, livestock and poultry.

Why do the countries of the Third World continue to be so short of food? This is a complicated issue involving agricultural science, economics, transportation, politics, climate and sociology. It is possible to state in very simple terms, however, that it is a matter of *corruption, poverty* and *ignorance*. The extent of corruption is difficult to judge; mention of it may be embarrassing but the following statement by India's Minister for Foreign Affairs and Labour in 1968 is significant:

> It is amazing how otherwise excellent studies on development problems in Asia and Africa avoid any serious reference to the fact of corruption. It is not that the writers do not know of its existence, but its relevance to the question of political stability and rapid economic development appears not to have been fully appreciated. It may also be that a serious probing of the subject has been avoided lest it should offend the sensibilities of Asians.[13]

The Indian national state of emergency in 1975 was called in order to tackle such corruption and other major issues.

### Poverty in the Third World

The Third World countries are often called 'underdeveloped' because of their poverty. People are undernourished because they cannot afford the food prices. Poverty seems to be connected with high birth rates,[14] so that it is a struggle even to maintain existing nutritional levels, let alone improve them. The cost of the agricultural development needed is enormous and often severely taxes available economic resources especially now in view of large balance of payment deficits since the raising of world oil prices in the 1970s.

The creation of new agricultural land, for example, is a most costly operation. Seven pilot schemes in the early 1970s had a

---

[11] M. Cepede, *op. cit.*, p. 116.
[12] L. R. Brown and E. P. Eckholm, 'Man, Food and Environment', in W. Murdoch (ed.), *op. cit.*, p. 85.
[13] G. Myrdal, *The Challenge of World Poverty* (Pantheon, 1970), p. 229.
[14] P. R. and A. H. Ehrlich, *op. cit.*, p. 114.

median per-acre cost of $218. Assuming that the average cost of clearing one acre of land for agricultural development is now $500 and that present levels of productivity can be maintained on the newly acquired soil, the annual world cost would be $35 billion simply to bring into production enough land to feed the increase in population at existing nutritional levels. The cost is due to the complexity of opening up new land for agriculture. This involves the provision of irrigation,[15] technical expertise, the creation of capital and labour for both farming and associated construction projects (mainly roads), machinery, land clearance, drainage improvement, social development (houses, schools, services) and human resettlement. Thus the creation of new agricultural land, while urgently needed, must be seen in economic perspective. In many parts of the world agricultural land is being lost due to urbanization and environmental threats brought about by land mismanagement. In lowland areas such as West Pakistan, the process known as *salinization* is rendering large areas of topsoil useless due to the upward movement of salt.[16]

The poverty of the Third World is such as to limit the effectiveness of fertilizer use. To make substantial increases in crop yields requires the addition of large amounts of fertilizers, especially when the soil is poor. Further, there are limits to the increase in production yields which can be achieved in this way. Experience has shown that fertilizer application does not necessarily lead to increased yields, probably due to ignorance on the part of local farmers; their lack of education is due to personal and national poverty and to the lack of agricultural technicians.[17] Poverty acts in other ways too; many cannot afford to buy fertilizer; the capital cost of a home-based fertilizer industry is such as to keep supplies low and expensive; the mechanized methods which utilize it best are beyond the meagre incomes of most.

## Ignorance in the Third World

The word 'ignorance' here means, simply, lack of knowledge, reinforced by cultural background. As already stated, one of the

---

[15] This is because in most cases land is already in use where rainfall is adequate.

[16] *Ibid.*, p. 116. They estimate that, in Pakistan, one acre of land is lost every five minutes.

[17] The Netherlands has 133 technicians and research workers per 100,000 people; India has 1.2. Research results are internationally circulated; implementation is the problem.

barriers to the efficient use of fertilizers is the lack of local knowledge. Paul and Anne Ehrlich quote a report by the Intensive Agriculture District Programme in Gujarat, India, which states that

> ... on the whole the performance of adjoining districts which have similar climate but did not enjoy the relative preference of input supply (*i.e.* fertilizer) was as good as, if not better than, the programme district.... A particularly disheartening feature is that the farm production plans, as yet, do not carry any educative value and have largely failed to convince farmers to use improved practices in their proper combinations.[18]

This report also suggests that there are cultural barriers to progress. The poorest and hungriest people, tragically, are the most resistant to change. They often cling to past customs, seeing them as their only security. Not only does this resistance to progress slow down the improvements potentially possible through the use of fertilizer; new strains of seed which, when harvested, need different cooking treatment or have a different taste, may need long periods before acceptance. It would certainly be wrong to condemn such inflexibility, due to malnutrition rather than causing it.[19]

## *The Green Revolution*

This is the popular name for the agricultural transformation made possible by the combined use of fertilizer and 'miracle grains', that is, high-yield and/or high-protein crops. For some, the Green Revolution is the answer to the world's food problem; for others the optimism is heavily qualified:

> The new genetic hybrids are not intended to solve the world food problem, but only to give us time to devise more permanent and realistic solutions.[20]

While food production has been significantly raised by the advent of these new grains, there are reservations about the ability to sustain the advance.

---

[18] *Ibid.*, p. 120.
[19] For other examples see M. Cepede, *art. cit.*
[20] 'The Ecologist', *Blueprint for Survival* (Penguin, 1972), p. 22.

(1) The increasing quantities of pesticides and fertilizers required constitute an environmental threat (see later section).

(2) The grains were rushed into production in areas with the most favourable climates, such as Pakistan, so that the limited field testing casts doubt upon their ability to grow under less favourable conditions.

(3) The lack of testing also means that resistance to pests and disease is an uncertain factor, especially where strains develop which are resistant to present methods of control and extermination.

(4) Genetic variability is being eroded as new grains are being developed and old ones discarded. The consequence of this could be the limitation of choices in the future.

(5) Higher levels of labour input are needed. This is costly and expense is sometimes reduced by covert or overt subsidization of mechanization.

## Food from the sea

In the past there have been optimistic forecasts that fish and other sea foods could supply all the food man needs. In 1950 the catch realized was 21 million metric tons and this increased annually to over 60 million tons in 1968. 1969 saw a 2% decline. Overfishing is now a problem in some areas and one recent estimate of the potential catch is 70 million tons per year by 1980.[21] In real terms, this would constitute a *per capita* decline as the world's population continues to rise.

Over-exploitation usually occurs when short-term economic considerations are allowed to override long-term environmental ones. The history of the whale industry is a case in point.[22] In 1933 nearly 29,000 whales were caught, yielding altogether 2.6 million barrels of whale oil; by 1966 the figures were 58,000 whales but only 1.5 million barrels; as larger and more profitable species were hunted to extinction, successively smaller and less productive varieties became the targets of the factory ships. The role of scientific advisers in this matter is an interesting one. It is suggested that the ship-owners ignored their advice,[23] while another account has concluded that the advice given was couched in terms of moral

---

[21] P. R. and A. H. Ehrlich, *op. cit.*, p. 127.
[22] *Ibid.*, pp. 127–131.
[23] *Ibid.*, pp. 127–131.

imperatives rather than giving a realistic assessment of the alternatives; in this case the method of presentation was the cause of its rejection.[24]

Exploitation has often been carried too far by the use of fine-mesh nets which catch not only the mature fish but also the immature which would, if left, breed and thus provide a better catch at a later date. It was in this way that the British east-coast herring stock was destroyed in 1969.

There are other stocks available which are yet little exploited. These cannot substantially raise the annual world catch but can help to maintain it as pressures on other stocks are eased. Close attention is being paid, however, to krill, shrimp and plankton, which are the organisms on which higher forms of marine life feed. To remove them would be to threaten the extinction of the fish as well. The behaviour of the world fishing industry over the past twenty years has provoked the following caustic comment:

> Judging from the fishing industry's behaviour towards the sea, one might conclude that if they were to go into the chicken-farming business they would plan to eat up all the feed, all the eggs, all the chicks, and all the chickens simultaneously, while burning down the henhouses to keep themselves warm.[25]

## Other sources of food

Novel sources of food are being developed with the aid of modern technology. Petroleum is being used for culturing single-celled protein-rich organisms (SCPs) which may provide a substitute for fishmeal as an animal feed; in theory, the fishmeal could then go to human consumption.

New kinds of protein-enriched wheat grains are being developed. Nourishing foods are being prepared by adding oilseed protein concentrate to cereals; examples include Incaparina (corn, cottonseed meal, vitamins A and B), and CSM (corn, soya, milk). At the moment there is some doubt about the economic prospects and the social acceptability of these foods. It is more than ten years since Incaparina was first marketed in Central America, but sales remain low. Although observers are puzzled the texture and bland taste may be the reason for its lack of popularity.[26] If this is correct

---

[24] J. Gulland, 'The Harvest of the Sea', in W. Murdoch (ed.), *op. cit.*, chapter 7.
[25] P. R. and A. H. Ehrlich, *op. cit.*, p. 134.
[26] *Ibid.*, p. 135.

it is a further example of resistance even to change in the best interests of those concerned.

## Food storage and distribution

Significant improvement could be effected in Third World countries through better storage and handling facilities. Attack by marauding animals may result in 10% or more of annual yields of grain being lost. Apart from control of these pests in the field, losses in storage are relatively easily eliminated by building rat-proof barns and by spraying the grain with carefully controlled amounts of selected pesticides.

Other reductions in wastage are possible through investment in more efficient transport; especially in hot climates, certain types of food go bad very quickly. As with so many other facets of improving agricultural production, cost is a controlling factor.

# The pollution problem

One of the greatest threats to world food supplies in the future is that of pollution, of which two types must be considered. There is agricultural pollution due to insecticides and pesticides, and industrial pollution, which affects agriculture in a number of different ways.

## Agricultural pollution

Huge amounts of pesticide and fertilizer are needed to push up crop production. The 34% increase in unit area yields during the period 1951–1966 necessitated the use of 146% more pesticide and 300% more fertilizer.

The use of pesticides disrupts the ecosystem, which functions by means of complex inter-reactions between numerous different types of plant and animal organisms.[27] Once pesticides start to kill off not only a pest but other components of the ecosystem as well, it is thought that its stability is put at risk. More and more pesticide is then required to protect it artificially from other pests.

The use of pesticide may also be double-edged in that not only the pest but also its enemies are killed, and the plant being 'protected' is in fact deprived of all its *natural* protection and is in

[27] E. Odum, 'The Strategy of Ecosystem Development', *Science*, 164, 1969, pp. 262–270.

greater danger of attack than at first. Some pesticides kill not only insects but also animals; others reduce their fertility. Thus the ecological imbalance may extend far beyond the decimation of one particular troublesome insect.[28]

Some recent studies have challenged the correlation between stability and complexity of ecosystems. Mathematical models developed by Robert M. Mays, for example, suggest that the opposite might be the case, and has pointed out that the complexity-stability equation 'has tended to become part of the folk wisdom of ecology'.[29] His work further suggests that the ecosystems in tropical and subtropical areas are more prone to instability than those of temperate climates.[30] It is these areas of the world where the food supplies are most critical and Mays' studies at least indicate that much work remains to be done before there is a really thorough understanding of the way in which ecosystems achieve stability.

Another pollution problem is linked with lack of 'biodegradability'; that is, pesticides break down very slowly. With some types, even the breakdown products are harmful. Thus, if DDT is sprayed on to a field, half of it might still be present in the soil ten years later; other lesser-known examples are even more stable. As a result of their longevity these substances become concentrated into the plants which grow in the polluted soil and thence may find their way into the human body. The concentrations measured in human tissue (20 parts per million and less) sound insignificant but are in fact high enough to cause physiological damage.

Effects of DDT on animals are already well documented,[31] but little except circumstantial evidence is available concerning effects on human beings. Certainly no immediate and drastic effects are known but there is little knowledge of long-term effects. Yet there are warning signs. DDT and its breakdown products have been found to be abnormally high in the fat of hospital patients who have died from such causes as brain softening, cerebral haemorrhage, hypertension and certain types of cancer.[32]

Another effect of its widespread use is the reduction of photo-

[28] R. Carson, *Silent Spring* (Hamish Hamilton, 1962).
[29] R. M. May, *Theoretical Ecology* (Blackwell, 1976), p. 158.
[30] *Ibid.*, p. 162.
[31] P. R. and A. H. Ehrlich, *op. cit.*, pp. 208ff.
[32] *Ibid.*, pp. 160ff.

synthetic activity by phytoplankton in the oceans. Reduction in photosynthesis means a reduction in food supply to other marine organisms, threatening an eventual reduction in the quantity of life the oceans could support and yield up for food.

Although a large amount of potential damage has already been done, use of DDT is now being severely restricted. More than this is needed because there are other pesticides of a similar nature, less widely known but equally dangerous, which are still widely used; at least one of the substances which has replaced DDT, namely methyl parathion, is even more toxic.[33]

Pollution is also a serious side-effect of the heavy use of certain types of fertilizer. Nitrogen is usually present in the soil in the form of organic humus and nitrate fertilizer is used to replace the amounts extracted during intensive agriculture. Only a small proportion of the nitrogen in the nitrate finds its way into the complex chemical processes by which plants grow. The remainder stays in the soil; being soluble in water, rain flushes it out into rivers, lakes and seas. Increasing nitrate levels are now being monitored not only in surface waters but also in the atmosphere and falling rain. The major effect of this nitrate is, however, a process known as *eutrophication*, which is exemplified by Lake Erie; the nitrate has contributed in large measure to the rapid growth of huge quantities of algae which, after their death, decay under the influence of bacteria. This decay process consumes all the available oxygen in the water, causing the death of most other forms of life present in the lake water.

In the case of Lake Erie the process has been compounded by the large amounts of phosphate fertilizer. The lake bottom is now covered with a layer 20–125 feet thick of rotted algal material rich in nitrogen and phosphorus, covered with a skin of insoluble iron compounds. This skin might eventually redissolve since its solubility increases in the absence of oxygen dissolved in the water. If this were to happen, more nitrate and phosphate would be released into the lake waters, making the eutrophication problem very much worse.[34]

---

[33] R. L. Rudd, 'Pesticides', in W. Murdoch (ed.), *op.cit.*, p. 336.
[34] W. T. Edmondson, 'Fresh Water Pollution', *ibid.*, pp. 266–267; see also P. R. and A. H. Ehrlich, *op.cit.*, pp. 230–233.

*Industrial pollution*

Industrial activity has introduced into the earth's surface waters large quantities of a wide variety of potentially toxic materials (chapter 2).

Mercury flushed into the oceans seems to have a similar effect to DDT. Around one Japanese bay where mercury-bearing compounds were flushed into the waters as an industrial by-product, a large number of people died of a strange 'disease' whose origins took many years to uncover.[35] The long-term effects of other metals building up in marine waters – lead, cadmium, zinc and chromium, for example, are not yet known, but the possibility exists of concentration into marine organisms and thence into human tissue.

Another threat to marine life is through oil pollution. One estimate puts the weight of annual spillage (accidental and deliberate) at 2.1 million tons per year.[36] Fortunately, oil is fairly volatile and most of it therefore evaporates. Small quantities of some components persist in the water, however. Of these, one group is relatively quickly broken down by bacterial action and oxidation, although it is toxic to animals and birds before chemical breakdown can take place. Another group is carcinogenic (cancer-producing) and extremely long-lasting. The effects on marine life could be very serious in the long term; the other potential hazard is the effect of these components if subsequently absorbed in human tissues. Such is the volume of oil spilt and the world-wide distribution of spillage incidents, together with the world's ocean current system, that no area of water remains uncontaminated.

## Physical disruption of the ecosystem

Apart from the threats caused by pollution, there are others, this time physically induced, due simply to the way in which the process of agriculturalization has been carried out.

One such threat to the stability of the ecosystem is the building of dams, which often turn out to be rather double-edged in their contribution to food production. The Aswan Dam in Egypt is an example in which the ecological consequences of building a dam

---

[35] E. D. Goldberg and K. K. Bertine, 'Marine Pollution', in W. Murdoch (ed.), *op.cit.*, p. 281.

[36] *Ibid.*, p. 288.

became apparent only after it was complete. Three major changes took place in the area:

(1) A drastic fall took place in the sardine catch at the eastern end of the Mediterranean Sea, where the River Nile drains into it. The reason for this is not fully understood although the connection seems clear.

(2) The change in the aquatic environment in the Aswan area has resulted in huge numbers of aquatic snails of a kind which carries a disease called *schistosomiasis*, infecting the liver and other organs.

(3) The downstream region has become covered in silt and its fertility is gradually decreasing.[37]

Thus even beneficial activity like dam construction can make inroads into acreage of good agricultural land, as well as bringing unwelcome side-effects. Another human activity with similar results is deforestation, which persists because of the pressure for more land and the demands of the paper industry. When the trees and plants are removed the soil is rapidly eroded by wind and running water. The removal of the soil can also result in loss of clear water downstream, the silting up of rivers and dams, and other effects. The net result is that the deforested area may be turned into wasteland.

It has been estimated that 50% of India's farmland is inadequately protected from erosion and in many places the complete removal of the topsoil is threatened. Elsewhere, deforestation and overgrazing have allowed the advance of desert sands blown by the wind. Parts of the Sahara desert have come into being in just this way and it is continuing its southward advance; similarly, the Thar Desert of western India was jungle two millennia ago. Inaccessible forest fell from 44% to 21% of total land area between 1882 and 1952 while the proportion of wasteland rose from 9% to 23%.[38]

Enough has been said to demonstrate threats to the adequacy of future world food supplies. While rising world human population is a key factor, environmental threats are also serious. The current battle is not to *improve* nutrition levels throughout the world but to *maintain* them. Many of the great advances which have been made in the field of agriculture are seen by experts as no more than

---

[37] P. R. and A. H. Ehrlich, *op.cit.*, p. 409.
[38] *Ibid.*, p. 202.

*Getting the Picture – The World's Food*

'holding operations', pending the advent of some more permanent solution.

## The world's climate

An already serious situation is further compounded by the prospects for future food production if there should be adverse changes in weather patterns. Droughts such as that of the Sahel region have brought starvation in their path. Until relatively recently it was assumed that climates are stable and predictable, but during 1975 and 1976 larger variations than usual were recorded world-wide, of which the two long, hot summers in Britain are just one example. Although climatic records do not go back far enough to be certain, it is now thought possible that the last fifteen to twenty years have been abnormally stable and that we may now be on the verge of a more typical phase in which larger variations will be experienced. What will be the effect of this on agricultural production?

Climatologists believe that, underneath these variations, the world's air temperature is slowly decreasing, possibly as the prelude to another glacial period. Rates of crop growth are extremely sensitive to temperature. In addition, there are some signs of a changing pattern of world rainfall distribution, with more now falling in the predominantly oceanic southern hemisphere and less in the northern, where most of the land surface is situated. The effects of water shortages have already been experienced in Europe during the summers of 1975 and 1976.

The reasons for these fluctuations are not yet clear but it is possible that atmospheric pollution is one contributory factor. Climates can be modified by *calcefaction* (the release of excess heat into the atmosphere, a side-effect of increasing world energy consumption), gaseous and particulate pollutants. The nature of climate and its variations is not yet well enough understood to predict firmly what the effects of these pollutants will definitely be.

A second hazard to climatic patterns is the possibility of a huge volcanic eruption somewhere in the world. The explosive eruptions of Mount Tambora in 1815 and Krakatoa in 1883 released into the atmosphere huge amounts of volcanic rock dust which caused world-wide atmospheric pollution. One result of both events was a marked fall in world-wide air temperatures and a fall-off in food production. While this kind of happening was obviously less critical in an age when population was much lower than at present, food prices rocketed upwards in response to shortages. The possible consequences of such an event happening in the modern world are serious.[39]

The atmosphere is also suffering depletion of the ozone content of its upper regions, due to the effects of supersonic transport flying at great heights and to the release of aerosol propellants into the air from household sprays. A fleet of 500 supersonic aircraft each flying for eight hours per day could reduce the ozone content by up to 20% by 1990.[40] The effect of this would be to allow a significantly increased amount of ultraviolet radiation to reach the earth's surface, against which we are protected by the ozone-rich layer, and such radiation could do great harm to a wide range of biological organisms.[41]

In summary, it is possible to say that various factors have combined to create the present critical situation. One is the rapid rise in the number of mouths which must be fed; this is, in itself, tied up with the issue of poverty in a complex way so that poverty actually drives population growth. Then there is the economic system which ensures the prosperity of the rich nations at the expense of the Third World. Another problem is the environmental disturbances caused by man's agricultural activities, allied to the pollution contribution from an increasingly industrialized resource-consuming world.

It has already been hinted that people in the West eat too much, and reference has already been made to our 'morbid craving' for meat. It is not just that we eat too much, but that the kind of food we like ties up other agricultural resources such as grain, which feeds our animals instead of hungry human mouths. To produce 1lb of beef, 7lbs of grain are needed. In the USA the *per capita* consumption of beef has risen from 55 lbs a year in 1940 to 116 lbs in 1972; for poultry the equivalent rise is from 18 to 51 lbs. There are similar trends in all the rich countries. Obesity has reached

---

[39] The 1980 eruptions of Mount St Helens volcano, USA, have recently added huge amounts of dust to the atmosphere, and scientists expect this material to have some effects on weather patterns from 1981.

[40] P. Fabian, 'How Critical is the Present-Day Threat to the Atmospheric Ozone Layer?', *Universitas*, 18, 1976, pp. 53–59.

[41] G. J. F. McDonald, 'Man, Weather and Climate', in W. Murdoch (ed.), *op.cit.*, p. 390.

## Getting the Picture – The World's Food

almost epidemic proportions and Britain spends upwards of £65 million a year on slimming foods, twice as much as is donated to relief agencies. As with other aspects of the environmental crisis there are no easy answers but at least one source of the trouble lies in the accustomed lifestyle of the western world.

# 6
# Getting it Wrong – The Effect of Sin on the Environment

This chapter seeks to explore the relationship between materialism and the environmental crisis. It would be superficial to make a simple equation between the two; rather they are both related to the sin-affected relationship between man and his physical world. What is our attitude towards nature meant to be? The creation narrative of Genesis helps us to answer this question and it also indicates how present wrong relationships between man and nature are to be explained.

## Materialism

Before examining the biblical material, however, it is necessary to examine carefully what is meant by 'materialism'. The strict definition is 'the philosophical doctrine that the only existents are material substances'.[1] But the term has acquired a much wider meaning which must necessarily be more loosely defined – 'the pursuit of wealth, luxury and sensual indulgence'.[2] The two definitions have much in common but are by no means identical.

In this second and broader idea of materialism we are no longer dealing with a carefully considered philosophical position but a behaviour system into which people simply drift. This may happen for a variety of reasons; there is the attraction of owning material wealth or aspiring to it and there is also the pressure to conform to the behaviour and standards of others.

It is in this sense that modern industrial society is materialistic. One of the dominant motives behind the direction in which this society moves is that of achieving higher standards of living. In a growth economy this is positively desirable; more jobs are created;

---

[1] R. W. Hepburn, 'Materialism', in A. Richardson (ed.), *A Dictionary of Christian Theology* (SCM, 1969), p. 209.
[2] *Ibid.*, p. 209.

## Getting it Wrong – The Effect of Sin on the Environment

but when demand falls, the result is unemployment. One of the principal tasks of trade unions is to negotiate higher wage rates for their members; politicians usually promise to increase living standards. A public statement of recent times is typical:

> We ought to have an automatic position of threshold agreements for cost of living, automatic increases in wages for increases in productivity and all that we would need would be topping-up processes every so often to make sure the earnings constituted a real increase.[3]

This is not to condemn the desire for a higher standard of living. Especially important in this respect is the plight of the poor. In this category are included the millions in the Third World who do not have enough to eat and those living in areas of deprivation even in the richest of nations.

In earlier years the trade-union movement was the champion of oppressed workers who lived in conditions of almost unbelievable poverty and deprivation. But most people in industrialized countries live in conditions of considerable affluence today. When the Board of Trade cost-of-living index was first published in 1900 it made no provision for the cost of butter or electricity: neither was considered essential.[4] Today the norm is home ownership,[5] a continental holiday, colour television, at least one car per family and numerous household gadgets.

Information from British shops during Christmas periods indicates that, in spite of widespread protestations of lack of spending power due to inflation, *per capita* expenditure runs into hundreds of pounds and increases annually. Nor is there any widespread lack of money for the January sales. It is, in general, no longer true that we need a higher standard of living to lift us from oppressive poverty.

There is nothing intrinsically wrong with hoping for a higher living standard, rather the opposite. The way the quest has been pursued has, however, put its continuance in danger. In the short

---

[3] Joe Gormley, President of the National Union of Miners, addressing the 1974 annual Union Conference, quoted in the *Daily Mail*, July, 1974.

[4] R. H. Fuller and B. K. Rice, *Christianity and the Affluent Society* (Hodder, 1966), p. 65.

[5] The Irish Republic, considered the poor partner in the EEC, has the highest proportion of home ownership of any country in the Community.

term, economic considerations restrict the possibility of further rises; in the longer term, the outlook is uncertain because of the possible environmental consequences of increasing consumption. We may have to forget about increasing affluence in the future.

*Prospects of increasing affluence*
Our motives for a higher standard of living are basically selfish rather than being based on a clear appreciation of the source of physical well-being. More money and more possessions often seem to be considered ours by right, while others are overlooked:

> The scriptural warnings about the corruption of wealth are coming home to the rich world today, not only in its hardness of heart and selfishness and its concentration on material values but also in its spiritual blindness to the claims of the hungry and underdeveloped peoples.[6]

The environmental side-effects of this quest are now clear but there are others. There are, firstly, economic side-effects. One major school of economic thought holds that our wealth is at the expense of increasing demands upon the world's finite resources, forcing prices upwards. The present inflationary spiral began at a time when all the major western economies were in 'boom' periods,[7] suggesting that inflation is due primarily to those with the greatest spending power; the effects, however, are greatest upon the economically weaker nations.

A second side-effect is that of the changes taking place in society. Prosperity often seems to go hand-in-hand with personal and social disorder:

> The things which are flourishing amidst our prosperity are venereal disease, mental disorder, bad debts, juvenile delinquency, drug addiction, strikes, bankruptcy, suicide and crime. And these 'signs of the times' are world-wide. We seldom love our present possessions. We must have more. We adore the things we do not own and look down on them as a source of happiness.

---

[6] F. R. Barry, *Christian Ethics and Secular Society* (Hodder, 1966), p. 270.
[7] C. Elliott, *Inflation and the Compromised Church* (Christian Journals Ltd, 1975), pp. 11–12.

## Getting it Wrong – The Effect of Sin on the Environment

Almost everyone is affected by this point of view. Most of us accept without question the idea that if only we owned things which we do not have, we should be much happier and more content.[8]

Yet, as F. R. Barry has pointed out, the economic system which has so transformed the standard of living in rich countries cannot be brought to a standstill without inviting disaster. Employment and stability depend upon an industrially oriented framework based on the manufacture and marketing of consumer goods; to create more jobs necessitates creating new demands:

It has become an unquestionable dogma that production is an end in itself. More and yet more must be produced, irrespective of the value of the product, in order to stop the machinery from stopping. This process cannot go on without the creation of artificial needs and a vast organisation to create them. Millions of people are being exposed to a subtly-directed suggestion that their primary aim is to keep up with the Joneses, that they will be social failures or even sub-status or doing something morally wrong if they do not acquire the latest gadget.[9]

When we consider the selfish kind of materialism which pervades the affluent society, we must avoid simply equating it with our economic system. If this system turns out to be disastrously inadequate to cope indefinitely with the increasing consumptive pressures upon it, it is the fault of the society which has allowed it to continue because of preoccupation with short-term personal gain. If economic growth has to decelerate or even cease, the barriers of selfishness must be overcome. Yet it is the thesis of many that it is the system which is wrong. If this were the case, it is astonishing that so little progress has been made over the years to put things right. Yet this kind of thinking persists, and Dennis Munby has assessed it as follows:

It is so easy to argue that because the modern world has seen a vulgarisation of taste, the wasteful destruction of social tissue in the emergence of a proletariat, the decline in Christian morals

[8] R. H. Fuller and B. K. Rice, *op. cit.*, p. 66.
[9] F. R. Barry, *op. cit.*, p. 269.

and the emergence of shallow this-worldly interpretations of human destiny – that *therefore* all these things are invariably linked with economic progress.[10]

Human pursuit of economic growth has been a selfish one which, because of the spin-offs, now puts the whole process in jeopardy through environmental and other threats. The problem lies within man himself. It is natural that Christians should think this way but one of the features of recent environmental writing has been the widespread expression that this is so. Similarly, problems within industry are moral ones which must be recognized as such before they can be succesfully tackled.[11]

Materialism as we see it is a result of the insecurity which pervades human existence and which stems from man's estrangement from God. Few people would, however, admit to conscious feelings of insecurity although most probably experience transitory moods of vague and indefinable unease. We may be seeing here the brief emergence of a subconscious awareness of things as they really are. It can be argued that the insecurity thus registered is a sort of sixth-sense warning signal.[12]

To understand how this insecurity has come about we must return to the opening chapters of Genesis in order to compare physical life before and after the fall. We will look first at some of the implications of the divine image in man and then at the effect of sin upon his relationship with God and with his environment.

## Man in the image of God

> Then God said, 'Let us make man in our image, after our likeness; and let them have dominion over . . . all the earth' (Genesis 1:26).

The issue of what it is in man's make-up which constitutes the divine image has occupied the minds of theologians for centuries and differing conclusions have been reached.[13]

From the days of Philo this likeness has been described in terms

---

[10] D. Munby, *God and the Rich Society* (Oxford University Press, 1961), p. 59.

[11] H. F. R. Catherwood, *The Christian Citizen* (Hodder, 1969), p. 67.

[12] Allied to this is the German *Angst* (anxiety). See E. Brunner, *The Christian Doctrine of Creation and Redemption* (Lutterworth, 1952), p. 128.

[13] For a summary see C. Westermann, *Creation* (SPCK, 1971), pp. 55–60.

## Getting it Wrong – The Effect of Sin on the Environment

of man's religious-moral life; Augustine, for example, mentioned powers of soul, memory and intellect and the capacity for love. Calvin, in his commentary on Genesis, made a similar point:

> The chief seat of the Divine image was in (man's) heart and mind, where it was evident.[14]

Karl Barth believed it necessary to think of the divine image in terms of the creation event itself, so that man's whole personal existence is an act of God's grace. Later, Claus Westermann wrote along similar lines:

> What God has decided to create must stand in a relationship to Him. The creation of man in God's image is directed to something happening between God and man.[15]

Emil Brunner refers, more specifically, to man's freedom and responsibility,[16] and Hugh Montefiore to 'freewill and moral sensibility'.[17] Derek Kidner also makes the point that the divine image is meant to enable God and man to communicate:

> Spiritual likeness . . . can be present only where God and man are in fellowship.[18]

Thus, considering the divine image in terms of man's totality is consistent with the creation narrative, while the idea of fellowship is true to the context of the whole self-revelation of God in Scripture. This vital relationship is emphasized in a slightly different way in Genesis 2:7:

> Then the Lord God formed man of dust from the ground and breathed into his nostrils the breath of life; and man became a living being.

---

[14] J. Calvin, *Genesis* (Banner of Truth, 1975), p. 95.

[15] C. Westermann, *op. cit.*, p. 56.

[16] E. Brunner, *op. cit.*, p. 57.

[17] H. Montefiore, *Can Man Survive?* (Collins, 1970), p. 60; *cf.* the same author, '(Man) alone of all creation can make a free and conscious response to God's creative word', *Man and Nature* (Collins, 1975), p. 45.

[18] F. D. Kidner, *Genesis* (IVP, 1967), p. 51.

This picture of man being formed from the earth itself recurs in the Old Testament (*e.g.* Job 4:19; 10:8; Psalm 90:3; 103:14; 104:29; 146:4; Isaiah 29:16). It is possible to see here a reference to God's skill (Psalm 139:14–16) and sovereignty (Isaiah 19:16; Jeremiah 18:4), but more than this, the verb *breathed* seems to allude to a warmly personal act in which self-giving was involved (*cf.* John 3:16; 20:22; Romans 5:8; 8:32; 1 John 4:9–10).[19]

When God made man in his own image, therefore, he bestowed on us some of his own characteristics, and it was not until this happened that man became alive (Genesis 2:7b):

> Man is capable of knowing God and incapable of true happiness without knowing Him. Man is made for the contemplation of Him in whose image he is made; all his perceptions and all his actions should work together to feed that contemplation or should flow from it as acts of love and worship. So living in the vision and love of God, man will become conformed to what he knows and loves and his whole being will become a 'reasonable, holy and lively sacrifice to God'.[20]

From this fellowship comes a deep understanding of the relationship between man and his physical world; both were created by God. Theological writing has often tended to view the God-man relationship without reference to the physical world, and one result of the environmental debate has been a new awareness of scriptural perspectives on this relationship. We are simply regaining a lost perspective; some early eucharistic prayers contained long thanksgivings for the whole created order and for man's place within it.[21] It is necessary to examine this man-world relationship, in order to understand more fully the consequence for nature of the fall of man.

## Man in his environment

And let them have dominion . . . over all the earth (Genesis 1:26).

---

[19] *Ibid.*, p. 60.
[20] H. A. Hodges, *The Pattern of Atonement* (SCM, 1955), p. 18.
[21] H. Montefiore, *Man and Nature*, p. 45.

Be fruitful and multiply, and fill the earth and subdue it (Genesis 1:28).

To environmentalists such as Lynn White and Ian McHarg, it is the outworking of such teaching that is largely responsible for the present trouble in the environment. To be fair to White, however, he is not necessarily criticizing the Genesis commission but rather the interpretation which, he feels, has been placed upon it.

The Genesis commission *can* be taken as seeing nature as of no inherent worth; its only function is then to satisfy man's material appetite. Confirmation for this view *could* be taken from the sense of the Hebrew *rādā* (subdue) which means literally to tread or trample, as in a wine press.

The creation narrative in its entirety suggests that this would be the wrong way to understand man's dominion over nature. There are three points to be made here.

(1) The commission comes directly after the statement about the divine image in man and must be understood in terms of it.[22] Without that image, therefore, he is not capable of exercising his dominion properly.

(2) It is difficult to see any biblical justification for an arrogant attitude towards nature, whose goodness is repeatedly pronounced in Genesis 1.

(3) Zimmerli has pointed out that in Psalm 8 there is a sense of wonder and awe as the psalmist thanks God for man's exalted place in the physical world.[23]

The Genesis narrative has other important implications for the present day. Rowland Moss, commenting on 'fill the earth . . .' sees in it the prescription of a range of human activity and the imposition of a limit:

> The expansion in number and the extent of migration should be limited by the resources of the home areas of the groups concerned.[24]

Another significant phrase is in Genesis 2:15, 'The Lord God

---

[22] W. Zimmerli, *The Old Testament and the World* (SPCK, 1976), p. 40.
[23] *Ibid.*, p. 41.
[24] R. Moss, 'Responsibility in the Use of Nature', *Christian Graduate*, 28, 1975, pp. 69ff.

took the man and put him in the garden of Eden to till it and keep it' (New English Bible translates *keep* as *care for*), which prompts Gerhard von Rad to comment:

> He is to work it and preserve it from all damage, a destiny that contrasts decidedly with the commonly accepted fantastic ideas of 'Paradise'.[25]

The theme of *caring for* creation occurs in other parts of the Old Testament; man is to care for the land (Leviticus 25:1–5), to treat domesticated animals properly (Deuteronomy 25:4) and respect wild life (Deuteronomy 22:6).

Dominion (Genesis 1:26) is also used in the Old Testament to describe the rule of a king over his subjects (Psalm 72:8; 110:2). It is not a matter simply of position and privilege but also of responsibility for the maintenance of righteousness (Isaiah 11:1–4; Jeremiah 33:15) and the observance of God's laws (2 Kings 23:2; *cf.* 2 Chronicles 17:7ff.; Judges 17:6). A similar concept must apply to man's dominion over nature:

> As lord of his realm, the king is responsible not only for the realm; he is the one who bears and mediates blessings for the realm entrusted to him. Man would fail in his royal office of dominion over the earth were he to exploit the world's resources to the detriment of the land, plant life, animals, rivers and seas. Only now, when there is a direct threat to the fertility of the land, the purity of the air, and to the state of the water, has there been awakened the long-delayed horror at the lethal consequences of the sweeping progress of the age of technology. Only now are some beginning to learn through the mistakes which show that something has gone wrong in the process.[26]

The story of the fall shows how badly things have gone wrong. Not only is man's relationship with God disturbed but also that with his environment; the words of Emil Brunner set the scene for what follows:

---

[25] G. von Rad, *Genesis* (SCM 1961), p. 78.
[26] C. Westermann, *op. cit.*, p. 15. *Cf.* H. Montefiore (ed.), *Man and Nature*, pp. 31–33; J. S. Hurst, 'Theology and Conservation', *Theology*, lxxv, 1972, pp. 197–205.

A civilisation and culture which has severed its connection with God, and thinks more of its achievement than of persons, necessarily becomes inhuman. It loses its true centre, and thus disintegrates into sectional spheres and sectional interests, each of which comes into conflict with the others, and tries to develop itself at the cost of the rest. True civilisation and true culture can only develop where the cultural creation and activity is directed and ordered from a centre which transcends culture. A culture or civilisation which is indifferent to morals and religion is bound to degenerate. Religion and morality however, are identical, where the God of Holy Love is known as the foundation of all being, and His will as the norm of all morality; that is, where man knows himself to have been created by God for love, and for communion with the God of love, in faith in Jesus Christ.

Upon this foundation alone, also, will man use his mastery of Nature aright; only thus will he be preserved from a selfish, arrogant exploitation of Nature – which is a perversion of his powers. Man is not called to an absolute, arbitrary mastery of Nature, but to a mastery of Nature which remains under the order of the Creator, and therefore honours and loves the created universe as God's creation.[27]

## The nature of man's disobedience

Genesis 3:1–7 portrays in a masterly way the severing of the ideal relationship between God and man. The serpent begins by asking a question which distorts what God commanded and obliquely casts doubt and scepticism on God's wisdom and authority:

Did God say, 'You shall not eat of any tree of the Garden'? . . . . . You will not die (verse 4).

It may be significant that the moral test comes in terms of man's relationship with nature;[28] certainly his moral responsibility is implied, and with it the moral significance of his relationship with the physical world. When the serpent says 'You will not die' the challenge is out in the open; the words are in flat contradiction of

[27] E. Brunner, *op. cit.*, p. 68.
[28] F. D. Kidner, *op. cit.*, p. 54.

God's warning in 2:16–17. Subsequent events show that physical death did not immediately ensue (3:7,22) but verses 22ff. suggest that death means here the end of life in the garden of Eden.

The serpent's statement in verse 4, however, is an invitation which sounds so appealing but which involves man's loyalty and ambition in a radical reorientation. There appears to be the possibility of being equal with God himself (*cf.* verse 22) and thus independent of him:

> The more that man is able to distinguish himself from the rest of creation, the more he becomes conscious of himself as subject, as an 'I', to whom the whole world is object, the more does he tend to confuse himself with God, to confuse his spirit with the spirit of God, and to regard his reason as divine reason.[29]

At that point the woman loses the battle with the serpent; she looks on the tree in a new light and decides that, independently of God, she can acquire moral, material and aesthetic enrichment.[30] Once the deed is done it is too late; there can be no return to the prior state because the tree is that of the knowledge of good and evil. *Knowledge* is used today in the sphere of intellect; in the biblical usage *to know* contains the idea of active involvement (*e.g.* sexual intercourse; Genesis 4:1). Here, the woman *knows* evil when she tastes of the tree; she becomes a participant in it, and knows too late that she can never be like God. The changes which follow from the act are therefore permanent.

The result is also seen in the woman's reaction and that of the man when he had tasted also. Shame ensues ('and they knew that they were naked') rather than the eagerly expected advancement. Von Rad speaks of this shame as:

> ... the most elementary emotion of a guilty feeling at the deepest root of human existence, the sign of a breach that reaches to the lowest level of our physical being.[31]

At another level, the woman's mistake was in listening to something *created* instead of to the Creator; it has been so ever since.

---

[29] E. Brunner, *op. cit.*, p. 54.
[30] F. D. Kidner, *op. cit.*, p. 68.
[31] G. von Rad, *op. cit.*, p. 88.

Already man has effected his own separation from God, and the idea is reinforced in the nature of the original prohibition (2:16–17), for death is then certain. The precise meaning of 'good and evil' – whether moral or sexual or aesthetic – is of secondary importance here; what stands out is the possibility of whole-hearted obedience to God and life therein (John 3:36). The tree represents the alternative – apparently attractive but ultimately disappointing – 'to be self-made, wresting one's values from the created world in defiance of the Creator'.[32] Materialism in its widest sense has now appeared.

## Man's new relationship with God

Genesis 3:8–13 makes a stark contrast with what has gone before. The relationship with God has changed, radically and tragically. In the garden of Eden this is seen in the way Adam reacts when God comes looking for him; he hides and is afraid. He even tries to blame God ('the woman *whom thou gavest* to be with me, she gave me fruit of the tree, and I ate'). Man starts to run away from himself as he really is, in insisting upon his independence. This point is important in the environmental debate; the problems cannot be properly discussed nor correct solutions found so long as we imagine that science and technology alone are to blame.

Man has changed. He may still possess something of the image of God (Genesis 9:6; James 3:9) but what is now lacking is sufficient to make the separation from God effective (Isaiah 59:1–2; Proverbs 15:29; Habakkuk 1:14; Colossians 1:21; Hebrews 1:13). It is not just that God's commands and ideals are inconsistent with what man thinks his requirements are; the problem is much deeper – it is no longer possible for fallen man to comprehend the wisdom of those commands. Thus his whole understanding of the physical world is wrong; and Paul writes:

> Claiming to be wise, they became fools, and exchanged the glory of the immortal God for images resembling mortal man or birds or animals or reptiles (Romans 1:22).

He refers elsewhere to man's darkened understanding (Ephesians 4:16) and John implies the same when he employs his favourite

---

[32] F. D. Kidner, *op. cit.*, p. 91.

metaphor of light and darkness. This is seen in various ways; many city children do not know where milk comes from (some have never seen the countryside); thalidomide caused untold human suffering; tower blocks still do. Modern urban life highlights the problem that, apart from basic biological necessities, we do not know what man's needs really are:

> It is commonly said that man cannot control the industrial juggernaut he has created, and we have daily evidences of how powerful forces that were once under human control seem now to have acquired a momentum of their own and to be dragging us along whether we like it or not. How could it be otherwise, if man no longer has any clear belief about who he is, or any vision of the direction in which he wants society to develop? Unfortunately man will use his powerful new weapons, industry and agriculture, to do violence to the world of nature, if he does not know what his relationship to that natural world should be.[33]

As a result the world is pervaded by many false and unrealistic ideas about man's needs.

> False beliefs and false systems of belief become established as an inseparable part of our cultural inheritance, false aims and perverted institutions propagate themselves through history. Within the individual soul the intellect is darkened, the imagination inflamed, the will perverted and subdued to the passions. Man lives as the ruin of what he should have been.[34]

Our material prosperity, so often seen as an end in itself and the cure for all ills, helps to blind us to the real situation; God is there and we are separated from him. Yet the ultimate consequences of the present trend in lifestyles could be disastrous. The seriousness of this separation is underlined in the New Testament, where sin leads to death (Romans 5:14; 6:23; 8:10; 1 Corinthians 15:56). This death, not only a future prospect but also a present reality ('the wages of sin *is* death'), manifests itself in a number of ways.

There is first a search for some sort of meaning to existence;

---

[33] H. Montefiore (ed.), *op. cit.*, pp. 72–73.
[34] H. A. Hodges, *op. cit.*, p. 20.

## Getting it Wrong – The Effect of Sin on the Environment

man insists there is no God but cannot face the logical consequences of this belief. He rebels against the idea that 'personal being is merely an irrelevant piece of flotsam on the vastness of space, time and the impersonal'.[35] This search for meaning lies behind many of the newly emerged features of modern society such as mysticism, drug culture and extremist politics.[36]

There seems to be a contradiction here; on the one hand man runs away from God, while on the other he is still searching. The history of religion is that of man's search for God.[37] In fact, there is no real contradiction. The source of all meaning and truth is there, but is rejected because of the fundamental conflict between God and man in his fallen state. So without divine aid the search only ends in despair or lack of resolve.

The second manifestation of the biblical idea of death is the pursuit of material wealth for its own sake. There is no desire to move beyond the bounds of an affluent lifestyle within which there is some semblance of satisfaction and security (*e.g.* Amos 6:4–6).

> The majority of the silent majority are those who really live in a post-Christian world. They may go to church, but they have no real absolutes in mind and they have only two values – personal peace and affluence.[38]

There are other possibilities open to people but this is the one for which most opt. The reason lies in the search for *security*, to which man aspires by the acquisition of material wealth. He has elevated these things to divine status whereas he was meant to be their master. Without God, therefore, he is insecure because he is in a totally wrong relationship with his physical world:

> Man rejects God's way and chooses his own pleasures, his own success, only to find that the self-centred life has forfeited all the values it sought to conserve. Thus it is a pleasure-seeking generation, but never before have so many men been jaded, blasé, bored and unhappy. Men have made success their ideal, and while their material achievements are impressive there is a wide-

---

[35] Michael Green, *Jesus Spells Freedom* (IVP, 1972), p. 18.

[36] F. Schaeffer, *The New Superspirituality* (Hodder, 1973); O. Guinness, *The Dust of Death* (IVP, 1973).

[37] H. A. Hodges, *op. cit.*, p. 17.

[38] F. Schaeffer, *op. cit.*, p. 10.

spread consciousness of failure at the deepest levels of life. In his fear man pursues security, and no generation has ever felt less secure. Sin carries with it a built-in frustration.[39]

Niebuhr has stated that the Christian view of man affirms his unwillingness to acknowledge his dependence and admit his insecurity – an unwillingness which simply accentuates the insecurity he seeks to escape:

> Greed . . . has become the besetting sin of a bourgeois culture. The culture is constantly tempted to regard physical comfort and security as life's final good and to hope for its attainment to a degree that is beyond human possibilities.[40]

The attempt through materialism to eliminate personal insecurity has failed; while a higher standard of living *is* worth striving for, frustration has resulted because the pursuit of material wealth has been pursued for its own sake. Further, because everything else has been relegated to a position of secondary importance, severe environmental problems have arisen which threaten to force us back to a lower standard of living. Even the environmental threats outlined in the previous chapters are heralded in a general way in the creation narrative, to which we now return.

## The effect of man's sin on his environment

Although the problems of the environment and man's effect upon it are only of relatively recent importance, the possibility of such an eventuality was suggested in theological writings of earlier years:

> Nature is offered up to God on the altar of man's worship. But how can man do this with darkened mind and twisted will, and alienated from God?[41]

Jurgen Moltmann recognized the same problem in his book

---

[39] L. Morris, *The Cross in the New Testament* (Paternoster, 1967), p. 184.
[40] R. Niebuhr, *The Nature and Destiny of Man: 1. Human Nature* (Nisbet, 1941), p. 203.
[41] H. A. Hodges, *op. cit.*, p. 22.

## Getting it Wrong – The Effect of Sin on the Environment

*Hope and Planning*,[42] while Emil Brunner pointed out that the conflict between man and his environment is deeper than his awareness of it.[43]

There is a complex relationship between God, man and the environment. If the relationship between two of them is disturbed in some way, the third is automatically implicated. Ideally, we should be able to look at the world and see it as God's handiwork (Psalm 8:1; 19:1), and then to grasp something of the nature of God himself (Job 12:7–9; Psalm 50:6; 148:1ff.; Acts 14:17; 17:27; Romans 1:20). But man's perception has been impaired (Romans 1:21; *cf.* Ephesians 4:17–18). In the Old Testament the prophets took the people to task for their failure to see God through his creation (*e.g.* Jeremiah 5:21–22). The inevitable conclusion is that man's ways and thoughts are not those of God (Isaiah 55:8–9; 65:2; 66:18; *cf.* 1 Samuel 16:7).

So it is inevitable that man should lose a sense of purpose and meaning with respect to the physical world. The naming of the animals in Genesis 2 can be interpreted as an exercise in understanding,[44] while Isaiah 28:23–29 shows the relationship between understanding God's ways and success in agriculture.[45] But man now fails to see that the world bears the stamp of its Creator. There are no absolutes that he can see to guide him in how to treat that world, so he makes them up as he goes along.

The new relationship between man and the earth is expressed by God to Adam in the garden of Eden:

Cursed is the ground because of you; in toil you shall eat of it all the days of your life (Genesis 3:17).

This is at the same time a pronouncement of divine judgment and a statement of the way things are bound to be. Other parts of this solemn judgment have come true in an alarming way through environmental mismanagement:

(1) To the woman he said,
  'I will greatly multiply your pain in childbearing;
  in pain you shall bring forth children,

---

[42] J. Moltmann, *Hope and Planning* (SCM, 1968), pp. 204ff.
[43] E. Brunner, *op. cit.*, p. 93.
[44] W. Zimmerli, *op. cit.*, p. 43.
[45] *Ibid.*, p. 46.

> yet your desire shall be for your husband,
> and he shall rule over you' (verse 16).

The reference here is not simply to childbirth but the wholesale disturbance of sexual relationships through promiscuity and lust. Moss suggests that 'this implies a root cause of population problems in the moral rather than the biological realm'.[46] This is certainly true to some extent; in many countries there is a 'natural' control of population through disease and starvation. Experience in underdeveloped countries where food is short shows that populations continue to rise, and birth control is rejected for a variety of religious and superstitious motives intimately connected with the very poverty which causes the problems to be so pressing.

(2) Thorns and thistles it shall bring forth to you;
 and you shall eat the plants of the field (verse 18).

The thorns and thistles are symbolic of the unproductiveness of the ground (*cf.* Proverbs 24:31; Isaiah 34:13; Hosea 10:8).[47] The truth of these words is now manifest. Increasing food production is achieved at the price of rural poverty, pollution, pesticides and increasing energy input; vital raw materials are being too rapidly consumed. The problems are not insuperable but there is doubt about man's ability to overcome them successfully. Donald Hay has argued that capitalism begins to break down here since it is concerned primarily with the most efficient use of resources and thus operates on financial principles to which human need is subservient.[48]

(3) In the sweat of your face
 you shall eat bread, till you return to the ground (verse 19).

Work has become a matter of grim toil, where it was intended that it should be part of man's very existence (2:15). The very nature of some jobs is monotonous and degrading. At a factory assembly line (often producing commodities whose only real purpose is to keep the economy running and prevent unemployment) people can lose their identity and become cogs in a machine. Urban living can have the same effect.

---

[46] R. Moss, *op. cit.*, p. 78.
[47] *Cf.* Isaiah 24:19–20 where the picture language is different.
[48] D. Hay, *A Christian Critique of Capitalism* (Grove Books, 1975).

## Getting it Wrong – The Effect of Sin on the Environment

The earth has become an enemy rather than a friend; it is little wonder that God's commission to Noah after the flood includes the observation that all creation would go in fear and dread of man (Genesis 9:2). Scripture warns us of the folly of materialism and its consequences. We are commanded not to covet (Exodus 20:17; Deuteronomy 7:25; Luke 12:15; Romans 7:7; 13:9), warned against love of money (Luke 16:14; 1 Timothy 3:3,8; 6:10; 2 Timothy 3:2), warned that we cannot serve God if material possessions take priority (Matthew 6:24; 19:22), which are transitory (Luke 12:19–20; 1 Timothy 6:7). There is no satisfaction in materialism (Ecclesiastes 5:10). God will turn our worldly standards upside down (Psalm 22:26; 107:9; 146:7; Matthew 5:6; Luke 1:53).

But in his insecurity man turns to the created order instead of to God and seeks security through material well-being alone. Niebuhr warns against the impossibility of this:

> Among those who are less obviously secure, either in terms of social recognition, or economic stability, or even physical health, the temptation arises to overcome or to obscure insecurity by arrogating a greater degree of power to the self. Sometimes this lust for power expresses itself in terms of man's conquest of nature, in which the legitimate freedom and mastery of man in the world of nature are corrupted into a mere exploitation of nature. Man's sense of dependence upon nature and his reverent gratitude towards the miracle of nature's perennial abundance is destroyed by his arrogant sense of independence and his greedy effort to overcome the insecurity of nature's rhythms and seasons by garnering her stores with excessive zeal and beyond natural requirements. Greed is in short the expression of man's inordinate ambition to hide his insecurity in nature.
>
> Greed as a form of the will-to-power has been a particularly flagrant sin in the modern era, because modern technology has tempted contemporary man to overestimate the possibility and the value of eliminating his insecurity in nature. Greed has thus become the besetting sin of a bourgeois culture. This culture is constantly tempted to regard physical comfort and security as life's final good and to hope for its attainment to a degree which is beyond human possibilities.[49]

---

[49] R. Niebuhr, *op. cit.*, p. 203.

## Bent World

Man has misunderstood the role of nature and has brought upon himself the threat of retaliation through impending exhaustion of physical resources, ecological imbalances and pollution. While some feel that this will enable man to see nature in its 'true' perspective and encourage him to treat it responsibly, it seems likely on the Christian view that, while we might learn to treat the world better, the fear and suspicion cannot be easily removed. Since nature is now marred and imperfect, it cannot be managed with complete success; even with proper insight, mistakes will always be made.[50]

At the same time, it is imperative that right solutions be sought and found; the longer the process takes, the less will be the margin for error as the situation deteriorates. Important scientific and technological advances have been made in recent years. This, however, is not enough unless the basic question is also answered – why does man behave as he does? The Christian view of man answers the question and states that part of the solution will involve seeking to remove man's insecurity. We may therefore ask the following question, which will be discussed in the chapter to follow: When God saves someone through Jesus Christ, does the change in his nature have any implications for the well-being of the physical world in which he lives? More particularly, the Genesis narrative has revealed that there are two separate issues which need to be resolved – can the broken relationship between man and nature be restored and can the deleterious effects of his sin in the environment be held in check?

---

[50] R. Moss, *op. cit.*, p. 79.

# 7
# Getting it Right – The Implications of Salvation

Salvation has been defined as 'the action or result of deliverance or preservation from danger or disease, implying safety, health and prosperity'.[1] In the Old Testament the emphasis is on a collective salvation involving rescue from slavery, famine, conquest and oppression. In the New Testament, while the theme of community remains strong, salvation comes first to the individual and is primarily moral and spiritual in content.[2]

The Old Testament emphasis invites application to the question of the environment, and there are two extreme views which could be taken. One is that salvation can be equated with physical liberation, while the other is that, since the New Testament meaning *transcends* that of the Old, the latter has no further relevance.

A middle path must be followed. The former view will be discussed later; the latter would imply that salvation as a biblical concept has little direct relevance to environmental problems. The need to investigate the physical dimension to salvation is an urgent one and is one of several meeting points of scientific inquiry and Christian faith. Jurgen Moltmann has written:

> Reduction of the contents of the Bible to the question of man's salvation – and at the same time the exclusion of its authority in all areas which do not relate to this personal, supernatural salvation – was then and is today felt to be a great liberation: it was the only possibility of affirming the Bible's validity. By this understanding, however, theology dissociated itself from the task of taking possession of the world through acquiring knowledge of the world. Its domain became a personal, supernatural

---

[1] 'Salvation' by G. Walters, in J. D. Douglas (ed.), *The New Bible Dictionary* (IVP, 1962), p. 1126.

[2] The whole issue of the relationship between the two Testaments in the context of salvation has been discussed in D. F. Wells, *The Search for Salvation* (IVP, 1978), pp. 24–28.

doctrine of salvation. It could interpret salvation only for the inner self-certainty of tempted man. In this way, science and the shaping of the world lost their place in the framework of the hope for possible salvation and the fear of possible condemnation. The more this salvation is thought of as being unrelated to the world, the less important and significant the knowledge and shaping of the world becomes.[3]

Any investigation of salvation must still centre on the individual and his spiritual need. This is the emphasis of the New Testament. The previous chapter showed how man's severed relationship with God has repercussions for the physical world through his broken relationship with nature and through the spoiling effects on the environment of his acts of sin. A new relationship with God will therefore have implications for the environment.

As already mentioned, a common view of the Old Testament is that it presents salvation in purely physical terms. This view must be examined before exploring the relationship between the Old and New Testament pictures.

## Salvation in the Old Testament

One of the Hebrew roots used for salvation is *hayah*, ('to be alive'). It carries various shades of meaning, most of which carry no salvific sense but occasionally it means 'to live a full and prosperous life':

> And Samuel said to all the people, 'Do you see him whom the Lord has chosen? There is none like him among all the people'. And all the people shouted, '*Long live* the king!' (1 Samuel 10:24).

*Hayah* has a similar meaning in the account of the famine which overtook the aged Jacob and his family in Canaan. When the brothers met Joseph in Egypt as they looked for food, Joseph revealed God's providential hand in everything which had happened:

> And now, do not be distressed or angry with yourselves, because

[3] J. Moltmann, *Hope and Planning* (SCM, 1971), pp. 201–202.

*Getting it Right – The Implications of Salvation*

you sold me here, for God sent me before you to preserve life. For the famine has been in the land these two years, and there are yet five years in which there will be neither sowing nor harvest. And God sent me before you to preserve for you a remnant on earth, and *to keep alive* for you many survivors (Genesis 45:5–7).

*Hayah* also occurs three times in the flood narrative, where it refers to preserving life on earth (Genesis 6:19–20; 7:3). Throughout the Pentateuch the idea of preserving life is important and man has the responsibility for preserving different kinds of plants and animals (*e.g.* Leviticus 22:27–28; Deuteronomy 20:19–20; 22:6–7). This may explain the aversion to castration (Leviticus 22:24; Deuteronomy 23:1; 25:11).

Another root word is *yasha*, ('to bring into a spacious environment') which comes to depict the state of being at ease, or of being free to develop without hindrance. The *yasha* idea runs right through the exodus story, where the Israelites were delivered from a state of hardship (1:11; 2:23) viciously multiplied after Moses and Aaron made their first representations to Pharaoh (5:7–19). The promised deliverance was not portrayed merely in terms of relief from their burdens; they would leave Egypt with great riches (3:22; *cf.* 12:35–36) and be guided into a spacious land flowing with milk and honey (3:8, 17; 13:5).

There is the temptation to apply this sort of picture directly to our environmental situation. But God delivered Israel because he 'remembered his covenant with Abraham, with Isaac and with Jacob' (2:24). The covenant had both a *content* – described in terms of political and economic security (Genesis 22:16–18; 26:2–5; 28:13–15) and a *purpose* – that the life of Israel would be devoted to serving the living God (Exodus 19:6). Furthermore, the Genesis references make it clear that the realization of the covenant *content* depended upon obedience; that is, the fulfilment of the covenant *purpose*. Thus already there are both spiritual and physical dimensions to salvation:

> The whole of the Old Testament faith is in a God who saves his people in history. It is a real material salvation that he brings, yet more than that. It is wholeness of life individually and in community, which contains a spiritual dimension as well. . . . Thus the Exodus was accompanied by the law and the sacrifices,

pointers to that right relationship with God which was intended to characterize the (politically liberated) people of God.[4]

Israel, as God's chosen nation, was able to experience political and economic security within the content of salvation because of that nationhood. It is for this reason that application of Old Testament ideas to the present day is not straightforward; the true Israel is the church (1 Peter 2:9), not a nation. Moreover, in the New Testament the exodus event becomes a picture of our redemption from sin through the work of Christ. It is from this starting point that we must later explore the relevance of salvation in the area of environmental issues.

In the Old Testament salvation, or deliverance, brings satisfaction (same root as *yasha*), which is experienced not only by the individual but also by the nation and is experienced partly on a physical level (*e.g.* Psalm 18:18–19; 91:16; Micah 4:10; Zechariah 8:7–8). This corporate experience of satisfaction raises the issues today of the influence of Christians upon society as a whole, not only through evangelism and the regeneration of individuals but also through active participation in the structures of industrial society. The environment is just one of many areas in which this participation is necessary (chapter 8) and which can contribute towards a marked improvement in the quality of physical life.

The Old Testament also has much to say about salvation as spiritual deliverance from the power and guilt of sin, even though the perfect deliverance has not yet come. The psalms frequently refer to the need for spiritual deliverance (*e.g.* 51:1–3; 119:155–156; 130:3–4) and this is an integral part of the teaching of the prophets (*e.g.* Isaiah 59:11–21; 61:10; 64:6; Ezekiel 36:25ff.).

Throughout the Old Testament there is a close link between national problems and Israel's sin. There were repeated cycles of decline (and fall) as the people turned away from God, followed by an act of divine salvation, a call to righteousness and another decline. This cycle is repeated several times, for example, during the period of the judges (2:11–12; 3:7–12; 4:1, *etc.*).

The prophets denounced all kinds of injustice, which were closely connected with the sin of the people and their rebellion against God. The opening verses of Isaiah speak of rebellion (1:2),

---

[4] *Jesus Christ the Only Saviour* by T. Wright and M. Sadgrove, in J. R. W. Stott (ed.), *The Lord Christ* (Hodder, 1977), p. 66.

iniquity (1:4), lack of purpose (1:3), corruption (1:4, 23), empty religion (1:11f.), injustice and oppression (1:7), lack of concern for human life (1:15, 21) and pervasive dishonesty (1:23). These same heralds were often bringing warnings of impending judgment, seen in terms of economic, politic and military disaster and in the failure of agriculture.

Judgment in the Old Testament goes back to the covenant curses of Leviticus 26 and Deuteronomy 28, in which the consequences of disobedience are clearly stated. Thus the prophets were simply declaring that God would do what he said he would do (*e.g.* Isaiah 24:1–6); the references to the curses are particularly clear in Jeremiah, Ezekiel, Amos and Hosea. The connection between Israel's sin and her disasters is, therefore, one of divine judgment:

> It was (Israel's) covenant with Jahweh which created, sustained and gave meaning to her nationhood. To disobey Jahweh was to betray and reject the very source of her life. The only way for Israel to live her peculiar life was to remain in fellowship with Jahweh. In that fellowship lay her whole 'peace' . . . the totality of her well-being. Out of fellowship with Jahweh she was cut off from life.[5]

God's dealings with Israel *as a nation* are unique in history but all have experienced what is called his common grace – that is, his creating and sustaining activity in nature and his goodness to all in terms of material gifts (Hebrews 1:3; 1 Timothy 4:1ff., *etc.*). The prosperity of the developed world is based on this common grace, so that if a nation's government, institutions and social structures are not subject to him, the instability which automatically ensues will jeopardize the maintenance of material prosperity through physical threats including environmental ones. Further, it will become more and more difficult to maintain such prosperity as the threats multiply. In this sense all nations are liable to judgment still.

## Salvation and eschatology in the Old Testament

An eschatological reality is one which is present and active but whose consummation lies in the future. Although the Old Testa-

[5] J. A. Thompson, *Deuteronomy* (IVP, 1974), p. 269.

ment sees God's salvation in acts of history and thus beginning in the past, that salvation is also in the present, as we have seen. But there is yet an eager anticipation of what is still to come; this is seen especially in the prophets.

In the Old Testament there is a pointing towards the final redemption of which the New Testament also speaks, in which the created order will participate:

> The biblical idea of redemption always included the earth. Hebrew thought saw an essential unity between man and nature. The prophets do not think of the earth as merely the indifferent theatre on which man carries out his normal task but as the expression of the divine glory . . . Salvation does not mean escape from bodily, creaturely existence. On the contrary, ultimate redemption will mean redemption of the whole man . . . creation in its entirety must share the blessings of redemption.[6]

The seeds of this idea, expressed supremely in Romans 8, are present throughout the Old Testament. The function of the physical world is not just to provide the environment in which men can live in peace and comfort; it is also to declare God's glory (Psalm 8:1; 19:1; Jeremiah 5:22; *cf.* Romans 1:19–20). Thus creation will still be declaring God's glory when he returns to judge the world (Psalm 96:11–13; 98:7–9) and its importance goes beyond the use man can make of it.

On the other hand, the physical world has been marred by sin, in which it then shares. This is a divine pronouncement (Genesis 9:2) and also a simple observation. So the prophets, especially Isaiah, look forward to the final and perfect redemption of which God's acts of salvation in history are 'matrix and type';[7] there will be a totally new order in which not only God's people but the physical world also will be renewed. Passages in Isaiah give different insights into the nature of this final world order. Thus 11:1–9 depicts a paradisical existence; in 49:5–13 (*cf.* Haggai 2:4–9; Zechariah 2:7–13) a new political world order centred on Jerusalem; in 65:17–25 and 66:22–23 a completely new heaven and earth.

---

[6] G. E. Ladd, *Jesus and the Kingdom: The Eschatology of Biblical Realism* (SPCK, 1964), pp. 54, 59.

[7] 'Salvation, Saviour' by A. Richardson in G. A. Buttrick (ed.), *The Interpreter's Dictionary of the Bible*, 3 (Abingdon Press, 1962), p. 173.

*Getting it Right – The Implications of Salvation*

These themes are continued into the New Testament, to which we must now turn.

## Salvation in the New Testament

In the New Testament, the main emphasis is on the redemption of the individual and on salvation as deliverance from the power and the guilt of sin; the repercussions extend to every aspect of a person's life and affect society as a whole. This active pervasion of society by Christian influence is the meaning of Jesus' words, 'You are the salt of the earth.'

From the outset, the ministry of Jesus was one of salvation. All that he said and did needs to be viewed in that light. His death and resurrection, the necessary climax of his ministry, were to secure salvation from sin. We cannot, however, isolate a purely 'spiritual' salvation; Jesus was concerned for every aspect of human existence. Among the many miracles which he performed, the only one to be recorded by all four gospels is that of the feeding of the five thousand (Matthew 14:13–31; Mark 6:32–44; Luke 9:10–17; John 6:1–4). This miracle is an acted parable illustrating spiritual truths (John 6:27ff.), but either by implication (John 6:5) or direct statement (Matthew 14:14), we are told that what he did was out of *compassion*.

We can explore the implications of salvation further by considering Jesus' words 'Your faith has saved you' which accompany various healing miracles (Mark 5:34; 10:52; Luke 17:19). There are two dangers to be avoided: one is to equate salvation with physical healing and the other is to assume that this is a sign of a purely spiritual deliverance. In the Old Testament, salvation had an essentially spiritual base but was grounded in historical reality. Sadgrove and Wright have therefore argued that while 'the miracles of healing were signs of something more than merely physical, it is surely also true that such miracles are not just visual aids but actually share something of the character of salvation.'[8]

A similar conclusion can be reached from looking at Jesus' teaching. Following the parable of the rich fool (Luke 12:13–21) and the Lord's comments, we are encouraged not to worry about material possessions; not only is this because they are not of primary im-

---

[8] T. Wright and M. Sadgrove, *op. cit.*, p. 69.

portance (verse 15) but also because God, in his love, will provide all that we need (verses 29–31).

Thus, while there may be different emphases in the Old and New Testaments concerning the nature of salvation, there is an essential continuity between the two. In both cases man's sinful nature has to be put right before there can be a right relationship between man and the physical world. We can now look in more detail at the way in which salvation, as described in the New Testament, has implications for the environment. These stem from the way in which human lives are liberated and blessed by God's grace through faith in Jesus Christ.

## What salvation frees us from

### From our former nature

In the previous chapter sin was described in terms of rebellion against God, but in order to understand how man's attitude towards the world has been affected, it is necessary to think in terms of the self-centredness and insecurity which are the natural outworkings of sin in terms of wrong relationships.

There are two aspects to self-centredness; one is a lack of concern for the needs and desires of others, and the other is a lack of concern for the consequences of our own actions. It is present in individual lives but is most starkly seen through national statistics. Thus, while the UN overseas aid target is 0.7% of gross national product, the actual figure for Britain in 1975 was only 0.4% and falling. Britain's aid budget in that year was £750 million, in contrast to the £6,300 million spent on alcohol and tobacco. In humanitarian terms it is very difficult to justify the colossal expenditure on prestige projects like Concorde and Apollo, in spite of the scientific discoveries made during their development.

Our lack of concern for the consequences of our actions is seen in the prospect of resources exhaustion and pollution. The implications of salvation are extremely relevant here; not only does man lack the power and the motivation to tackle the environmental problem at its roots but he cannot even see where those roots are. They lie within the corruption of human nature. It is because of man's inability to accept the consequences of his own actions that we must reject as inadequate J. S. Black's ethic for the proper care of the earth's resources:

## Getting it Right – The Implications of Salvation

It seems to me that almost the only course open to western man is based on the vision of all mankind stretched out along the dimension of time. As a general rule, most of us are prepared so to manage our affairs that we and our contemporaries do not suffer; self-interest sees to that. It is the transfer of this interest in the general good of mankind to the future – particularly the remote future – that raises difficulties. By expanding our view of the general good of mankind, by redefining 'mankind' in terms of the whole of humanity, dead, living or as yet unborn, we may perhaps be able to assess what we do in terms of the good of mankind, regardless of the position of the individual along the time axis of the world.[9]

Akin to selfishness is the spirit of conformity, which easily serves as a reason for selfish actions and attitudes. It is seen in 'keeping up with the Joneses', and can motivate such issues as pay negotiations and our material expectations in general. This derivation of standards from the world around us instead of from God himself, is what Paul called 'the spirit of this present evil age' (Galatians 1:4); he and Peter warn against it (Romans 12:2; 1 Peter 1:14). One of the most pathetic figures in the New Testament is Demas who, complains Paul, 'in love with this present world, has left me and gone to Thessalonica' (2 Timothy 4:10).

Much is made today of the spirit of dissent exhibited by many young people. It is to be welcomed in so far as it challenges the materialistic presuppositions which pervade society.[10] Yet it would be dangerous to pin too much hope on it. Almost inevitably the alternatives turn out to be no better and people drift back into materialism, especially when professional and family commitments replace the freedom of student days. They can be trapped in this state as thoroughly as ever their parents were.

Yet the Christian can, as God's grace works through his life and transforms it, be released from selfishness and all its manifestations and be transformed by the renewal of his mind (Romans 12:2).

### From our former habits

Selfishness leads to greed and covetousness, which form habits. Crimes on personal property are the tip of the iceberg, representing

[9] J. S. Black, *The Dominion of Man* (John Black, 1970), p. 123.
[10] C. Derrick, *The Delicate Creation* (Tom Stacey, 1972), p. 112.

*Bent World*

the 'unacceptable' manifestations of a widespread and deep-seated attitude. Most people do not succumb to greed in the form of outright crime but everyone knows other temptations, such as tax evasion, customs dodging and working short hours.

On another level, greed and covetousness are partly responsible for the drain on the world's physical resources. We tend, however, to take such sins less seriously than, for example, murder, because the immediate consequences are less serious. Scripture does not allow such a distinction (James 2:8–13; *cf.* 1 Corinthians 5:11, where the greedy were barred from fellowship); in any case, the environmental consequences of greed *are* serious. It is simply that they are less obvious and immediate. Both because of its serious nature and its serious consequences we need to be – and can be – freed from covetousness.

## *From our former fears*

This is the main emphasis of 2 Timothy 1:7, in which salvation is described as a past event. Michael Green comments:

> In saving us, God has replaced the old spirit of . . . 'cowardice and dread in the face of the unknown' . . . by the Holy Spirit, who brings love and power and self-control.[11]

The Graeco-Roman world of the first century was a time when people longed for some sort of salvation. The imperical cult, demanding at least a nominal worship of the Roman emperor who had brought a period of sustained political stability, did not satisfy; the people were free to follow the popular religions (*superstitiones*) which had wide popularity:

> Their astonishing success is due to the hunger in men's hearts for wholeness, emotional release, security, in a word, for salvation in this world and the next. This salvation was what the *superstitiones* offered. Indeed the very instability of the times helped to make men conscious of their needs and ready for a religion which would save from the emptiness and insecurity of life.[12]

The coming of Jesus was, then, to a world deeply affected by

---

[11] M. Green, *The Meaning of Salvation* (Hodder, 1964), p. 160.
[12] *Ibid.*, p. 77.

*Getting it Right – The Implications of Salvation*

insecurity – by people's fear of finding their lives and destinies controlled by circumstances over which they had no control and by fear of death. It can be argued that similar thoughts prevail today; many retain bitter memories of two World Wars; terrorist bombs go off without warning; we are all affected by, but have no control over, economic forces which give rise to chronic inflation and unemployment while in the environmental debate there are some who claim that man is close to doom.

Meanwhile advertisements present financial schemes offering security against the ravages of inflation; people react to publicized commodity shortages (real or illusory) by panic buying, and violence may ensue. In spite of our wealth we are no less insecure and afraid than the people of the first-century Roman world.

Fear makes it difficult to find real answers to the problems caused by excessive consumption of physical resources. Thus, fear of rising prices will militate against the kind of economic justice which demands a fair price for imported commodities. It will also act in direct opposition to the necessity of building into manufacturing industries extra costs which will enable them to operate with less environmental impact, mainly in terms of pollution. Fear of rising prices affects government policies since, in a democracy, a government can continue to govern only by the consent of the people. Insecurity ensures that prices remain an important election issue, with the effect of relegating to a minor place such issues as environmental wholeness and economic justice for developing nations and the poorer sections of our own society.

Our old *nature*, our old *habits* and our old *fears* have largely determined the materialistic pattern of the present age, both in the life of the individual and in society. When we look at the man who has been recreated by Christ we may expect to see something of the way in which God deals with these problems of the old life and something of the response of the new man to God as Creator and to the physical world in which God has placed him. We will look at three aspects of this new nature: at the new *mind*, the new *security* and the new *power*.

## What salvation creates in us

### *A new mind*
While there is always the danger of reducing Christian faith to intellectual propositions, and discipleship to doctrinal conformity,

there is also the danger of a mindless faith, unstable and insensitive to new situations and challenges.

The first and great commandment is 'to love the Lord your God with all your heart and with all your soul and with all your might' (Deuteronomy 6:5). In Hebrew psychology the heart was thought of as the seat of the mind and of many emotions.[13] The commandment thus shows how intellectual devotion is an integral part of discipleship. When the New Testament talks about the renewal of personal life in Christ (*e.g.* 2 Corinthians 4:16; 5:17) the renewal of the mind is implied. This is stated explicitly in Romans 12:2 and Ephesians 4:22–24.

The renewal of the mind, a need stated explicitly by the Lord (Matthew 15:18–20; Mark 7:20–23), is an integral part of salvation. It is connected not only with mental activity but with the words and deeds this gives rise to (*cf.* Job 42:1–6). With new minds created in us by God we can begin to see the world as he sees it and to appreciate it as such:

> . . . to choose the Giver rather than His gifts. Having chosen Him, and having been drawn into a relationship of faith and love with Him alone, man finds that all the things that he had renounced are given back to him again, transformed because they are now seen and known precisely as God's gifts.[14]

Such ideas are also inherent in the wisdom concept of the Old Testament. Wisdom has a number of meanings derived from various Hebrew roots;[15] included among these are *understanding* and *insight* (Proverbs 1:2; 2:2) and *knowledge* (1:5; 2:5; 3:6). It comes to those who fear God and results in a hatred of evil (8:13), which is itself a result of being able to tell good from evil (the same Hebrew root as *understanding*; 1 Kings 3:9).

The divine gift of the new mind is to be used to assess political, social and economic ideologies and to explore directions in which we must move to solve the problems our technology and lifestyle have raised for the future of the environment. This is a sphere of activity in which Christians can make individual and corporate contributions to the wider debate:

---

[13] J. A. Thompson, *op. cit.*, p. 122.
[14] H. Montefiore and others, *Man and Nature* (Collins, 1975), pp. 51–52.
[15] F. D. Kidner, *Proverbs* (IVP, 1968), pp. 36–38.

Because we are convinced that Christian theology can provide a unifying vision which we believe society must recover if attitudes are to change, it follows that theologians should meet with others to share and discuss problems concerning the environmental crisis . . . Our argument therefore forces us to urge the pressing importance of inter-disciplinary discussions in which theologians will join with moral philosophers, economists, agriculturalists, environmentalists, industrialists, sociologists, politicians and others. Such attitudes should show how changed attitudes could result in changed policies at regional, national and international levels.[16]

*A new security*
The pursuit of a higher standard of living by a society which is already making heavy demands on the environment is part of a search for some sort of security against what is beyond its control or comprehension. This search has been counter-productive in large measure.

Throughout Scripture God is seen as the only source of real security. One of the divine names in the Old Testament expresses this certainty; it is *El Shaddai* (God who is sufficient). In the book of Genesis this is first used at 17:1, where God reassures the doubting Abraham that he will be the father of a great nation. Kidner comments that this and subsequent uses of *El Shaddai* occur in situations where his servants are hard-pressed and needing reassurance.[17] The most often used name *Jahweh* expresses the changelessness and faithfulness of the One upon whom we may rely (*e.g.* Exodus 3:14–15; Malachi 3:6). It is this God who assures those who love him of security and satisfaction (Job 24:23; Psalm 37:3; 81:16; 102:28; Jeremiah 31:14, 25; 33:6).

Other Old Testament pictures express the same certainty. God is a refuge (*e.g.* 2 Samuel 22:33), a source of strength (*e.g.* Psalm 46:1), a fortress (*e.g.* 2 Samuel 22:2) and a rock (*e.g.* Deuteronomy 32:15). The beginning of Psalm 23 expresses the quiet confidence of a man who has found security in God. Similarly Zechariah is told in a vision that the new Jerusalem will need no fortifying walls because God will protect the city himself (Zechariah 2:4–5; *cf.* Revelation 21:16–17).

---

[16] H. Montefiore and others, *op. cit.*, pp. 81–82.
[17] F. D. Kidner, *Genesis* (IVP, 1962), pp. 128–129.

*Bent World*

In the New Testament this security is seen as one of the blessings of salvation. Through the redeeming death of Christ we have security because we are brought into God's very presence (Romans 5:1ff.). So the Lord warns his disciples about being anxious for their material needs (Matthew 6:25ff.); the reason for this is simple but many-sided. We cannot serve God effectively while being anxious (verse 24); there is more to life than food and clothing (verse 25); anxiety is by its very nature counter-productive (verse 27); God knows our needs better than we do (verse 32). Epistle writers urge their readers to be content with what they have (1 Timothy 6: 6–8; Hebrews 13:5–6).

But salvation is not free insurance against difficulty. Inflation can be seen as one of the symptoms of our folly in chasing more material wealth.[18] Economic recession and environmental threats may force us to share the sufferings of a sinful world; we can only be effective servants of Christ in so far as we, like him, are willing to identify with the plight of others.

The Christian's security lies in the fact and experience of being 'in Christ' (2 Timothy 2:10; 3:15; *cf.* Ephesians 1:4), and no amount of suffering or lack of certainty can alter that fact:

> (The phrase) is intended to express the very practical truth that the Christian, if faithful to his calling, will not try to be self-sufficient, or to move beyond the limits of the purpose and control and love of Christ, nor will he turn to the world for guidance, inspiration and strength. He finds all his satisfaction and his every need met in him, and not in any other place or from any other source.[19]

Our security lies in God's sustaining power enabling us to overcome all that might befall us and there is no need for supplementary sources of security. A notable biblical example of this is the life of Paul. God brought him safely through various tribulations (*e.g.* 2 Timothy 3:10–11; 2 Corinthians 1:9–10; 11:21 – 12:10; 2 Thessalonians 3:1–2). But because of the real security of being 'in Christ' he insists that there is no need for anxiety (Philippians

---

[18] C. Elliott, *Inflation and the Compromised Church* (Christian Journals Ltd, 1975), and J. F. Sleeman, *Economic Crisis: A Christian Perspective* (SCM, 1975) give detailed explanations of the causes of inflation.

[19] F. Foulkes, *Ephesians* (IVP, 1963), p. 43.

4:6); the peace of God can override worries (Philippians 4:7, 9; *cf.* John 14:27). More than that, when hard times do come, they are permitted by God for the purpose of strengthening (Romans 5:3–5; Hebrews 12:3–10; James 1:2–4).

Especially relevant here is the theme of poverty. Paul's privations brought him into more intimate fellowship with his Lord (Romans 8:17; Galatians 6:17; Philippians 3:10), so that we are encouraged to take seriously Jesus' poverty during his earthly life (Matthew 8:20; Luke 8:58). Paul was not ashamed to talk about the poverty he accepted for the sake of Christ (1 Corinthians 4:11; 2 Corinthians 6:10), but in the following passage he explains his attitude towards it:

> Not that I complain of want; for I have learned, in whatever state I am, to be content. I know how to be abased, and I know how to abound; in any and all circumstances, I have learned the secret of facing plenty and hunger, abundance and want. I can do all things in him who strengthens me (Philippians 4:11–13).

Contentment here is independent of material circumstances, so that Paul can tolerate poverty. The reality of his security in Christ is such that he considers poverty and abundance as of equal status; both have their dangers and both have to be faced (*cf.* Proverbs 30:6), but both can be mastered.

The challenge here for Christians with high standards of living is that we will have to rely upon this security in order to tackle effectively various environmental problems. Consider, for example, the chronic needs of inner-city areas. For any Christian to make a deliberate decision to move back into an inner-city area will mean counting the cost in terms of the security offered by suburbia. Consider too the need to evaluate fearlessly what we need and what we do not. We may find that much of what we consider essential is not really so. On another level, Christians must be willing to ask awkward questions, such as whether we *need* another pay rise.

So far we have considered the relevance of salvation to environmental questions in purely individual terms and while it is certainly right to begin with Christ's saving work in the life of the believer, we cannot end here. We are all members of his church, which is 'nothing less than the visible expression of Christ's salvation . . .

the normal sphere of Christ's saving ministry and the instrument of his salvation in the world.'[20]

## The corporate dimension to salvation

There is also a *corporate* dimension to salvation. In the Old Testament this was connected with a national identity; God saved Israel as a nation from Egypt. The true Israel is the church (Phil. 3:3; Rom. 2:29; Gal. 6:15–16), into which believers are incorporated. This corporate dimension is present throughout the New Testament, which uses such phrases as 'the body of Christ' (Ephesians 1:22) and 'the people of God' (*cf.* Hebrews 8:10).

In addressing the church in terms formerly used of Israel, Peter immediately speaks of its function:

> . . . that you may declare the wonderful deeds of him who brought you out of darkness into his marvellous light (1 Peter 2:10).

It is not immediately clear whether the 'wonderful deeds' refer to the saving work of Christ on the cross, or to *all* of God's wonderful deeds including creation. But since creation and redemption are linked, it is best to understand Peter's phrase in its widest sense. Certainly at Athens, Paul's sermon contained a proclamation of God as creator (Acts 17:24–28).

This brings us to the need to consider a corporate response to the environmental crisis, as related to the biblical nature and function of the church. Various studies have attempted to define *models* of the church;[21] we will consider three such models, the first a structural one and the others functional.

### The mystical communion model

This model is based on the nature of God himself as a unity (John 17:20–23; 1 Corinthians 12:4–6, 11–13; Ephesians 4:4–6) and leads to a concept of the unity of all believers. Ephesians 2 expounds the unifying consequences of the Lord's death in terms of breaking down dividing walls of hostility so that the church, as a mystical

---

[20] *The Nottingham Statement*, p. 14.
[21] Reviewed in R. Nixon, 'Ecumenism, Models of the Church and Styles of Authority', *Churchman*, 91, 1977, pp. 229–241.

communion, is a structure displaying the unity which redemption makes possible.

Since the Old Testament portrays a broken relationship between man and nature, it is valid to inquire whether the New Testament says anything about a new co-operation between man and nature. There is little stated explicitly about the subject since the emphasis lies elsewhere. There are various hints, however, such as the clear recognition that God is the giver of all good gifts (Matthew 6:25ff.), the concept of stewardship and the need for thanksgiving for all material blessings (1 Timothy 4:1–4).

In Colossians 1, however, the cosmic significance of Christ's redeeming death provides more than a hint; it is in Christ that 'all things hold together' (verse 17), and the object of that death was that all things should be united to God, whether in heaven or on earth (verse 20).

There is, therefore, an environmental dimension to the gospel. The unity which is in God himself and which he makes possible in human relationships through reconciliation extends not only to the way we relate to other people but also to the world. There are consequences here for the way that the church lives (chapter 8) and for the content of the gospel message which that church proclaims to the world.

## *The herald model*

The purpose of the church is to proclaim God's wonderful deeds (1 Peter 2:10) and this is the great commission given by the Lord to the disciples (Matthew 28:16–19; Luke 24:44–47). It has been suggested that it is impossible to do justice to the message of God the Saviour apart from its containing the message of God the Creator.[22] Theologians separate special and common grace because the recipients of the latter do not necessarily receive the former, but there is always the danger of completely divorcing the two in a way which Scripture will not allow. Alan Richardson may err slightly in the other direction when he states that 'in the prophetic view salvation is also virtually synonymous with creation',[23] but the point is well made. Creation and redemption are integral aspects of God's over-all plan for the universe and need to be seen

---

[22] D. Watson, *I Believe in Evangelism* (Hodder, 1976), p. 65.
[23] A. Richardson, *op. cit.*, p. 173.

in each other's light.[24] In proclaiming the gospel, the church must also recognize that attempts to promote better social attitudes towards the environment cannot simply be educative but must be addressed to man in his spiritual, as well as physical and mental, dimensions; it is sin which is the root cause of the trouble:

> These changes in attitudes, values and policies will not come about otherwise than through the deep pervasive influence of a world-view which ties together man and nature in a unity and which we believe will also lead society as well as individuals to acknowledge their accountability before God for their stewardship and trusteeship of the world. Here again we stress the importance of deep commonly-held convictions as the precondition for imaginative and effective policies.[25]

The theme of this section includes worship, which is both a feature and a function of the church. We need to proclaim God as Creator because we worship him as such. He is addressed as Creator in many of the intercessions of the *Book of Common Prayer* ('we bless thee for our creation, preservation, and all the blessings of this life . . .'). And, strangely enough in an increasingly materialistic world, the service of harvest thanksgiving is often the best-attended church service in the year!

Arthur Peacocke has drawn attention to the use of physical objects (bread, wine and water) in the sacraments.[26] He argues that these objects perform two functions: a *symbolic* function in that they express God's mind and an *instrumental* function in that they are the means by which he effects his will and purpose. Science, he continues, has underlined the Christian understanding of God's cosmic purposes as expressed symbolically and effected instrumentally through nature. There is, therefore a sense in which we are worshipping God as Creator as well as Saviour in the sacraments.

## The servant model

This functional model starts with Jesus as the servant washing the disciples' feet (John 13:15) and with the early church's understand-

---

[24] Thus an interesting comparison has been made between the opening chapters of Genesis and John's gospel; see, for example, E. K. Lee, *The Religious Thought of St John* (SPCK, 1962), pp. 113–116.
[25] H. Montefiore and others, *op. cit.*, p. 79.
[26] *Ibid.*, pp. 132–142.

ing of him in terms of the Suffering Servant (Isaiah 53). It is from this understanding of the Lord's life that we derive our understanding of the church as the servant of society; that is, our concerns are to be the needs of society (*e.g.* Matthew 25:35ff.; Galatians 6:10).

Thus a picture of the church as servant should help us to speak and act on environmental issues. The history of missionary work shows that this will be in essential continuity with what has already been done:

> Called to follow the example of Jesus Christ in his mission, the church must not only bring the message of eternal life, but must also feed the hungry. In that sense the blessings that the *world* enjoys are the fruits of the *church's* salvation.[27]

The church will continue to send out not only preachers but also agronomists, doctors, teachers and funds for famine relief. Through these and other activities by which God's love is proclaimed, the world comes to share in the *blessings* of salvation, although it does not come into salvation in its fullest sense. The teaching of the Bible is, rather, that since people come to see something of God's love through the ministries of the church, they are without excuse if they reject the Source of that love. Wright and Sadgrove draw the analogy of the blessings of salvation as like servicing a car; if the driver of the car is going in the wrong direction, the service will simply enable him to arrive sooner at the wrong destination.[28]

## The cosmic dimension of salvation

We have already seen that although common and special grace must be distinguished, they may not be completely divorced. God's salvation is recreative and reconciliatory and his concern is cosmic in scale. Most of the teaching of the New Testament is about the individual's experience of salvation but the essential continuity between creation and redemption demands that we explore the cosmic dimension to salvation.

In Old Testament times, God's promise to Abraham was a

---

[27] T. Wright and M. Sadgrove, *op. cit.*, p. 85.
[28] *Ibid.*, p. 86.

universal one (*e.g.* Genesis 12:3), even though Israel was a special and a chosen race (Deuteronomy 7:6; Isaiah 49:7). Thus his concern for Israel did not imply a limit to his concern for others. The law made provision for the well-being of strangers (Exodus 23:9, *etc.*); Israel was to be a light to the nations (Isaiah 42:6). Prophecies of the coming of the Lord (Isaiah 49:6; 60:3, *etc.*) pictured salvation reaching to the ends of the earth and including the recreation of nature (Isaiah 65:17–18).

In the New Testament this universal concern is more explicitly stated (*e.g.* Luke 2:32; 24:47; Acts 1:8). In the death of Jesus, who is not only our redeemer but the agent of creation (Colossians 1:15; Hebrews 1:3), God was reconciling not only people of all nations but also fallen nature to himself (Colossians 1:20). A new relationship between man and nature is therefore possible, to be realized by the church as we realize our solidarity with nature (*cf.* Genesis 2:7), and made available to society at large by Christian influence (Matthew 5:13):

> We recognise . . . that individual efforts, valuable though they are, must be somewhat ineffective in the face of such gigantic problems, so that public opinion has to be mobilized and there must be pressure for such legislature and other controls as are needed.[29]

We must beware of imagining that God has ceased working in nature; his creative and renewing activity is involved in the world at all levels. Old Testament references to the Spirit (Genesis 1:2, 5; Job 33:4; Psalm 33:6; 104:30) probably refer to the energizing function of the Spirit in creation,[30] while in the New Testament Christ is portrayed as still active in this role – 'in him all things were created . . . all things were created through him and for him. He is before all things, and in him all things hold together' (Colossians 1:16–17); 'He reflects the glory of God and bears the very stamp of his nature, upholding the universe by his word of power' (Hebrews 1:3). Paul's sermon at Mars Hill refers specifically to this continuing activity in creation (Acts 17:25), and in part of the sermon on the mount (Matthew 5:44–45), Jesus makes the point

---

[29] H. Montefiore and others, *op. cit.*, p. 66.
[30] Michael Green, *I Believe in the Holy Spirit* (Hodder, 1975), pp. 28–29.

that we must show active love to everyone, for the simple reason that God's activity in creation is for the benefit of all.

The message of salvation we proclaim, therefore, must include God as the world's Creator, still at work therein, concerned for it and for the whole of mankind living in it. As the environment shares in the salvation won by Christ, so the material blessings potentially won can be shared by the whole of society, which also needs to be continuously warned of the dangers to the environment. Those blessings made available to mankind through salvation are to show the love of God and bring a crisis to man's life in that he is then confronted with the need to make a decision concerning his attitude to that love.

## The eschatological dimension of salvation

The main eschatological emphasis of the New Testament is that believers will receive eternal life in all its fullness, while those who have refused salvation will permanently forfeit it. It is this anticipation which is, in Scripture, a motive for complete commitment and growth in holiness here and now. But the pressing nature of the environmental crisis and the materialistic world view of our age can preoccupy us enough to forget this Christian hope.

Sadly, it is often true that the church has only a hazy idea of what it is moving towards, while hope gives impetus, direction and energy. In this respect there is much to learn from Marxist and other revolutionaries; their goals are clearly defined and their strategies are worked out in terms of these goals. They are utterly dedicated, often willing to undergo prolonged and intense deprivations for the sake of those goals.

The Christian hope is based not on what man is going to achieve but on what God has promised to effect. This hope should spur Christians to act, not to relax. What part does the physical world order play in this hope? The question is important because the answer to it will guide us towards an estimation of how important the environment should be on the agenda of the church.

We have seen how, in the Old Testament, the idea of redemption always included the earth. In the New Testament too the final redemption of creation is clearly foretold:

For the creation waits with eager longing for the revealing of the sons of God; for the creation was subjected to futility, not of its own will but by the will of him who subjected it in hope; because the creation itself will be set free from its bondage to decay and obtain the glorious liberty of the children of God (Romans 8:19–21).

Creation, then, is included in the goal towards which history is inexorably moving.[31] This must indicate to us something of our priorities and concerns in this life. Christians are called to have a deep concern for every aspect of man's existence and well-being, including the issue of the environment. There is also a challenge not to make material possessions the motivation for our actions. The Lord warned his disciples not to 'labour for the food which perishes, but for the food which endures to eternal life' (John 6:27; *cf.* Isaiah 55:2); likewise Paul reminded Timothy that 'we brought nothing into this world, but if we have food and clothing, with these we shall be content' (1 Timothy 6:7–8).

It is not that the physical dimension of human existence is of no importance but that our hope gives it its correct perspective. It *is* important and salvation has implications for it. We have seen in this chapter, therefore, that while the Old Testament forms a backcloth to the New Testament climax of salvation as deliverance from sin, the physical terms in which that salvation is portrayed in the Old Testament are intensely relevant if viewed in the right way.

[31] G. E. Ladd, *op. cit.*, pp. 327–329.

# 8
# Getting on with the Job – A Christian Contribution to the Solution

It is because of the reality of salvation that Christians are different and have a distinctive contribution to make in helping mankind to face environmental problems. There is the new understanding of the world, realized through the renewal of the mind (Romans 12:2; Ephesians 4:23); the power which releases men from slavery to sin generates a new moral influence in society and the possibility of a persuasive new lifestyle. There is a new security, found by the believer in Jesus Christ, which can release him for the costly obedience always necessary for effective discipleship.

This, briefly, is the framework within which we can formulate the Christian contribution to environmental understanding. Being a framework, it does not provide ready-made answers but rather guidelines.

## Sinful structures

Before discussing positive contributions, it is necessary to remember that we are dealing with sin not only at the personal level but also within the structures which express human values and hopes in society. While it is easy to find scapegoats, this ignores the fact that the materialism which is so pervasive is the fault of all. Some may be more to blame than others but we are all guilty at least of acquiescence in the 'good life'. In the Old Testament the prophets identified themselves with the sinfulness of the society God called them to denounce. For this reason it is not easy to see the way forward – how do we deal with sin in the structures?

At this point there is the temptation to complain of helplessness and feelings of despair, but there are ways forward. The rest of this chapter is concerned, therefore, not only with how to live more simply, but with confronting the structures, and given the difficulty of the task, four preliminary points need to be made.

First, despair must not lead to inactivity. This is further to acquiesce in the sins which need purging, and also to deny the goodness of the Creator's handiwork. It is also to deny the power of the Holy Spirit, who convicts the world of sin (John 16:8) and through whom the early Christians made such a great impression on the contemporary world. The course of the last two thousand years of history has much to encourage us:

> We should not underestimate the ability of small groups to get things done, certainly on a national scale. The modern missionary movement is a story of too few people, pitifully small resources and much prayer. Can anyone looking at Africa today deny the enormous impact that it has had on the nations of that continent? There is no limit to the power of God.[1]

Secondly, Jesus told his disciples, 'You are the salt of the earth' (Matthew 5:13). Salt signifies a restraining, cleansing presence which is as much the result of what the Christian *is* as what he *does*. Jesus did not say, 'You can be the salt of the earth *if* . . . ', because he was telling them their function in the world. To take these words seriously is an antidote to despair.

But optimism must not be utopian. It must take realistically the persistence of sin in the world until God's final and decisive intervention which will redeem creation (Romans 8:19ff.) and usher in the new heaven and the new earth (Revelation 21:1ff.). What we are to look for now, therefore, is the limited possibility of improving structures, not perfecting them.

Thirdly, the church is well able to face the task because it is an international body capable of responding to problems on all levels. It certainly needs an international moral force to make the nations see the seriousness of environmental problems when national self-interest may be in direct conflict with broader considerations. It is also because of the international nature of the church, and the wide spectrum of views encompassed by its members on many matters, that it will probably never be possible to look back and single out the contribution which Christians made on these problems. Our concerns overlap here with those of many individuals, organizations and institutions with whom we co-operate. But does it matter?

Fourthly, to feel helpless is to miss the real issue of the

---

[1] Unpublished paper by Donald Hay.

Christian's calling to involvement in the world. The motivation is compassion, which springs from love and obedience; it is not a case of getting involved only when we see that results can easily be obtained. It is possible to argue that Jesus achieved little in terms of influencing people during his earthly life, although he did promise his disciples that they would achieve much more (John 14:12). His aim was not to influence people but to bring salvation to the world through suffering and rejection (John 1:12), while his compassion was there for all to see.

Thus we are faced with the possibility of not accomplishing much in attempting to change structures, but obedience and compassion motivate at a deeper level. This was what spurred on the prophets, notably Jeremiah, who spent his whole life at the task at great personal cost and yet was, at the end, almost totally unsuccessful in influencing the people of Jerusalem. He was, in fact, as much a herald of judgment as of salvation. This leads us to the vital truth that God is not only Creator and Redeemer but also the Lord of history. The results of our obedience are in his hands and it is not always open to us to know what will ensue; but in the long term we know that history is moving towards its divinely appointed goal, and here is our hope and the sustenance of our commitment.

Opposition to the structures which demand the pre-eminence of economic considerations aims to do two things: to demonstrate their sinfulness, and to improve them. It is the nature of our salvation which provides guidelines on how this may be done: through a persuasive example; a new way of thinking; and a new moral dimension.

## A persuasive example

Words on their own carry little weight. In February 1979 a much-publicized sermon on acquisitiveness by Dr Donald Coggan, then Archbishop of Canterbury, drew the retort from one MP that here was hypocrisy. Whether or not this reaction was justified, it highlights the need for an example in non-acquisitive living – of a simpler lifestyle.

It is often argued, of course, that simpler living on the part of a few makes no difference and that, if followed, it would lead to unemployment in manufacturing industry. The reply to this briefly takes two parts: first, results are secondary to truth, and second, the argument actually *points to* the need to change the structures. What kind of prosperity is it which can survive only by the perpetuation of consumerism?

We are engaged, in the matter of simple living, in a ministry of persuasion, demonstrating an alternative to high-consumption materialism. The economic history of recent times, together with gloomy prognoses and the inability of the nations to maintain control of economic events, has left many with the vague feeling that all is not well, and some wonder if there is an alternative way of living. Thus a simple lifestyle can perhaps be called prophetic in the sense that it demonstrates something of what the kingdom is like which Jesus inaugurated. Since the fall brought about a cosmic chain of broken relationships, this kingdom is concerned with restoring those relationships, at least in part, and with announcing the new creation still to come:

> With its different lifestyle the church points to the lifestyle that will one day transform creation. The church has a different lifestyle not because it is holy and unblemished but because it has a relationship with the future kingdom and experiences in part the quality of the life of the final kingdom . . . How will men know that God will create all things new and has begun to, unless they see what a new creation will look like? The church, despite its failings, is to demonstrate what the kingdom looks like and since the kingdom will be the perfect human society, the church is to be the microcosm to society of what it ought to be like.[2]

## The example of the individual

There are numerous books giving advice on the use of our possessions and on how to move towards a simpler lifestyle.[3] But equally important are attitudes; one definition of a simple lifestyle is that it 'demonstrates a joyful sharing of material and spiritual resources, on the principle that our abundance is for the benefit of others'.[4]

Thus in the Old Testament, possession of private property was

---

[2] C. Sugden, *Social Gospel or No Gospel?* (Grove Books, 1977), pp. 15–16.

[3] R. J. Sider (ed.), *Living More Simply: Biblical Principles and Practical Models* (Hodder, 1980); B. Bye, *What About Lifestyle?* (Paternoster Press, 1978); J. Holliman, *Consumer's Guide to the Protection of the Environment* (Pan/Ballantine, 1970).

[4] *The Nottingham Statement* (Falcon, 1977), p. 75.

## Getting on with the Job – A Christian Contribution to the Solution

set in the context of a properly exercised social responsibility – a model rediscovered by the early church (Acts 2:44ff.; 4:32ff.). Criticisms are made that the Acts experiment failed, but this is by no means certain;[5] it should also be pointed out that the principle of joyful sharing must be capable of demonstration in a wide variety of ways, of which that depicted in Acts is only one.

Simple lifestyle can too easily be equated with lists of 'ecotrivia', but Klaus Bockmuehl has emphasized its more costly aspect:

> We might expect Christians to show a sense of sufficiency in claims for material goods and raw materials which, in the environmental and resources crisis, has acquired such central significance. A pioneering effect in the struggle against inflation might be expected from Christians precisely because of their heritage in seeking to overcome materialism.[6]

If we believe in challenging the *status quo*, then why not begin by questioning the need for the next inflationary pay increase? In Canada there is a Christian trade union which has adopted such a policy; it is claimed that their policy has moderated the demands of other Canadian labour unions. Here is where suffering might begin, because to speak with such a voice could prove more than merely unpopular, but it recalls us to our vision of the future and our experience of the kingdom:

> The presence of the kingdom now means that while disciples look to the future and can be critical of the present, they can take the pain of the present on themselves knowing that glory only comes through suffering.[7]

The theme of sharing leads on to the practical ministry of hospitality, referred to by Jesus (Matthew 25:35) and drawn out explicitly in the epistles (Romans 12:13; 1 Timothy 3:2; Titus 1:7–8; Hebrews 13:2; 1 Peter 4:9). In Timothy and Titus it is bishops who are to be hospitable, but since Paul is enumerating the qualifications of those *worthy of* the office, he is explaining the respon-

---

[5] This criticism is discussed in detail in R. J. Sider, *Rich Christians in an Age of Hunger* (Hodder, 1977), pp. 91–93.

[6] K. Bockmuehl, *Conservation and Lifestyle*, translated by B. N. Kaye (Grove Books, 1977), p. 24.

[7] C. Sugden, *op. cit.*, p. 14.

sibilities of all; *philoxenos* and *philoxenia* carry the sense of 'loving to give hospitality' and 'given to hospitality', so that the New Testament picture is one of Christian homes opened gladly and habitually.

Apart from the use of the home in evangelism, it is the place where the lonely and insecure can find comfort and friendship. The city, as we saw in chapter 4, can include large numbers of such people. If you *want* to practise hospitality, then (for example) prepare enough food next Sunday to be able to invite the new person in the morning congregation back to lunch. The offer may be refused, but does it matter? Beware of feeling that your home is 'not nice enough' – if you do, it may be that you have been trapped by your possessions.

Stewardship of our homes involves their location. Inner-city churches lament the seemingly inevitable transfer of all their young people to the suburbs after marriage, and some survive only with imported leadership.[8] Yet in such areas are the problems which call compassionate Christians as the salt of the earth. To live in an inner-city area is a possibility which can be sacrificial but which must be taken seriously.

## *The example of the church*

From the examples of the previous section, it is clear that realistic responses to environmental problems are not easily made and can be sacrificial. This brings us to the example of the church, which is to be seen first in the support the fellowship can (and must) give to those whose commitment is especially costly. Here too is part of the practical answer to helplessness, which may at least in part be synonymous with alone-ness. But this support presupposes that the church is fully informed of the situation and united in its conviction that such support must be given.

## *Joyful sharing*

In practical terms there are three different ways in which the church can persuade by the example of its lifestyle. The first is through joyful sharing, which can be expressed in a number of ways. There are, for example, possibilities of a more imaginative use of Sunday, since worship is most properly set in the context of fellowship (*e.g.* Acts 2:42ff.; 20:7; 1 Corinthians 16:2). Many churches follow

---

[8] D. Sheppard, *Built as a City* (Hodder, 1974), pp. 52-53.

morning worship with a shared meal, often a simple one from which the proceeds go to relief or missionary agencies or world development.

There are also many possibilities for economic co-operation in the church; stewardship teaches that our possessions are for the benefit of others. Consider what most people now possess – car, TV, washing machine, lawnmower and much else; on a purely financial level, a development of economic sharing could release financial resources much needed elsewhere. The importance of this kind of practice is partly in the standing rebuke it delivers to egalitarian consumerism and partly through the joy which can be generated through sharing (2 Corinthians 8:2).

The concept of sharing leads into the subject of Christian communities. The scope of this is vast, but some of the considerations which have led to the setting up of some communities fall within the scope of this chapter. Sometimes they have come about through the concern of families and individuals to share possessions, reduce consumption and release financial and other resources for the service of others. This is a much more radical kind of economic sharing than that mentioned above.

Some communities are located in city centres, enabling transport requirements to be cut and further finances released by sharing cars or doing away with them altogether. They often seem to make a greater impression upon the social needs and problems of their areas than is achieved by more conventional methods.[9] Some writers feel that communities succeed here while the nuclear family home cannot, because of the fragmentation society has forced upon it:

> In its present restricted form, the family fails to meet many of the new demands of its role: insularity has increased the problem of loneliness among the elderly, the single mothers of young children; domestic roles have become devalued; there are few opportunities for effective relationships in the larger society dominated by specialist roles; and the relative remoteness of kin reduces the chances of successfully coping with emergency situations such as sickness and death.[10]

[9] See, for example, M. Harper, *A New Way of Living* (Hodder, 1973).
[10] H. Davis, 'Christian Freedom and Communities', *Christian Graduate*, 28, 1975, p. 2.

In so far as communities meet these pressures, they fulfil their role effectively and provide a healing atmosphere. But it is suggested that the ordinary Christian home can achieve this too, particularly if linked to a caring church fellowship. Communities themselves are of a wide variety of conceptions, structures and purposes, and are part of the wider need for experimentation in corporate lifestyles:

> In a variety of ways, therefore, Christians continue to demonstrate the need for and the possibilities of alternative forms of human relationship. And this variety will persist if the God-given freedom to create and enjoy social structures and relationships is to be enjoyed to the full. Since freedom is not defined as a relationship between thought and action, between ends and means rather than desire and satisfaction, community living will never be the only, or for that matter the best, mode of experience. Prevailing material and social circumstances are the precondition for the exercise of choice; conformity to God's will may mean choosing either a traditional and ordinary way of life or one which asserts a more distinctive rationale.[11]

## Use of the church's resources

The local church has three types of resource – people, money and buildings; it is the latter which form the major concern of this section. Apart from the house in which the ordained minister lives, and possibly a school, there is the church building itself and probably also a church hall, used for a wide range of activities.

The church's concern for its neighbourhood is often revealed in the way it uses its buildings. A common line of reasoning says that since the church possesses a church hall, it must be used, and therefore a range of clubs and activities has to be devised. An alternative line of reasoning states that, since the proclamation of the love and concern of God for his creatures is the main business of the church, the use of its resources must be related to the needs of the community, and that it is therefore right to 'invite in' organizations which may already exist – old folks' clubs, toddlers' clubs and others. There is no real need for the worry often expressed, that unless such activities are specifically 'Christian' they are not really suitable for church premises. Rather, here is a way

[11] *Ibid.*, p. 5.

## Getting on with the Job – A Christian Contribution to the Solution

for the church to minister to the community by promoting and getting involved in the work of 'need' organizations. Probably there will be a balance between the two types of activity – the church's own organizations, and those of the wider community; each has its rightful place under the roof of the church hall, or even that of the church itself.

A particular problem concerns the disposal of surplus buildings. Admittedly the situation is often complicated by legal regulations, but it is sad to see such plant being disposed of by public auction to the highest bidder. In the short term this policy may make financial sense, but at the same time the church is seen to neglect its responsibility towards the continued physical well-being of the area, and of its local people, who then have no control over the use of the property being disposed of. Badly needed resources can then become the object of financial speculation, often ultimately of great harm in both rural and urban areas.

### Involvement in environmental organizations

Environmental organizations include conservation bodies such as Friends of the Earth, but the scope is far wider. Included also in this category are groups such as neighbourhood associations and various levels of government.

To grasp the nettle of Christian involvement in such groups is to face squarely the dichotomy often seen between the sacred and the secular. The need to care for creation demands involvement in all structures involving its stewardship. Consider the local neighbourhood association, for example; a healthy structure, with a good relationship with authority, can help to give to local people a measure of real power in the government of local affairs, and deserves every encouragement the local churches can give it. Christian individuals are, rightly, actively involved; and the church can give practical support in a number of ways, including the promotion of neighbourhood initiatives and active opposition to bad planning applications. It is wrong to see these activities as 'taking people away from' church life. But even these structures can be corrupted, and Christian involvement then acts as salt where, for example, such an association acts simply to preserve the monetary value of its own members' private property.

Christians are already involved in politics at all levels and rightly so, because political decisions affect human life at all levels, not least through local authority decisions which influence environmental quality. For some this is a spare-time voluntary involvement, while for others it is a career and a job. In either case, those involved find themselves in major decision-making processes such as planning and legislation.

The mechanism by which planning decisions are made and inquiries operate can be a cause of major frustration and anger; in spite of all reasonable precautions vested financial interests can hinder the progress of planning towards its best ends. When such forces win the day, power is being effectively removed from the authorities whose role it is to exercise it on behalf of the electorate. Christian salt is needed here.

Important in this field too is the legislative process, which must seek to produce laws to protect the environment from abuse and exploitation and to restrain greed, arrogance and ignorance in man's dealings with nature:

> Such laws would deal with the problems of resource depletion, pollution and the like in ways whose combined cumulative effect would be to move society gradually along the road to a new order. For example, a tax might be imposed on the depletion of raw materials, thus making recycling comparatively less expensive, and perhaps stimulating employment – creating reclamation and recycling activities of considerable magnitude. Such a tax would also place a higher value on thrift and durability, a lower one on rapid product obsolescence. . . . The possibilities for imaginative and enlightened government are endless; and while we probably cannot know in advance which ideas will work well, surely such creative experimentation is worth our best public efforts.[12]

This involvement in the legislative process is a vital one, and is hinted at in the New Testament, where the eschatological breakdown of creation is seen in conjunction with increasing lawlessness (Matthew 24:12; 2 Thessalonians 2:6ff.). But in a sense this is a negative argument; laws restrain evil but do not promote positive thinking; if that is to happen the public conscience must also be mobilized to think seriously about the future in a way which has so far been only partly successful. Governments have failed to do

---

[12] T. S. Derr, *Ecology and Liberation: A Theological Critique of the Use and Abuse of our Birthright* (WSCF, 1973), p. 101.

it,[13] and, curiously, the Archbishop of Canterbury's 'Call to the Nation' in Britain in 1976 was later judged to be naive, although it met with an enormous response from ordinary people.[14]

Legislation is really effective only when it is linked closely to public opinion; good law-making should, in restraining greed and exploitation, encourage the wisdom and unselfishness necessary to help avoid making unreasonable demands on the environment in the years ahead. But how can we help people to think in this way?

## A new way of thinking

Pragmatic ways of thought are insufficient if ecological issues are to be successfully dealt with. Even the church can fall into this trap when, for example, its decisions are governed solely by economic arguments. The danger is that pragmatic thinking cannot *sustain* motivation and action. It has been argued, for example, that the social concern of nineteenth-century evangelicals, in spite of the enormous good it achieved, eventually ran out of steam for precisely this reason, and that we continually face the same danger today:

> Current standards by evangelicals on social issues are usually *ad hoc* reactions . . . We lack a coherent political theory or philosophical perspective and so by default all we can do is to react against evil in the direction of restoring the past rather than acting positively towards the future. Since we have no developed theory of how society works or changes, we tend to moan that things are changing, and we want to restore the *status quo* of ten years ago![15]

Our first task, therefore, is to be one of critical self-examination in order to reveal just how much of the *status quo* we have accepted, and we need to face the conclusion of Klaus Bockmuehl:

> The growth in material things occupied us as well and we were concerned with ourselves. The church of Jesus Christ was no

---

[13] *The Nottingham Statement*, p. 47.

[14] J. Poulton, *Dear Archbishop* (Hodder, 1976).

[15] J. A. Walter, 'Social Concern: 2. Some Lessons from the Past', *Christian Graduate*, 29, 1976, pp. 11–14.

longer a centre of integrity and discipline, which gave men illumination. The reason for this lies very deep, not only in practice, but also in thought we sought unknowingly to copy our surroundings. Our theology resembled an intellectual cargo cult; whatever the tide of time spilt on the beach was eagerly taken up and venerated.[16]

One of the basic assumptions of modern life only now being questioned is that we are all entitled to an ever-increasing standard of living measured in material terms. We have already considered the possible influence that simpler personal and corporate lifestyles can have in terms of persuasion; we are here concerned with the slightly different task of engaging people in the examination of presuppositions on what constitutes a good life, and of the structures which perpetuate them.

In part this problem can be tackled at an everyday level through personal contact. It is true, as we have seen, that many contacts are superficial, but there is an enormous potential here because such conversation openers as the cost of living are almost as popular as the weather! Not only will personal conversation occasionally open up the way to deeper discussions, but there is much to learn from the insights and situations of other people.

Another personal way of persuasion is through resistance to the persuasiveness of advertising. This industry exists to help sell products, and a common practice is to *create* needs in people's minds. We are continually being persuaded that we *need* more than we have:

> Today we are likely to suffer all seven assaults upon our consciousness at once, by TV commercial, by posters, by coupons through the letter box, by national newspaper advertisements, by lead-line display in several local shops, by local newspaper ads with cut-out coupons for cash-off enticements to quicker sales, and by actually seeing the product on a neighbour's kitchen table. Somewhere along the line we have lost the ability to say 'why?' any more. Why must my sights be raised constantly beyond what would be sufficient for me and mine? Why must

[16] K. Bockmuehl, *op. cit.*, pp. 23–24.

I continue to be edged along into expecting more and more of life quantifiably measured in goods and services?[17]

John Taylor suggests that we can begin what he calls the 'cheerful revolution' with three slogans to help us rethink our attitudes – 'The price tag is too high', 'Who are you kidding?' and 'You can't take it with you'.[18] Thus we may decide to stop buying a product which is marketed through a particularly persuasive type of advertising or which we find we can do without; to boycott firms with a bad record in the fields of pollution or exploitation, or which have justifiably acquired a bad record for industrial relations in the Third World.

This resistance needs to be vocal, not silent. Simply to stop buying certain commodities will achieve something, but not so much as if accompanied by a letter to the manufacturer explaining the decision. The well-chosen words of concerned individuals or groups can be effective in an area such as this which is very sensitive to public opinion.

But how far do these attempts to change opinions in the developed world go towards ameliorating a problem which is international? The answer is that they go a long way, for two reasons. The first is that environmental problems are largely the fault of the western world although their extent is world-wide; the second is that the developing nations of the world will not be persuaded that ecological awareness is more than the device of the rich to preserve the balance of economic power, unless international economic justice becomes more of a reality. So long as we are preoccupied with personal affluence this will be impossible to achieve.

## Economic growth

It is impossible to discuss the environment without taking in this vital subject because of the way that our demands upon the resources of the earth are so rapidly increasing. In most, if not all, of the nations the major political issues and goals are economic ones. Lord Keynes has, however, urged us not to 'overestimate the importance of the economic problem, or sacrifice to its supposed necessities other matters of greater or more permanent significance'.[19]

---

[17] J. Poulton, *People Under Pressure* (Littleworth, 1973), p. 103.
[18] J. V. Taylor, *Enough is Enough*, (SCM, 1975), pp. 70–77.
[19] Quoted in E. F. Schumacher, *Small is Beautiful* (Sphere Books, 1974), p. 34.

*Bent World*

This is not to condemn economic growth as such. One of the easy ways out of any complex problem is to find a scapegoat to explain all our ills, whether it be economics or technological progress (the trap which awaits the unsuspecting conservation society). What is necessary is to question the role of economic growth, and its priority with respect to other issues. If the assumption of its pre-eminence is found wanting then this must be stated, and an alternative suggested.

Professor Charles Elliott argues that the economic crises of the 1970s, with their inflation, stagnation and unemployment carrying through to the following decade, reflect a deep malaise in the system, caused by man's failure to manage the earth's resources in a reasonable way:

> We are facing the prospect of a much lower rate of growth of national and individual wealth; the possibility of frequent periods, some of them perhaps prolonged, of zero growth and falling employment and, most important of all, the nigh-certainty that the ability of the rich countries to make the rules of the international economy is going to be challenged with increasing ferocity.[20]

We must therefore attempt to question the *status quo* of modern economics and its presuppositions, not so much to confront the practitioners as to help them. It is not just that economists need help, but they are often asking for it:

> They realize, sometimes acutely, that they who in many respects are least competent to make value judgments are faced with difficult normative decisions . . . What they are often looking for is some kind of ethical criterion by which to judge the possibilities presented to them.[21]

## Economics and presuppositions

There are a number of different views among Christian specialist writers on the subject of economic growth. Those who consider

---

[20] C. Elliott, *Inflation and the Compromised Church* (Christian Journals Ltd, 1975), p. 109.

[21] C. Elliott, 'Ethical Issues in the Dynamics of Economic Development', in D. Munby (ed.), *Economic Growth in World Perspective* (SCM, 1966), p. 346.

it basically correct but who appreciate at the same time the need for proper human behaviour to make it work include J. F. Sleeman, Simon Webley and Sir Fred Catherwood (who states his belief that almost *any* system can be made to work).[22]

Others believe that, since all of life was affected by the fall, and since much modern economic theory has been moulded by a naturalistic world view, Christians cannot accept it uncritically. This point is made notably by Tony Cramp, who has traced the following steps in the development of economic thought.[23]

(1) By the second half of the nineteenth century, a system of utilitarian economic theory had been developed which relied heavily upon the materialistic (*sensu stricto*) sensory psychology of the seventeenth-century political philosopher Thomas Hobbes. This psychology is summarized by Cramp as follows:

> All psychological phenomena are the outcome of bodily conditions, and may be divided into feelings held desirable . . . and feelings held undesirable . . . All of an individual's actions are naturally, and ought to be rationally, directed towards promoting his own interests, preserving his life, increasing his pleasures and/or reducing his pains.[24]

The utilitarians realized man's moral nature but held that education would promote reasonable behaviour since concern for others would be reciprocated and be in his own best interests, so that Hobbesian thinking served as a reasonable basis for economic theory.

(2) This system, although its influence is still felt, has now been largely superseded, partly because of changing ideas in the field of human psychology and partly because of the observable gap between man's actual behaviour and how, according to utilitarianism, he *ought* to behave. The rise of 'scientific behaviourism', which argued that only people's *actions* can be taken as primary data, paved the way for a new kind of economic thinking which is empirically neutral and has no room for ethics and morality. It is

---

[22] J. F. Sleeman, *Economic Crisis: A Christian Perspective* (SCM, 1974); S. Webley, 'Can Christians Support Economic Growth as a Policy Objective?', *Christian Graduate*, 30, 1977, pp. 1–5; Sir Fred Catherwood, *A Better Way* (IVP, 1975), p. 109.

[23] A. B. Cramp, *Notes Towards a Christian Critique of Secular Economic Theory* (Institute for Christian Studies, Toronto, 1975).

[24] *Ibid.*, p. 36.

both empty and unpractical because it rests on an unreal model of human nature (man now becomes merely a 'consumer machine'), and because it is sustained by circular arguments relating the customer's behaviour to market preferences.[25]

It is thus possible to argue that an economic analysis based on an unreal view of man and which is ethically empty cannot *sustain* economic activity in a real world, and it is instructive to go back to the Old Testament to see certain principles governing the economic life of Israel, through a series of laws divinely given. These principles challenge certain modern presuppositions, and since they are part of God's revelation to his chosen nation they can be taken as resting on a proper view of man. The three presuppositions which are particularly challenged are that the pursuit of efficiency via profit-maximization is both rational and right; that efficiency in production takes priority over justice in distribution; and that accumulation of capital in large units is acceptable if the pursuit of efficiency leads in that direction.[26]

But Leviticus 19:9–10 emphasizes that human well-being is more important than efficiency, and Exodus 23:9–10 shows the importance of allowing resources to 'rest'. (Perhaps the distinction can then be made between exploitation and short-term efficiency on the one hand and careful stewardship and long-term efficiency on the other.) When efficiency is paramount, other considerations have to be relegated, including economic justice;[27] this is closely related to environmental well-being in a number of ways, including the belief among the developing nations that ecological concern is a weapon of the rich countries to retain their supremacy. The link is also seen in the alleged process of 'high-grading' during ore extraction,[28] and in the transformation of Britain from a nation supporting low oil prices to one in favour of high prices, a switch necessitated by huge capital investment in the North Sea.

In the Old Testament and in the Talmud, there are laws which insist that distribution of wealth is more important than efficiency in production; Talmud 'welfare benefits' were, for example, designed to guarantee their recipients dignity and a reasonable stan-

---

[25] *Ibid.*, pp. 50–51.
[26] A. B. Cramp, 'Cutting the Cake', *Third Way*, 28 July 1977, pp. 3–5.
[27] J. F. Sleeman, *op. cit.*, p. 121.
[28] 'High-grading' refers to rapid extraction of the richest ore for quick profit; a more sensible practice is to mix the richest ore with lower-grade material, thus prolonging the life of the mine.

dard of living, and, through these means, a reasonable opportunity to use personal initiative to escape their poverty. The well-known sabbatical and jubilee laws of Leviticus 25 and Deuteronomy 15 were designed to prevent the very kind of large-scale accumulation of capital which is so necessary to economic life today.

This is not to construct a system of 'alternative economics' or to argue that the pursuit of efficiency is wrong. Rather it is to suggest that there are more important priorities, related to human need, and that there are biblical principles to help us. Nor is this to suggest that there are particular ways of putting principles into practice; the Old Testament pattern is manifestly inapplicable today. What is being suggested is that proper management of world resources and the attainment of economic stability will only be approached as these principles are reflected in whatever economic structures pertain in the future.

Professor Elliott has questioned Christian awareness on these issues. He is extremely pessimistic of any real response from the ranks of the institutional church, partly because he believes it to be too deeply bound up in the injustice of economic structures.[29] Andrew Kirk shares his view:

> Many Christians, in all honesty, are playing the game in deadly earnest, personally committed to its success, even when this may endanger our health and cause suffering to others, for we are literally and metaphorically up to our eyes in debt to the system. As a result, despite what we may claim about liberty in Christ, we are not free from bondage to a form of life based fundamentally on a non-Christian, immanent view of man and his relationship to the world. Development, progress and the whole future of man are seen in terms which relate almost exclusively to man's possession and manipulation of things. Affluence has dulled our ability to look critically at the ideology of the modern state and its political mentors and made us vulnerable to the propaganda indiscriminately flung at us with their blessing.[30]

Such pessimism may turn out to be too extreme in the long run, but much depends on how effectively Christians can be taught the

---

[29] C. Elliott, *Inflation and the Compromised Church*, p. 145.
[30] J. A. Kirk, 'The Kingdom, the Church and a Distressed World', *Churchman*, 94, 1980, pp. 127–128.

relationship between biblical revelation and the economic life of the nations. There is much scope here for further study, and from this, for persuading the wider world to review its economic and moral priorities.

## The teaching ministry of the church

The sheer complexity of modern life and its structures is just one reason for urgently stressing the need for a teaching ministry within the church today. There must be exhortation (Romans 12:8) but also information and instruction, because action has to have a firm foundation in man's mind and will (Matthew 22:37; Deuteronomy 6:5). Meaningful responses to environmental and economic problems presuppose some appreciation of their nature, and of the guidelines which Scripture provides.

To this end, some churches plan their preaching programmes not on a weekly basis but months or even years ahead, so that their members receive integrated courses of biblically based instruction. These may include sermons devoted to important secular issues. But many problems of modern life are too complex to be tackled satisfactorily in this way, and are better suited to Christian study centres which are becoming an increasingly important part of the Christian life of many urban communities. It is suggested that the environment and economic issues are subjects well suited to this kind of extended treatment. Local churches could actively encourage their members to attend, or even *ask* certain members to attend, with financial assistance where necessary. Attending members could then report back to their congregations in order to promote discussion of the issues raised and the formulation of appropriate local responses.

Informal midweek meetings also provide the kind of setting for extended discussion of complex issues, and suitable study guides are available. In such ways it is possible to bridge the gap between faith and action which is so evident to the economist J. F. Sleeman:

> We need to know not only the facts of the situation, but their inner meaning, in terms of men's hopes and fears and aspirations, in terms of what we believe to be the truth about the nature of the universe and of men and women in it. As Christians we have a great need to make our faith come alive in these terms. So often there is a big gap between the theology we profess in

church and try to live by in our personal conduct, and our actions and beliefs in the economic and political fields.[31]

## A new moral dimension

Morality is concerned with right and wrong and therefore with choice. When men deny God, they do more than deny his existence; they deny any absolute criteria for making moral judgments and are forced to derive their guidance from a world which cannot be fully apprehended apart from the One who created it.

This highlights the moral influence Christians can bring to bear in the field of environmental decision-making. Given that the future use of the world's physical resources involves choice, what moral guidance is available? Since the threats are so serious, and the pervasiveness of sin in the structure so inclusive, the question is a vital one; moreover, as we have already seen, economists are among those actually requesting ethical criteria on which to base their decisions.

Man's God-given status is one of dominion (Genesis 1:26ff.), which reflects not only privilege but also responsibility. The idea of stewardship reflects the same thought. This responsibility is continuous in that it is concerned not only with the well-being of present generations but also with those yet unborn, and it is inclusive in that we are responsible for the use and care of the whole of the created order, of which we are part. Dominion encompasses in addition the vital dimension of justice, which is so prominent in the Old Testament.

Let us see how important these concepts are in making responsible choices in environmental and economic issues, by examining three particular questions – industrialization in Third World countries, nuclear decisions, and the distribution of wealth in times of economic non-growth.

### Industrialization in Third World countries

It is often assumed that the way to bring much-needed economic self-determination to Third World countries is through large-scale industrialization of a western type. But many express doubts over this kind of policy, since it can be argued that proliferation of environmental problems ensues and that it does little to solve the

---

[31] J. F. Sleeman, *op. cit.*, p. 178.

enormous problems of poverty, unemployment and malnutrition. E. F. Schumacher described what can happen: a European government 'gave' a textile factory to an African country and built it in a rural area with a particularly severe unemployment problem. The factory cost £1.5 million but employed only 500 people. When it opened for production armed guards were needed to protect it from crowds of young people desperate for work.[32]

As a means of job creation, this kind of strategy is very expensive and inefficient, and examples could be multiplied. It also serves to exacerbate the gap between the 'haves' and 'have-nots' by bringing it right into the local community.

In response to these issues, the concept of 'intermediate technology' has arisen – a concept whose basis is encapsulated in four propositions: work has to be made available where people are *now*, rather than in the cities, with all the ensuing problems of uncontrollable urban migration; work has to be made available cheaply and simply enough to avoid the need for large-scale accumulation of capital and importation of resources, inevitably increasing external financial dependence; production methods and associated activities (creation of finance, stockpiling of raw materials and marketing) have to be simple enough to avoid the need for a high degree of training; and production should use local materials and be for local use.

Examples of what can be done are numerous. A simple and foolproof water-raising pump for use in arid areas has been designed which can be made exclusively from easily available local materials, and a simple machine developed to make egg cartons from pulped waste paper, for Zambia's poultry farmers. Much work of this type is promoted by the Intermediate Technology Development Group, an organization composed of people in the professions, industries and administration who have returned to Britain from overseas. Various projects are also being promoted in the local extraction of ores and other physical resources by the Geoscientists for World Development group.

Intermediate technology will not change the Third World overnight and is certainly not the answer to all its problems but it can make significant contributions. It makes smaller demands upon the environment in terms of resources, transportation, pollution and population movement. It is also more likely to contribute

---

[32] In J. V. Taylor, *Enough is Enough*, p. 89.

towards economic justice by helping to alleviate the worst kinds of inequality and suffering. It leaves the West with a choice which is therefore a moral one – whether to help the developing nations in a way which is, arguably, best suited to their real needs but which provide little economic benefit in return, or to persist in promoting the exportation of expensive high-grade technology, personnel and materials.

## *Nuclear decisions*

The main question confronting us in the issue of nuclear power concerns the risks involved and whether they are worth taking. A broader question has already been considered: namely, the presupposition of continued rapid economic growth (in a high-technology setting, growth in energy requirements occurs simultaneously).

First, the issue of risks needs to be put into its wider context, in that human endeavour and progress have always entailed taking risks. In terms of history up to 1980, however, the nuclear industry has been a great deal safer than, for example, coal-mining. The Rasmussen Report (chapter 3) has predicted mathematically that the chances of a major disaster at a nuclear power station are extremely small, although the assumptions contained in the report are now being challenged.

Certain qualifications, however, need to be made concerning the use of accident probability figures. They do not tell us when figures point to risks which are acceptable and when to those which are not. Given that the likelihood of a major nuclear disaster is small, it has been argued that to take nuclear decisions on the basis of the figures alone is akin to a 'calculated gamble.'[33] It is also argued that to put a high arithmetical probability against such an accident is to encourage us to think that it could never happen, simply because it is then so difficult to *imagine* it happening at all.

So risk figures on their own reveal little; they have to be interpreted according to accepted normative values in society. For the Christian one of the major questions which will guide in the direction of a proper moral choice is – is this the most *responsible* way to proceed? Thus alternatives need to be carefully considered: how much can be contributed in the future by serious energy

---

[33] J. Ravetz, 'Public Perceptions of Acceptable Risks', *Science and Public Policy*, October 1979, pp. 298–306.

conservation programmes? How much research and development into alternative energy sources has taken place, and how far has it been financed in comparison with the enormous amounts funnelled into the nuclear option? How fast does energy consumption *need* to grow? These are serious questions which must always be asked, because the answers may show that our preoccupation with nuclear power development has not left us with free choice – the huge amounts of money devoted to its development may leave us under some kind of pseudo-moral obligation to persist with it, while the underfinancing of alternative energy sources may leave us without the knowledge necessary to make a free and responsible moral choice in the matter.

Then there is a question concerning man himself. Is he morally capable of handling his new capability? Even the most enthusiastic nuclear proponents are fully aware of this question:

> It may well be that we will show ourselves to be too sinful a civilisation to be entrusted with the knowledge of nuclear power – and to say that is perhaps also to say that we are obviously and in an unprecedented way experiencing the terrible judgement of God, not for discovering nuclear fission, but for being ill-prepared when by his providence it came.[34]

> But the price that we demand of society for this magical energy source is both a vigilance and a longevity of our social institutions that we are quite unaccustomed to.[35]

This is merely to show that nuclear decision-making is a complex and difficult business, and that it is simplistic to argue that since we have always managed in the past we will always manage in the future. But the right questions must be asked, and Christians must insist that they be properly answered as a proper prelude to advancement in the field of nuclear power.

## Distribution of wealth

Some economists are now predicting a sustained period of non-growth or, at least, very slow growth.[36] This prognosis is usually

---

[34] E. Jenkins, 'Fruit of the Atom', *Third Way*, 18, August 1977.
[35] Alvin Weinberg, quoted in J. Francis and P. Abrecht (eds.), *Facing up to Nuclear Power* (St Andrew Press, 1976), p. 148.
[36] C. Elliott, *op. cit.*, p. 109.

## Getting on with the Job – A Christian Contribution to the Solution

made on the grounds of present economic trends, but ecological considerations point to the possibility of such a period also. It has been argued, however, that zero economic growth is undesirable because it will lead to a politically rigid society.[37] Yet if everyone continues to demand more when there is nothing left to give, what are the alternatives? Herman Daly, discussing the state of affairs which would pertain under a steady-state economy[38] where growth is impossible, pinpoints the major issue:

> The important issue in the steady state will be distribution, not production . . . increased income in the form of leisure will result from continued technological progress. How will it be distributed if not according to some ethical norm of equality? The steady state would make fewer demands on our environmental resources but much greater demands on our moral resources.[39]

So long as everyone is becoming wealthier, equality is not a major issue in practice. But as soon as growth in material wealth becomes impossible, equality becomes a matter of major importance. This is a moral question, which has already raised its head in various pay comparability studies. If there are no absolutes in ethical matters, it is difficult to see how society can cope with its moral problems, and it is here that the Christian contribution is again vital:

> The Churches must strive to produce a moral atmosphere in which imaginative programmes of restraint and mutual sharing become politically possible.[40]

Herman Daly referred to an ethical norm of equality as a guide to the distribution of goods in a steady-state situation. Unless accompanied by a marked change in moral climate it would, even if attainable, be a matter not of voluntary restraint but of suspicious watchfulness. Attainment looks, in any case, to be far beyond what is practically possible on any scale, and there are further problems

---

[37] S. Webley, *op. cit.*, p. 2.
[38] H. Daly, *Towards a Steady-State Economy* (Freeman, 1973), pp. 12–27.
[39] *Ibid.*, p. 19.
[40] *The Report of the Lambeth Conference 1978* (Church Information Office, 1978), p. 67.

of trying to quantify the unquantifiable qualities of a truly prosperous lifestyle.

The pentateuchal laws of the Old Testament seem to take account of the impossibility of arriving at a situation of absolute equality, even in such an early, simple and homogeneous type of community as Israel. What those laws provide, however, is a framework within which inequality can be restrained within limits; but the successful operation of those laws, and many other legal codes since, was always dependent on the voluntary subordination of the individual to the needs and well-being of his society and particularly the needs of its poorest members. This is the pattern already noted in the life of the early church (Acts 2:44ff.; 4:32ff.; 2 Corinthians 8:1ff.).

The creation of the moral climate within which these issues can be brought to light and successfully tackled cannot be divorced from evangelism. It is not a case of evangelism *or* involvement in the world; here is an urgent matter which illustrates the stance of Scripture: that evangelism and involvement in society are equally valid parts of what God calls his people to do. The Lord of our salvation is also the Lord of creation, and our relationship with his world is close to the heart of Christian living. Although this is not the *motive* for evangelism, we should have a vision of a gradually increasing number of committed, informed and concerned Christians pervading society at all levels, bringing salt-like influence and helping to generate a new moral climate which will help us to deal successfully with problems of distribution of wealth in the future.

## Judgment

There have already been references to judgment in this chapter, and this is the final theme; it is fitting since the events leading in the final judgment are seen, even though (arguably) metaphorically, in terms of a wholesale disruption of the created order. Some of the details given in the book of Revelation are chillingly parallel to aspects of our present dilemma. There are still some who believe, however, that science and technology will guarantee our continued well-being. But E. F. Schumacher's famous dictum, 'A breakthrough a day keeps the crisis at bay,' is a reminder that such an argument is merely to refuse to face the truth of what is essentially a moral problem, lying within man himself. Because of who he is, man is capable of making choices; he is also responsible for those choices in terms of their consequences, and this ultimately is a matter of salvation or judgment at the hand of a merciful but holy Creator.

Judgment came to Israel and Judah because of their material prosperity, which mattered more to them than the divine covenant which was the basis of that wealth:

> Woe to those who lie upon beds of ivory,
>> and stretch themselves upon their couches,
> and eat lambs from the flock,
>> and calves from the midst of the stall;
> who sing idle songs to the sound of the harp,
>> and like David invent for themselves instruments of music;
> who drink wine in bowls,
>> and anoint themselves with the finest oils,
>> but are not grieved over the ruin of Joseph!
> Therefore they shall now be the first of those to go into exile,
>> and the revelry of those who stretch themselves shall pass away (Amos 6:4–7).

This is not a condemnation of affluence as such but of a society whose preoccupation with wealth had blinded them to the troubles in their midst. Today's world is similar; there is a rich society, whose riches always threaten to disengage it from the very problems caused by the amassing of that wealth.

There are also relevant warnings in the prophets about the dangers of uncertain allies:

> Is Israel a slave? Is he a homeborn servant?
>> Why then has he become a prey?
> The lions have roared against him,
>> they have roared loudly.
> They have made his land a waste,
>> his cities are in ruins, without inhabitant.
> Moreover, the men of Memphis and Tahpanhes
>> have broken the crown of your head.
> Have you not brought this upon yourself,
>> by forsaking the Lord your God,
>> when he led you in the way?
> And now what do you gain by going to Egypt,
>> to drink the waters of the Nile?
> Or what do you gain by going to Assyria,

> to drink the waters of the Euphrates?
> Your wickedness will chasten you,
> and your apostasy will reprove you.
> Know and see that it is evil and bitter for you to forsake the Lord your God;
> the fear of me is not in you,
> says the Lord God of Hosts! (Jeremiah 2:14–19).

Here Judah is informed of judgment, partly already realized and partly still to come, because she seeks security in political alliances with fickle allies instead of in the living God. In our present situation there is a parallel with the hunt for economic security in fragile political alliances; there is also a warning that science cannot save us from our problems without reference to the Creator.

Whatever scientific options and economic choices we take up, there are no moral alternatives; we are required to act responsibly towards creation. And judgment may have already begun in the ecological and economic disruptions of the 1970s. In so far as it is only partial it serves as a warning to take us back to the right way, but when Israel and Judah ignored the warnings it worked through to completion.

Compassion for men and concern for creation demand that the church keep before the world this picture of judgment. There are real decisions to be made in order to ensure continued physical survival, let alone well-being, of the human race. There are enough biblical pictures to persuade us that judgment is a real, inevitable, divine process. Repentance must come now; one day, as for Judah and Israel, it will be too late.

> Then the kings of the earth and the great men and the generals and the rich and the strong and everyone, slave and free, hid in the caves and among the rocks of the mountains, calling to the mountains and the rocks, 'Fall on us and hide us from the face of him who is seated on the throne and from the wrath of the Lamb. For the great day of their wrath has come and who can stand before it?' (Revelation 6:15–17).

# Index

Abrecht, P., 158
Adamson, J., 42
Adriatic Sea, pollution of, 20
Advertising, 125, 148f.
Affluence, 35, 72, 98ff., 108, 129, 137, 148, 161
Agricola, 29
Agricultural land, 40, 84
　technicians, 84
　workers, 62
Agriculture, 30, 111
Airports, 30f.
Alcoholism, 75
Alexander, W., 24
Alexandria, 61
Algae, 56, 90
Allen, D. R., 44
Alternative energy sources, 57f., 157f.
Alternative lifestyles, 60
Aluminium, 19, 21, 26f., 29, 33
American Arms Control and Disarmament Agency, 54, 57
American Association for the Advancement of Science, 10
American Atomic Energy Commission, 52
*Amoco Cadiz*, 47
Anaemia, 81
Anderson, J. N. D., 13
Andrews, B., 42
Anglesey, 46
Animal feed, 27
Antimony, 22
Antioch, 61
Anxiety, 100, 121, 128
Apathy, 73
Archbishop of Canterbury, 139, 147
Argentina, meat exports, 83
Asbestos, 69

Ashby, E., 20
Aswan Dam, 91
Atlantic Ocean, 55
Augustine, 101
Averitt, P., 39

*Bacteriophages*, 56
Bankruptcy, 98
Bantry Bay oil refinery, 44ff.
Barlow Report 1974, 64
Barry, F. R., 98f.
Barth, K., 101
Bascom, W. F., 26
Batisse, M., 22
Beauty spots, congestion at, 66
Behaviourism, 151f.
Behrens, W. W., 17
Beriberi, 80f.
Bertine, K. K., 91
'Biodegradability', 21, 89
Birmingham, inner-city area, 65
Black, J. S., 9, 16, 122f.
Blindness, 80
Blowouts, oil rigs, 44
Blue Circle Group, 27
Bockmuehl, K., 141, 147f.
Brain size, 82
　softening, 90
Brazil, meat exports, 83
Breeder reactor, 48f.
Breese, G., 61
Brickworks, 45
Brighton, 66
Britain, 18
　coal, 39
　oil, 38, 152
Brobst, D. A., 39
Bronchitis, 69
Brown, L. R., 83
Brunner, E., 100f., 104ff., 111

163

Buchanan, C., 60
Bunyard, P., 51
Bureaucracy, 60, 64, 67, 72
Burner reactor, 48
Buttrick, G. A., 120
Bye, B., 140

Cadmium, 21, 91
Calcefaction, 58, 93
Calcium, 20, 79
Caldwell, M., 11
California, 22, 30, 43f.
'Call to the Nation' 1976, 147
Calvin, J., 101
Cambridge, 66
Cancer, 89
  lung, 50, 69f.
Canvey Island oil refinery, 44
Capitalism, 112
Carbohydrate, 79
Carbon dioxide, 47, 69
Carbon monoxide, 47, 69f.
Care for nature, 104, 117
Carson, R., 89
Carthage, 61
Castration, 117
Catherwood, H. F. R., 100, 151
Caulcott, T., 66
Central Electricity Generating Board, 53
Cepede, M., 81, 85
Cerebral haemmorhage, 90
China, antimony resources in, 22
Christian study centres, 154
Christ's death, cosmic significance, 131
Chromium, 19, 26, 33
Church, 138, 140, 142ff., 147, 153
  attendance, 71
  buildings, 142f.
  lifestyle of early, 159
  models of, 130ff.
  teaching ministry of, 154f.
Church of England, 14
Cities, 60ff.
  geographical divisions of, 65
Civil disobedience, 73
Clacton, 66
Climate, 33, 58, 93f.
Cloud, P., 32
Coal, 37ff.
  environmental effects of mining, 40
  estimation of future demands, 39
  mining, 40
  reserves of, 39
Cobalt, 19, 26, 31f.
Cocking, R., 44
Coggan, D., 139, 147
Columbium, 19
Communities, 143f.
Commuting, 66, 69
Compassion, 15, 139
Compost, 27
Conformity, 123
Congestion, 66, 69
Consumer durables, 17, 99
Contentment, 129, 136
Copper, 23, 26, 29, 33
Corn, 79
Cornwall, tin deposits, 25
Corruption, 72, 83, 119
Council of Europe, Soil Charter, 30
Covenant, 117, 119
Covetousness, 123f.
Cox, W. H., 72
Cramp, A. B., 151ff.
Creation, 10, 103, 120
Crime, 66, 71, 73f., 98, 123
Crowe, P., 15
CSM, 87
Cupitt, D., 20
Curse, 119
Cut-off grade, 25

Dairy products, 79
Daly, H., 159
Darling, F. F., 11
Davies, K., 61
Davis, H., 143
Davis, K., 81
Death, 105f.
  Christ's, 131
DDT, 89ff.
Deficiency diseases, 80
Deforestation, 12
Derr, T. S., 12f., 16, 146
Derrick, C., 123
Despair, 137
Detweiler, R., 11
Dietary needs, 79
Disease, 80, 112
Disobedience of man, 105
Divorce, 75

*Index*

Dominion, 103, 155
Douglas, J. D., 115
Drug addiction, 98
  culture, 109
Dublin Docks, petrol spillage, 46
Dubos, R., 65, 68, 71, 74
Duhl, L. J., 76
Dysentery, 80

Earth Resource Technology
  Satellites, 24
Eckholm, E. P., 83
Economic collapse, 17
  depression, 33
  growth, 20, 35, 149ff.
  justice, 125, 149, 152
  presuppositions, 150ff.
  theory, 151f.
Ecosystems, 88ff., 92
'Ecotrivia', 141
Edmondson, W. T., 21, 90
EEC fuel imports, 19, 38
Egypt, 91
Ehrlich, A. H., 57, 69, 71, 78, 80, 82f., 85ff., 89, 90, 92
Ehrlich, P. R., 11, 18, 57, 69, 71, 78, 80, 82f., 85ff., 89, 90, 92
Electricity, 37, 97
Elliott, C., 98, 128, 150, 153, 158
Energy, 17, 37, 57f.
  conservation, 157
  consumption, 37, 42, 58, 112
Enrichment factor, 29
Environmental crisis, 9
Environmental organizations, 145
Equality, 157f.
Erosion, 30, 40, 92
Eschatology, 13, 119f.
Etté, A., 12f.
European Nuclear Energy Conference 1975, 49
Eutrophication, 90
Evangelism, 118, 135, 142, 160
Exhaustion of resources, 17, 21ff., 28, 34, 39, 43, 112, 124
Exploitation of nature, 10, 104f., 149
Exploration, oil and gas, 41f.
Exponential growth, 21, 28

Fabian, P., 94
Families, 143f.
Fat, 79f.

Fawley Island oil refinery, 44
Fear, 124
Fellowship between God and
  man, 101
Fertilizer, 19, 32, 83ff., 88ff.
Findlow, J., 14
Firebaugh, M. W., 52
Fish, 44f., 79, 86f.
  stocks, 44f.
Fleming, D., 42
Floods, 9
Fly-ash, 41
Food production, 78
  transport of, 79, 88
Foot, P., 46f.
Foulkes, F., 128
Francis, J., 158
Fuller, R. H., 97, 99
Future generations, responsibility
  towards, 15, 123

Gans, H. J., 72ff.
Garnish, J. D., 58
Gas, 32, 37, 39, 41ff.
Gasification of coal, 41
Geochemical haloes, 31
Geographical mobility, 62
Geophysical exploration, 32
Geoscientists for World
  Development, 156
Geothermal energy, 37, 57f.
Gold, 29
Goldberg, E. D., 91
Gordon, K. K. and R. E., 76
Gormley, J., 97
Govett, G. T. S. and M. H., 23, 31f., 34
Granville, A., 26
Grade of metal ores, 25, 29
Grain, 79, 94
Gravel, 32
Great Lakes, pollution of, 90
Greece, 18
Greed, 110, 123f.
Green, E. M. B., 109, 124, 134
Green Revolution, 85f.
Grossling, B. F., 25ff.
Growth, economic, 20, 35, 149ff.
  zero, 150, 158f.
Guinness, O., 109
Gulland, J., 87
Gunther, M., 76

165

Half-life, 54
Hall, P., 62, 65
Harper, M., 143
Hay, D., 112, 138
Heart disease, 70
Helium, 24
Hendricks, S. B., 79
Hepburn, R. W., 96
Herring, 87
Hettena, P. H. G., 11
High-grading, 152
High-rise flats, 74 (*see also* Tower blocks)
Hobbs, T., 151
Hodges, H. A., 102, 108ff.
Holdren, J. P., 57
Holiness, 135
Holl, K., 56
Holliman, J., 140
Holy Spirit, 134, 138
Home ownership, 97
Hope, 135
Hospitality, 141f.
House, J. W., 63
Houser, R., 67
Hurst, J. S., 104
Hydroelectric power, 37, 39
Hydrogen, 54
Hypertension, 90


Iceland, geothermal energy, 57
Ignorance, 84f.
Ilke, F., 54
Image of God, 100, 107
Incaparina, 87
India, state of emergency 1975, 83
Industrial Revolution, 39, 61, 81
Industrialization, Third World, 155ff.
Inflation, 35, 42, 75, 98, 125, 128, 150
Injustice, 118f.
Inner-city areas, 65, 73, 129, 142
Insecurity, 100, 113, 122, 124f.
Intermediate technology, 156
Intermediate Technology Development Group, 156
International Atomic Energy Agency, 57
International Fusion Research Council, 58
International relations, 18
Involvement in society, 15f., 118, 137f., 145ff., 160
Iodine, 54
Iran, 38
Irish Conservation Society, 45
Irish Republic, 97
  waste disposal, 21
Iron, 21, 29, 90
Irrigation, 84
Isolation, 60, 71, 76
Israel, OT economic life of, 152f.
Italy, mercury resources, 21
  waste disposal, 20


Jamaica, 19
Jenkins, E., 158
Jones, W. J., 40, 46, 48, 50ff.
Judgment, 119, 160ff.
Justice, economic, 125, 149, 152


Kaye, B. N., 15, 141
Keynes, Lord, 149
Kidner, F. D., 101, 105ff., 126f.
King, P., 15
Kirk, J. A., 153
Knowledge, 106, 126
Krakatoa, 93
Krill, 87
Krypton, 54
Kwashiorkor, 80


Ladd, G. E., 120, 136
Lambeth Conference 1978, 159
Landscaping, 31
Landslides, 40
Laporte, L. F., 29, 33
Laskey's Law, 25, 29
Lausanne Congress 1974, 15
Law and order, 60
Law of the Sea conferences, 32
Lead, 21, 23, 29, 33, 69, 91
Lebeaux, C. N., 67
Lee, E. K., 132
Legislation, 146f.
Ley, D., 73
Lifestyle, 137, 139, 141, 160
*Limits to Growth, The*, 17
Lindh, H., 62
Liverpool, inner-city area, 65
London, inner-city area, 65
Loneliness, 60
Loomis, W., 81
Love, 139

## Index

Low Pay Unit, 62
Lung cancer, 50, 69f.
Lung, R., 44

MacDiarmid, R. A., 22
McDonald, G. J. F., 94
McHarg, I. L., 11, 103
McIntyre, A., 71
McKelvey, V. E., 24, 32
Macquarrie, J. S., 12
Maddox, J., 18
Man in image of God, 100, 107
Manganese, 32f.
Magnesium, 33
Malnutrition, 78, 112
Marasmus, 80
Marion, J. B., 40, 42
Materialism, 96, 107, 110, 113, 140, 151
May, R. M., 89
Mayuga, M. N., 44
Meadows, D. H. and D. L., 17
Measles, 80
Meat, 79, 83, 94
Mechanic, D., 70
Mediterranean Sea, 92
Megalopolis, 71
Mental illness, 70, 75, 82, 98
Mercury, 21ff., 29, 91
Metal resources, 17ff., 24
Methyl parathion, 90
Mica, 19
Middle East, 18
Migration, 62
Milford Haven oil refinery, 44
Milk, 79
Milton Keynes, 66
Mineral nutrients, 79f.
Mining, 29f., 32, 40
Miracles, 121
Mobility, geographical, 62
  social, 62, 65, 67
Molotch, H., 44, 64
Moltmann, J., 110f., 115
Molybdenum, 23, 26, 33
Montcrief, L., 12
Montifiore, H., 10, 20, 101f., 104, 108, 126f., 132, 134
Moral responsibility, 100. 104, 150, 155ff.
Morris, L., 110
Moss, R., 103, 112

Mount St Helens volcano, 94
Mount Tambora, 93
Munby, D., 99f., 150
Murdoch, W., 21, 64, 83, 90f., 94
Myrdal, G., 83
Mysticism, 109

National Academy of Sciences, 10, 22
National Coal Board, 39
National Evangelical Anglican Congress 1967, 14
National Evangelical Anglican Congress 1977, 15
National Research Council, 10
Netzer, D., 60
Neutrons, 48
Nevada, mercury resources, 22
Newell, J., 27
New Zealand, geothermal energy, 57
Nicholson, M., 11
Nickel, 23, 26, 29, 31f.
Niebuhr, R., 110, 113
Nile, 92
Niobium, 26
Nitrogen, 90
Nixon, R., 130
Nodules, ocean-floor metallic, 26, 31ff.
Noise, 45, 66, 68f.
Non-Proliferation Treaty, 57
Norman, C., 22
North Africa, 19
North Sea oil and gas, 38, 41, 43, 152
Northampton, 66
Nuclear decision-making, 157ff.
  fission, 48ff.
  fusion, 58f.
  parks, 51
  power, 37, 39, 48ff.
  processing plants, 51
  reactor accidents, 51f.
  reactor design, 52
  security, 53
  technology, sale of, 57
  waste disposal, 54ff.
  waste storage, 51
  waste transport, 50
  weapons, 57
Nuclear Regulatory Commission, 51, 54

Obedience, 15, 139
Ocean-floor mining, 25, 31
Odum, E., 88
OECD, 38
O'Hagan, D. J., 22
Oil, 32, 37, 39, 41ff., 47, 91
  refineries, 44ff.
OPEC, 19, 35, 37
Open University Course Team, 38, 48
Osborn, E. F., 19, 30, 40
Osteomalacia, 81
Overcrowding, 74
Overgrazing, 12
Overseas aid, 122
Oxford, 66
Ozone, 94

Pacific Ocean, 32
Packer, J. I., 13
Palmer, A., 53
Panic buying, 125
Paor, L. de, 72
Paper, 27
Paraguay, meat exports, 83
Park, C. F., 22
Passmore, T., 11
Pawley, B. C., 14
Permissiveness, 67
Pesticides, 86, 88, 112
Petroleum, *see* Oil
Phosphate, 90
Pietism, 13
Plankton, 87, 90
Planning, 44f., 146
Plastics, 26
Platinoid metals, 19
Platinum, 31
Plutonium, 48f.
Pneumonia, 80
Polonium, 50
Pollution, 12, 17, 20, 22, 44f., 47, 68ff., 90, 93, 112, 114, 122, 125
  atmospheric, 41
  deliberate, 47
Population, growth, 78, 112
  world, 17
Potassium, 33
Potatoes, 79
Poulton, J., 147, 149
Poultry, 79
Poverty, 60, 66, 73, 83ff., 88, 97, 112, 129, 153
Pragmatism, 71, 147
Pratt, W. P., 39
Prayers of thanksgiving, 102, 132
Private property, 140ff.
Proctor, R., 44
Protein, 78ff.
Psychology, 151

Rad, G. von, 104, 106
Radetzki, M., 34
Radioactive isotopes, 54
Radon, 54
Rasmussen, N. C., 52
Rasmussen Report, 52, 157
Randers, J., 17
Ravetz, J., 157
Rebellion, 118
Recession, 21, 128
Reclamation of land, 31, 40
Reconciliation, 131, 134
Recovery rates, oil and gas, 42
Recycling, 26f., 33f., 146
Red Sea, 33
Redemption, 120f., 135f., 138, 140
Rees, E., 15
Reserves, metal, 23
  oil and gas, 38f., 42
Residents' associations, 46f., 73, 145
Resources, discovery of new, 22
  exhaustion of, 17, 21ff., 28, 34, 43, 112, 124
  pressure on, 35
Rhine, pollution of, 20
Rice, 79, 81
Rice, B. K., 97, 99
Richardson, A., 96, 120, 131
Richter, R., 61
Rickets, 81
Righteousness, 104, 118
Risk, 157ff.
Rivers, P., 60
Rome, 61
Rubbish, 21, 27
Rudd, R. L., 90
Ruedisili, L. C., 52
Rural community, 63
  depopulation, 60ff.
  transport, 63
Russia, 18

Sacraments, 132

*Index*

Sadgrove, M., 118, 121, 133
Sahara Desert, 92
Sahel drought, 93
Salinization, 84
Salvation, 16, 115ff.
  cosmic dimension, 133ff.
  eschatological dimension, 135ff.
  in NT, 121ff.
  in OT, 116ff.
San Francisco, smog in, 47
Santa Barbara oilfield, California, 43
Satellite imagery, 31
Satellite towns, 66
Saudi Arabia, 37
Scandinavia, hydroelectric power, 37
Schaeffer, F., 11, 109
Schistosomiasis, 92
Schumacher, E. F., 149, 156, 160
Scotland, hydroelectric power, 37
SCP, 87
Scrap metal, 27
Sea floor, ownership of, 32
Sea water, metal content, 32f.
  thermal properties, 33
Seabed mining, 25, 31
Search for meaning, 108ff.
Searle, G., 30
Seaside resorts, congestion at, 66
Second Vatican Council, 14
Security, 109f., 117f., 127ff.
Selfishness, 122f.
Sennett, R., 72
Separation of man from God, 107ff.
Sermons, 154
Shame, 106
Sharing, 140ff.
Sheppard, D., 142
Shrimp, 87
Sider, R. J., 140f.
Silica fibres, 26
Silver, 21, 23
Simmons, I. G., 11
Sin, effect on environment, 110ff.
Skinner, B. J., 42
Skylab, 24
Slag heaps, 40
Sleeman, J. F., 128, 151f., 154
Smith, P. J., 30, 46
Smog, 47
Snowdonia, 30
Social mobility, 62, 65, 67
Sodium, 33

Soil, 30, 45, 84
Solar energy, 37, 57
'Spaghetti Junction', 69f.
Spain, mercury resources, 21
  nuclear reactors, 38
Starvation, 17
Steady-state economy, 159
Stewardship, 131, 142f., 152
Stott, J. R. W., 15, 118
Street, A., 24
Stress, 70, 73
Strikes, 98
Strontium, 19
Subsidence, 30, 40, 42
Substitution, 26, 33
Suburbs, 66, 75
Sugden, C., 140f.
Suicide, 75, 98
Sulphur dioxide, 41, 45, 47
Supersonic transport, 94
*Superstitions*, 124
Sutherland, J. N., 11
Svensson, L. E. O., 34
Syer, G. N., 11

Talmud, 152f.
Tank, R. W., 44
Tantalum, 19, 23
Taxes, environmental, 146
Taylor, J. V., 149, 156
Television, 67, 148
Terrorism, 53f., 125
Thalidomide, 108
Thanksgiving, 131
Thar Desert, 92
Third World, 19
Thomas, C., 27, 33
Thompson, J. A., 119, 126
Thorium, 48
Three Mile Island, 51
Tidal power, 37, 57
Tin, 21ff., 33
Titanium, 23
Tokyo, smog in, 47
*Torrey Canyon*, 47
Tower blocks, 108 (*see also* High-rise flats)
Town and Country Planning Act 1947, 64, 71
Toynbee, A., 11
Transport, personal, 143
  supersonic, 94

uranium, 50
Tuberculosis, 70
Tungsten, 22f.
Typhus, 56

Ultraviolet radiation, 94
UN Conference on Human Environment 1972, 14
Undersea prospecting, 26, 31
Understanding, 108ff., 122, 125, 137
Unemployment, 45, 75, 97, 125, 150, 156
UNESCO Biosphere Conference 1968, 9
Uranium, 48ff.
  transport of, 50
Urban environment, 67
  planning, 63, 67, 72, 146
Urbanization, 60ff.
Uruguay, meat exports, 83
USA, 18
  Energy Bill 1979, 37
  Geological Survey, 42
  metal imports, 19
  National Academy of Sciences, 10, 22
  Nuclear Regulatory Commission, 51, 54
Utilitarianism, 151

Vanadium, 23f., 26
Vandalism, 73
Vegetables, 79
Venereal disease, 98
Verney, S., 60, 67
Viljoen, R. P., 31
Violence, 73, 75
Vitamins, 79f.
  deficiency, 80
Volcanic eruptions, 9, 93f.
Volcanoes, 37, 94

Wage increases, 97, 129, 141
Waller, R., 12f.
Walter, J. A., 147
Walters, G., 115
Wang, F. F. H., 32
War, 20, 38
Ward, B., 61, 65, 68, 71, 74
Warren, H. V., 69
Waste disposal, 20f., 33, 68, 71
Watson, D., 131
WCC Commission for Churches in International Affairs, 15
Wealth, distribution of, 158ff.
Weather patterns, 93f.
Webley, S., 151, 159
Weekend exodus, 66
Weinberg, A., 18, 158
Wells, D. F., 115
Werthman, M. S., 11
West, R., 46f.
Westermann, C., 100f., 104
Whales, 86
White, L., 11f., 103
Wilensky, H. L., 67
Willmott, P., 74
Wilmington oilfield, California, 43
Wilson, R., 40, 46, 48, 50ff.
Wiltshire, P., 61
Wind energy, 57
Wolf, P. C., 70
Wood, 38
World Council of Churches, 15, 53
World Health Organization, 21
Worship, 132, 142f.
Wright, J. B., 31
Wright, T., 118, 121, 133

Young, M., 74

Zimmerli, W., 103, 111
Zinc, 23, 32, 91
Zirconium, 54

COMSEWOGUE PUBLIC LIBRARY

3 0620 00346 1281

**For Reference**

**Not to be taken from this room**

Coleman, William L. *You and Your Aging Parents*. Discovery House, 1994. [biblical]

Kirkland, Kevin H., and Howard McIlveen. *Full Circle: Spiritual Therapy for the Elderly*. Haworth Press, 1999.

McLeod, Beth Witrogen. *Caregiving: The Spiritual Journey of Love, Loss, and Renewal*. J. Wiley & Sons, 1999.

Meckelson, Doug. *The Elder Wisdom Circle Guide for a Meaningful Life: Seniors across America Offer Advice to the Next Generations*. Plume, 2007.

## SUICIDE

*Depression and Suicide Facts for Older Adults*. National Institute of Mental Health, 2000.

Leenaars, Antoon A., et al. *Suicide and the Older Adult*. Guilford Press, 1992.

McIntosh, John L., et al. *Elder Suicide: Research, Theory, and Treatment*. American Psychological Association, 1994.

Softly, Pat, producer. *A Desperate Act: Suicide and the Elderly*. Films for the Humanities and Sciences, 2001.[videorecording]

## SUPPORTIVE EMPATHY FOR ELDERS

Koch, Tom. *Age Speaks for Itself: Silent Voices of the Elderly*. Praeger, 2000.

Kriseman, Nancy L. *The Caring Spirit Approach to Eldercare: A Training Guide for Professionals and Families*. Health Professions Press, 2005.

Pipher, Mary Bray. *Another Country: Navigating the Emotional Terrain of our Elders*. Riverhead Books, 1999.

Solomon, Deborah, and Tom Kidder, producers. *Depression and the Elderly: Mental Health and Aging*. Aquarius Health Care Videos, 2003, 2004. [videorecording]

Matthews, Joseph L. *Long-term Care: How to Plan and Pay for It.* Nolo Press, 2004, 2006, 2008.

Namazi, Kevan H., and Paul K. Chafetz, eds. *Assisted Living: Current Issues in Facility Management and Resident Care.* Auburn House, 2001.

Nassif, Janet Zhun. *The Home Health Care Solution: A Complete Consumer Guide.* Harper & Row, 1985.

Rubenson, Ellen F. *When Aging Parents Can't Live Alone: A Practical Family Guide.* Lowell House, 2000.

U.S. Department of Health & Human Services, Eldercare Locator, http://www.eldercare.gov/Eldercare/Public/Home.asp

Yeh, Elizabeth T. *How to Achieve Quality of Life and Care in a Nursing Home.* Rosenwasser Pub. Co., 1996.</ER>

**SEXUALITY**

Aging Wisely, Sexuality in Later Life, http://agingwiselypro.lifeledger.com/library/index.cfm?fuseaction=article&art_id=134&CFID=32288380&CFTOKEN=51993006

Gross, Zenith Henkin. *Seasons of the Heart: Men and Women Talk about Love, Sex, and Romance after 60.* New World Library, 2000.

Health Media. Producers. *The Heart Has No Wrinkles* (NSW Dept. of Health, 1988). [videorecording, elder sexuality]

Helpguide.org, Lifelong Sexuality, http://www.helpguide.org/elder/sexuality_aging.htm

Lenz, Elinor. *Rights of Passage: How Women Can Find a New Freedom in Their Midyears.* Lowell House/Contemporary Books, 1992.

DeNoon, Daniel J. Older Americans Have Active Sex Lives, http://www.medicinenet.com/script/main/art.asp?articlekey=83439

Winer, Lucy, and Karen Eaton, producers. *Golden Threads.* Women Make Movies, 1900.[videorecording, older lesbians]

**SPIRITUAL CONCERNS**

Alters, Sandra. *Death and Dying: End-of-life Controversies.* Cengage Learning, forthcoming, 2009.

Barnett, Libby. *Reiki Energy Medicine: Bringing Healing Touch into Home, Hospital, and Hospice.* Healing Arts Press, 1996.

Sankar, Andrea. *Dying at Home: A Family Guide for Caregiving*. Bantam Books, 1995.

Schloss, Sima Devorah. *Taking Care of Mom, Taking Care of Me: Coping with a Relative's Illness and Death*. Judaica Press, 2002.

Shannon, Joyce Brennfleck. *Death and Dying Sourcebook: Basic Consumer Health Information about End-of-life Care and Related Perspectives and Ethical Issues, Including End-of-life Symptoms and Treatments, Pain Management, Quality-of-life Concerns, The Use of Life Support, Patients' Rights and Privacy Issues, Advance Directives, Physician-assisted Suicide, Caregiving, Organ and Tissue Donation, Autopsies, Funeral Arrangements, and Grief*. Omnigraphics, 2nd ed., 2006.

Shemmings, Yvonne. *Death, Dying, and Residential Care*. Aldershot, Hanks/Avebury, 1996.

## SELECTING CAREGIVERS, ASSISTED-LIVING RESIDENCES, AND LONG-TERM CARE FACILITIES

Bausell, R. Barker, et al. *How to Evaluate and Select Nursing Homes*. Addison-Wesley Pub. Co., 1983, 1984, 1988.

Bornstein, Robert F., and Mary A. Languirand. *When Someone You Love Needs Nursing Home, Assisted Living, or In-home Care: The Complete Guide*. Newmarket Press, 2002.

Cassidy, Thomas M. *Elder Care: What to Look For, What to Look Out For!* New Horizon Press, 3rd ed., 2004.

Davis, Ruth. *The Nursing Home Handbook: A Guide to Living Well*. Adams Media, 2000.

ElderCareLink, http://www.eldercarelink.com/

Horne, Jo. *The Nursing Home Handbook: A Guide for Families*. AARP/Scott, Foresman & Co., 1989.

Ilminen, Gary R. *Consumer Guide to Long-term Care*. University of Wisconsin Press, 1999.

Kranz, Marian R. *The Nursing Home Choice: How to Choose the Ideal Nursing Home*. Branden Pub. Co., 1998.

Matthews, Joseph L. *Beat the Nursing Home Trap: A Consumers Guide to Assisted Living and Long-term Care*. Nolo Press, 1999.

Matthews, Joseph L. *Elder Care: Choosing and Financing Long-term Care*. Nolo Press, 1990.

Sheehy, Gail. *Passages in Men's Lives: New Directions for Men at Midlife*. Simon & Schuster, 1999.

Sheehy, Gail. *The Silent Passage: Menopause*. Pocket Books, Revised, 1998.

University of Florida, IFAS Extension, EDIS, Elder Health (en espanol), http://edis.ifas.ufl.edu/topic_spa_elder_health

Van Kanegan, Gail, and Michael Boyette. *How to Survive Your Hospital Stay: The Complete Guide to Getting the Care You Need, and Avoiding Problems You Don't*. Simon & Schuster, 2003.

## HOME SAFETY AND DESIGN

Altman, Adelaide. *Elderhouse: Planning Your Best Home Ever*. Chelsea Green Pub., 2002.

Home Safety Council, http://www.homesafetycouncil.org

National Fire Protection Association, http://www.nfpa.org

U.S. Department of Health & Human Services, Centers for Disease Control and Prevention, Elders' Health & the Built Environment, http://www.cdc.gov/HEALTHYPLACES/healthtopics/elders.htm

## HOSPICE AND GRIEVING

Ahronheim, Judith C. *Final Passages: Positive Choices for the Dying and Their Loved Ones*. Simon & Schuster, 1992.

Beresford, Larry. *The Hospice Handbook: A Complete Guide*. Little, Brown & Co., 1993.

Buckingham, Robert W. *Among Friends: Hospice Care for the Person with AIDS*. Prometheus Books, 1992.

Chase, Deborah. *Dying at Home with Hospice*. C.V. Mosby Co., 1986.

Glavan, Denise. *Hospice, A Labor of Love*. Chalice Press, 1999.

Home Box Office. *Letting Go: A Hospice Journey*. Films for the Humanities & Sciences, 2003. [videorecording]

Kübler-Ross, Elisabeth. *On Death and Dying*. Scribner Classics, 1997.

Lattanzi-Licht, Marcia E. *The Hospice Choice: In Pursuit of a Peaceful Death*. Simon & Schuster, 1998.

Munley, Anne. *The Hospice Alternative: A New Context for Death and Dying*. Basic Books, 1983.

Russo, Richard, ed. *A Healing Touch: True Stories of Life, Death, and Hospice*. Down East, 2008.

Helpguide.org, Senior Citizen Driving: Warning Signs and Helping an Unsafe Driver to Stop Driving, http://www.helpguide.org/elder/senior_citizen_driving.htm

Helpguide.org, Senior Fitness and Sports, http://www.helpguide.org/life/senior_fitness_sports.htm

Harvard Medical School. *Home Safety for Older Adults*. Harvard Health Publications, 2005.

"Is Your Home Safe for the Holidays?" *Health* 124 (December 2007).

National Family Caregivers Association (NFCA). *The Resourceful Caregiver: Helping Family Caregivers Help Themselves*. Mosby Lifeline, 1996.

U.S. Department of Health and Human Services, Centers for Disease Control and Prevention, Heat Stress in the Elderly, http://www.bt.cdc.gov/disasters/extremeheat/elderlyheat.asp

"Winter Safety Tips for Older Adults." *Geriatrics* 15 (February 2007).

**FRAUD ON ELDERS**

Camille, Pamela. *Getting Older, Getting Fleeced: The National Shame of Financial Elder Abuse and How to Avoid It*. Fithian Press, 1996.

Smith, Ron. *Scambusters!: More than 60 Ways Seniors Get Swindled and How They Can Prevent It*. Collins, 2006.

**HEALTH ISSUES**

Depression in the Elderly, http://www.medicinenet.com/depression_in_the_elderly/article.htm

Garnett, Carla. Senior Health: Successful Aging, http://www.medicinenet.com/senior_health/article.htm

Horrigan, Bonnie J. *Red Moon Passage: The Power and Wisdom of Menopause*. Harmony Books, 1st ed., 1996.

Margolies, Luisa. *My Mother's Hip: Lessons from the World of Eldercare*. Temple University Press, 2004.

Mayer, Brenna, et al., eds. *Better Elder Care: A Nurse's Guide to Caring for Older Adults*. Springhouse Corporation, 2002.

Medicinenet.com, Senior Health Center, http://www.medicinenet.com/senior_health/focus.htm

Sharon, Thomas A. *Protect Yourself in the Hospital: Insider Tips for Avoiding Hospital Mistakes for Yourself or Someone You Love*. Contemporary Books, 2004.

Huber, Ezra. *Eldercare: The Legal Issues of Aging.* American Institute of Certified Public Accountants, 2003.

Platt, Harvey J. *Your Will and Estate Plan: How to Protect Your Estate and Your Loved Ones.* Allworth Press, 2003.

Strauss, Peter J., and Nancy M. Lederman. *The Complete Retirement Survival Guide: Everything You Need to Know to Safeguard Your Money, Your Health, and Your Independence.* Checkmark Books, 2003.

Strauss, Peter J. *The Elder Law Handbook: A Legal and Financial Survival Guide for Caregivers and Seniors.* Facts on File, 1996.

*TheStreet.com Ratings' Consumer Guide to Long-term Care Insurance.* Grey House Pub., 2007.

Wold, Lucy F., and Ann F. Andersen. *Family Realities: Helping Aging Parents, Closing the Family Home, Dividing Family Possessions, Putting Affairs in Order.* Harmony House, 1989, 1998.

**ETHNIC AND CULTURAL AWARENESS**

Bengston, Vern L., and Ariela Lowenstein, eds. *Global Aging and Challenges to Families.* Aldine de Gruyter, 2003.

Olson, Laura Katz, ed. *Age through Ethnic Lenses: Caring for the Elderly in a Multicultural Society.* Rowman & Littlefield Publishers, 2001.

Olson, Laura Katz, ed. *The Graying of the World: Who Will Care for the Frail Elderly?* Haworth Press, 1994.

**FAMILY/HOME HEALTH CARE**

ACEP Foundation, Emergency Care for You, http://www.emergencycareforyou.org

Ball, Karlene K. "Driving in an Aging Society: Innovations in Technology." *Generations* 31 (Summer 2006).

Caruso, Ellen M. *Keeping Them Healthy, Keeping Them Home.* Health Information Press, 1998.

Garry, Ronald. *Living Better, Living Longer.* Harvard Health Publications, 2005.

Garry, Ronald. *Living Independently.* Harvard Health Publications, 2005.

Helpguide.org, Age-Related Memory Loss: Recognizing, Reducing and Preventing Symptoms, http://www.helpguide.org/life/prevent_memory_loss.htm

Piver, Susan. *The Hard Questions for Adult Children and Their Aging Parents: 100 Essential Questions for Facing the Future Together with Courage and Compassion*. Gotham Books, 2004; Thorndike Press, large-print edition, 2005. [workbook]

Taylor, Dan. *The Parent Care Conversation: Six Strategies for Transforming the Emotional and Financial Future of Your Aging Parents*. Penguin Books, Revised ed., 2006.

## COMPREHENSIVE GUIDES

A Place for Mom, A Place for Mom's Family: An Online Community about Eldercare, http://elder-care-community.aplaceformom.com/forums/48.aspx

Beerman, Susan, and Judith Rappaport-Musson. *Eldercare 911: The Caregiver's Complete Handbook for Making Decisions*. Prometheus Books, Revised ed., 2008.

Breitung, Joan Carson. *The Eldercare Sourcebook*. Contemporary Books, 2002.

Harris, Dan R., ed. *Aging Sourcebook: Basic Information on Issues Affecting Older Americans, Including Demographic Trends, Social Security, Medicare, Estate Planning, Legal Rights, Health and Safety, Elder Care Options, Retirement Lifestyle Options, and End of Life Issues*. Omnigraphics, 1998.

Morris, Virginia. *How to Care for Your Aging Parents*. Workman Publishing, 1996.

Rhodes, Linda M. Colvin. *The Complete Idiot's Guide to Caring for Aging Parents*. Alpha Books, 2001.

Richards, Marty. ed. *Eldercare: The Best Resources to Help You Help Your Aging Relatives*. Resource Pathways, Inc., 1999.

Sharpe, Charles C. *Online Resources for Senior Citizens*. McFarland & Co., 2nd ed., 2006.

Weisstub, David N., et al., eds. *Aging: Caring for Our Elders*. Kluwer Academic Publishers, 2001.

## ESTATE AND FINANCIAL PLANNING AND WILLS

Bove, Alexander A. *The Medicaid Planning Handbook: A Guide to Protecting Your Family's Assets from Catastrophic Nursing Home Costs*. Little, Brown & Co., 2nd ed., 1996.

Burda, Joan M. *Estate Planning for Same-sex Couples*. American Bar Association, 2004.

Karr, Katherine L. *Promises to Keep: The Family's Role in Nursing Home Care*. Prometheus Books/Golden Age Books, 1991.

Kenny, James, and Stephen Spicer. *Elder Care: Coping with Late-Life Crisis*. Prometheus Books, 1989.

Koch, Tom. *Mirrored Lives: Aging Children and Elderly Parents*. Praeger, 1990.

Manning, Doug. *Aging Is a Family Affair: Planning the Care of Elderly Loved Ones*. In-Sight Books, 1998.

Marcell, Jacqueline. *Elder Rage, or, Take My Father ... Please!: How to Survive Caring for Aging Parents*. Impressive Press, 2001.

Norris, Jane, ed. *Daughters of the Elderly: Building Partnerships in Caregiving*. Indiana University Press, 1988.

Quill, Timothy E. *Death and Dignity: Making Choices and Taking Charge*. W.W. Norton, 1993.

Roots, Charles R. *The Sandwich Generation: Adult Children Caring for Aging Parents*. Garland Pub., 1998.

Satow, Roberta. *Doing the Right Thing: Taking Care of Your Elderly Parents Even if They Didn't Take Care of You*. Jeremy P. Tarcher/Penguin, 2005.

Schiff, Harriet Sarnoff. *How Did I Become My Parent's Parent?* Viking, 1996.

Silin, Jonathan G. *My Father's Keeper: The Story of a Gay Son and His Aging Parents*. Beacon Press, 2006.

Silin, Peter S. *Nursing Homes: The Family's Journey*. Johns Hopkins University Press, 2001.

Strong, Maggie. *Mainstay: For the Well Spouse of the Chronically Ill*. Little, Brown & Co., 1988.

Zal, H. Michael. *The Sandwich Generation: Caught between Growing Children and Aging Parents*. Insight Books, 1992.

**COMMUNICATION**

DiGeronimo, Theresa Foy. *How to Talk to Your Senior Parents about Really Important Things: Specific Questions and Answers and Useful Things to Say*. Jossey-Bass, 2001.

Edinberg, Mark A. *Talking with Your Aging Parents*. Shambhala, 1987.

Norlander, Linda, and Kerstin McSteen. *Choices at the End of Life: Finding Out What Your Parents Want Before It's Too Late*. Fairview Press, 2001.

The President's Council on Bioethics. *Taking Care: Ethical Caregiving in Our Aging Society*. September 2005.

U.S. Administration on Aging, http://www.aoa.gov

U.S. National Institutes of Health, National Institute on Aging, http://www.nia.nih.gov/

## ALZHEIMER'S AND DEMENTIA

Callahan, Sally. *My Mother's Voice*. Elder Books, 2000.

Kinney, Jennifer M., and Cary S. Kart. "Not Quite a Panacea: Technology to Facilitate Family Caregiving for Elders with Dementia." *Generations* 64 (Summer 2006).

Mace, Nancy L., and Peter V. Rabins. *The 36-Hour Day: A Family Guide to Caring for Persons with Alzheimer Disease, Other Dementias, and Memory Loss in Later Life*. Johns Hopkins University Press, 4th ed., 2006.

Moskowitz, Bette Ann. *"Do I Know You?": A Family's Journey through Aging and Alzheimer's*. Taylor Trade, 2004.

Raymond, Florian. *Surviving Alzheimer's: A Guide for Families*. Elder Books, 1994.

Rox, Robert, and Scott Rudin, producers. *Iris* (Miramax/Buena Vista, 2001, 2002). [videorecording]

## CAREGIVER ISSUES

American Library Association. *Library Services to the Sandwich Generation and Serial Caregivers*. Association of Specialized and Cooperative Library Agencies, 2001.

Ball, Avis Jane. *Caring for an Aging Parent: Have I Done All I Can?* Prometheus Books, 1986.

Carlin, Vivian F., and Vivian E. Greenberg. *Should Mom Live with Us?: And Is Happiness Possible if She Does?* Lexington Books, 1992.

Chearney, Lee Ann. *Visits: Caring for an Aging Parent: Reflections and Advice*. Three Rivers Press, 1998.

Gould, Jean ed. *Dutiful Daughters: Caring for Our Parents as They Grow Old*. Seal Press, 1999.

Greenberg, Vivian E. *Children of a Certain Age: Adults and Their Aging Parents*. Lexington Books, 1994.

Hargrave, Terry D. *Loving Your Parents When They Can No Longer Love You*. Zondervan, 2005.

# BIBLIOGRAPHY

*Following is a topical list of resources dealing with elder, elder-care, and safety issues. Inclusion or exclusion of any resource from this list does not imply approval or disapproval by the author.*
~ Bibliography compiled by James T. O'Reilly, J.D. and Holly L. McEntyre, M.A. ~

**ABUSE DETECTION AND PREVENTION**

Aitken, Lynda, and Gabriele Griffin. *Gender Issues in Elder Abuse.* SAGE, 1996.

Breckman, Risa S. *Strategies for Helping Victims of Elder Mistreatment.* Sage Publications, 1988.

Johnson, Tanya F. *Elder Mistreatment: Deciding Who Is at Risk.* Greenwood Press, 1991.

Sandell, Diane S., and Lois Hudson. *Ending Elder Abuse: A Family Guide.* QED Press, 1st ed., 2000.

Wolf, Rosalie S. *Helping Elderly Victims: The Reality of Elder Abuse.* Columbia University Press, 1989.

**ADVOCACY/ORGANIZATIONS**

AARP. *Aging/Parents & Adult Children Together (A/PACT).* Federal Trade Commission, 1999.

American Association of Retired People (AARP), http://www.aarp.org

ElderWeb, http://www.elderweb.com/home/

Nolo, Health Care & Elder Care Resource Center, http://www.nolo.com/resource.cfm/catID/84404409-3882-4800-81764383AA66993B/118/207/

**NOSOCOMIAL INFECTION**—A viral or other infection caused by the elder's contact with the hospital or nursing home.

**NURSING HOME**—Shorthand for a "skilled-nursing facility" in which trained nurses provide for the medical needs of residents, while certified nursing aides provide activities of daily life such as bathing and feeding.

**PHYSICAL ABUSE**—Use of force that may result in impairments such as bodily injury or physical pain.

**REIMBURSABLE COST**—A cost for service given to an elder by a Medicare or Medicaid provider; these are individual bills for reimbursement or, in the nursing home, a monthly report of the costs of care of covered individuals.

**REVERSE MORTGAGE**—Owners of a residence agree to use the equity in the home to receive monthly payments; when the residence is sold, the lender is paid the face amount of the loan, plus interest.

**SELF-NEGLECT**—Behavior of an elderly person who consciously threatens his or her own health or safety by refusing to acquire or consume food, shelter, and other necessities, excluding the conscious choice by a competent elder to forego a particular matter.

**WANDERING**—The unauthorized pedestrian movement of a person with dementia, outside of the zone of their home or residence, usually with confusion and an inability to remember how to return to the home.

**GENERIC DRUG**—A drug modeled on an already-marketed pharmaceutical product, which is used for the same purpose as a "pioneer" name-brand drug, but which costs less because its owner does not advertise and does not perform extensive research.

**HOME HEALTH CARE**—Assistance programs to provide personal care, to aid the elder to remain at home. The home health aide assists with the activities of daily life, including routine taking of medication.

**HOSPICE**—Residential or in-home services to provide comfort and relieve pain during the last weeks of a dying person's life.

**INDEPENDENT LIVING**—A residential arrangement without structured care or supervision; a "normal" adult-living program, perhaps with visiting-nurse service to continually examine signs of aging.

**INSPECTOR GENERAL**—The office within the federal Department of Health and Human Services that examines potential fraud by providers of Medicare and Medicaid services.

**INSTITUTIONAL ABUSE**—Actions by an employee or agent of a residential-care institution that constitute physical, psychological, or financial abuse.

**LONG-TERM CARE**—A broad term intended to cover health care provided through residential programs; typically used for a skilled-nursing facility.

**MECHANIC'S LIEN**—When a home-repair company works on your residence, you may disagree about their charges; they will threaten to place a lien on the title for your home so that before it can be sold, they will have to be paid. If you intend to pay them, this threat will not be carried out. If it is, ask an attorney to assist you in contesting and removing the lien.

**MEDICAID**—A federal program for health care for vulnerable persons; eligibility is dependent on poverty-level status and medical needs; Medicaid has a primary role in funding of long-term care for indigent elders.

**MEDICARE**—A federal program for hospital and medical services for elderly and disabled persons; Medicare provides limited inpatient benefits for nursing homes.

**NEGLECT**—Conscious refusal of necessary food, water, medicine, shelter, or other care to an elder; or failure to fulfill one or more obligations to an elder by a person who has some special responsibility and duty of care.

# GLOSSARY

**ABUSE**—Maltreatment of an elderly individual by another person who has a special duty of care or other responsibility toward the elder; this includes physical, psychological, and financial abuses.

**ACCREDITATION**—The voluntary private process by which entities like the Joint Commission (JCAHO) evaluate the adequacy of services and programs at hospitals and nursing homes.

**A.D.A. ACCESSIBLE**—The Americans with Disabilities Act requires ramps, rails, and other physical means of allowing mobility-impaired persons to enter public places such as government offices.

**ASSISTED LIVING**—A residential arrangement with services and care, including food and other assistance with activities of daily living.

**CENTER FOR MEDICARE AND MEDICAID SERVICES**—Part of the federal department of Health and Human Services responsible for two large health-care systems affecting elders.

**CONTINUING-CARE CENTER**—A residential community that offers several levels of care for elders.

**DEMENTIA**—A medical diagnosis of brain disease, manifested by behaviors that are abnormal in the majority of adults.

**DEPOSITION**—A structured interview with questions, used in preparation for a trial; the questions are asked by the opponent of the person who is being "deposed."

**DEPRESSION**—A medical diagnosis of a mental illness.

**ENTRY FEES**—Charges due at beginning of residence in a continuing-care center.

**FINANCIAL ABUSE**—Unlawful or improper withdrawal or removal of funds or assets of an elder, e.g., sudden unexplained closure of an account or changes to a signature card and transfer of funds.

# APPENDIX 4:
# HOME FRAUDS PROTECTION CHECKLIST

__ Contractor is bonded and insured (for your protection if workers are hurt)

__ Contractor is willing to name local references of satisfied customers

__ A trusted friend or relative has read the contract and agrees it is appropriate

__ You obtained one or two other bids on the identical work, to evaluate prices

__ Contractor has local license, e.g., plumber, heating, etc.

__ Contractor is listed by local Better Business Bureau (phone white pages or bbb.org)

__ Contractor will allow you time to consider the contract before signing it

___Contractor does not demand 100 percent payment before work starts

___ If the work is to be financed (not paid in cash), you have information about the lender, the payment term, and the disclosures of Annual Percentage Rate

# APPENDIX 3:
# ELDER SELF-NEGLECT: ADULT PROTECTIVE SERVICES CHECKLIST

If the elder is reported by neighbors or friends to be in need of intervention to provide health or supportive services, then Adult Protective Services representatives are likely to:

___ Visit and interview the elder

___ Interview adult children, relatives, and caregiver(s) regarding conditions

___ Obtain a medical assessment of the elder

___ Admit the person to the hospital if the condition warrants hospital treatment

___ Contact local police if evidence of physical abuse warrants investigation

___ Contact Agency on Aging or other social services agencies for home health aide

___ Contact energy-supply company to assure heat/power will remain on

___ Obtain "Meals on Wheels" or comparable local food delivery assistance

___ Contact local volunteer home-repair organization, if any

# APPENDIX 2: EVALUATION OF POSSIBLE ABUSE CLAIMS

What has suddenly changed? What seems to be unlike an elderly person's longtime conduct? If you are a close relative or friend, have a conversation with the elder; a close friend or relative of the same gender should be able to check him or her for indications of physical abuse. Remember that "abuse" includes psychological and financial abuse as well.

___ Bruises visible and evident

___ Untreated injuries: explanation of how they occurred is suspicious

___ Unclean, unsanitary conditions, with no explanation by the caregiver

___ Broken eyeglasses

___ Arms show signs of restraint straps or ropes

___ Refusal by caregiver to allow conversation alone with elder

___ Underclothes bloody, torn, or stained

___ Refusal by caregiver to allow trusted family member to see the elder's financial statements or checking-account statements

___ Unexplained closure or cash-out of existing bank accounts

___ Calls from the family lawyer to confirm changes being made to the elder's will

___ Confirmation letters from financial institution re changes to account ownership or addresses

## STATE ELDER-CARE OR LONG-TERM CARE CONTACTS FOR PROBLEMS

| Vermont | 802–241–2401 | dail.vermont.gov |
|---|---|---|
| Virginia | 800–552–3402 | vda.virginia.gov |
| Washington | 360–236–4700 | fortress.wa.gov/doh/hpqa1 |
| West Virginia | 800–352–6513 | wvdhhr.org/bcf/children_adult/aps/report.asp |
| Wisconsin | 800–815–0015 | longtermcare.state.wi.us/home/complaint.htm |
| Wyoming | 800–442–2766 | wdh.state.wy.us/aging |

## STATE ELDER-CARE OR LONG-TERM CARE CONTACTS FOR PROBLEMS

| Kansas | 800–860–5260 | agingkansas.org |
| --- | --- | --- |
| Kentucky | 502–564–7372 | chfs.ky.gov/dms/ |
| Louisiana | 800–259–5301 | dhh.louisiana.gov/offices/?id=105 |
| Maine | 800–750–5353 | maine.gov/dhhs/dlrs |
| Maryland | 800–243–3425 | mdoa.state.md.us |
| Massachusetts | 800–922–2275 | masslongtermcare.org |
| Michigan | 800–803–7174 | michigan.gov/ltc |
| Minnesota | 800–882–6262 | dhs.state.mn.us |
| Mississippi | 800–948–3090 | msdh.state.ms.us/msdhsite/_static/30,0,83.html |
| Missouri | 800–390–3330 | dhss.mo.gov/aaa |
| Montana | 800–362–8312 | dphhs.mt.gov/sltc |
| Nebraska | 800–942–7830 | dhhs.ne.gov/ags |
| Nevada | 775–687–4210 | aging.state.nv.us |
| New Hampshire | 800–442–5640 | dhhs.nh.gov/dhhs/oltco |
| New Jersey | 800–792–9770 | state.nj.us/health/healthfacilities |
| New Mexico | 800–752–8649 | dhi.state.nm.us/hflc |
| New York | 888–201–4563 | nyhealth.gov/facilities/nursing |
| North Carolina | 800–662–7030 | ncdhhs.gov/olderadults |
| North Dakota | 701–328–2352 | ndhealth.gov/hf |
| Ohio | 800–342–0553 | odh.ohio.gov/odhprograms/dspc |
| Oklahoma | 405–271–6868 | ok.gov/health/protective_health/long_term_care_service |
| Oregon | 800–522–2602 | oregon.gov/ltco/contact_us.html |
| Pennsylvania | 877–724–3258 | dsf.health.state.pa.us/health/cwp |
| Rhode Island | 401–222–2566 | dea.ri.gov/programs/nursing_homes.php |
| South Carolina | 803–545–4370 | sdhec.gov/health/licen/complaint.htm |
| South Dakota | 800–738–2301 | doh.sd.gov/licensure/complain.aspx |
| Tennessee | 877–287–0010 | health.state.tn.us |
| Texas | 800–458–9858 | txabusehotline.org |
| Utah | 800–662–4157 | health.utah.gov/hflcra |

# APPENDIX 1: STATE ELDER-CARE OR LONG-TERM CARE CONTACTS FOR PROBLEMS

| State | Phone | Web site |
|---|---|---|
| Alabama | 800–243–5463 | adphnotes.state.al.us/ncfweb.nsf |
| Alaska | 866–465–3165 | hss.state.ak.us/dsds/ |
| Arizona | 602–364–2690 | azdhs.gov/als/ltc/index.htm |
| Arkansas | 800–852–5494 | arhspa.org |
| California | 800–434–0222 | aging.ca.gov |
| Colorado | 800–544–9181 | cdphe.state.co.us/hf/ncf |
| Connecticut | 800–994–9422 | ct.gov/agingservices/site |
| Delaware | 800–336–9500 | dhss.delaware.gov/dhss/dltcrp |
| District of Columbia | 202–676–3900 | dcoa.dc.gov |
| Florida | 800–963–5337 | ahcaxnet.fdhc.state.fl.us |
| Georgia | 800–669–8387 | aging.dhr.georgia.gov/portal/site/dhr-das |
| Hawaii | 808–586–0100 | hawaii.gov/health/elder-care/health-assurance/licensing |
| Idaho | 800–488–5731 | idahocareline.org/elibrary |
| Illinois | 800–548–9034 | health.illinois.gov/seniors |
| Indiana | 800–452–4800 | in.gov /isdh/23260.htm |
| Iowa | 800–351–4664 | dia-hfd.iowa.gov/dia_hfd/home |

## MANAGING THE INTERACTION WITH OFFICIALS

Ask for the office handling the particular type of help you need, and ask for an appointment with the appropriate person to discuss your elder's application or status. Ask what documents you need to bring.

3. Do not be intimidated by long waits on the phone; be patient and persistent. The benefits process is like a race over hurdles, and waiting is one of the hurdles to be overcome. Bureaucracies win if applicants wander away.

4. Bring a pen and a notebook with you. Write down the names of the persons with whom you have dealt, not in an accusatory way, but because you will need to include names when you write any subsequent letters.

5. Sometimes government-office "intake" workers are overstressed, rude, or difficult. Smile and be very patient. If they persist in being difficult, ask to speak with the supervisor of their department. Do not be intimidated by their unfriendly attitude, if you observe it. Don't respond in the same manner ("you work for us, the taxpayers").

6. Frustrating waits are part of the system. Remember that people like you convinced your legislators to create this program and this benefit. If you (or the elder you assist) have the income, health, or other qualifications that match those of this program, then you have rights to fair consideration of your qualifications by the agency. Don't give up.

7. If you don't get a satisfactory response in person, ask, "To whom shall I address my letter when I write about what you're telling me here?" This polite inquiry stimulates managers to want to avoid dealing with paperwork, and incoming complaint letters generate paperwork.

8. If $10,000 or more is at stake, consider having an elder-law attorney handle all of this for you. The hassles you save will be worth it, and the attorney's experience will speed up a favorable decision.

9. Don't let the experience of friends create unreasonable expectations about how the agency process should work.

10. Finally, do not do the typical counterproductive things, such as protesting that "I'll have your job for this!" or "I'm going to call my legislator!" or using expletives. Your mission is to get the benefits, not to permanently alienate the people who decide on those benefits.

# CHAPTER 14: MANAGING THE INTERACTION WITH GOVERNMENT OFFICIALS

This chapter assumes that the federal, state, or local office has some role in assisting you in dealing with the elder's problem, and that you have been able to understand what specific problem is being or has been encountered by the elder whom you seek to assist.

Most of your meetings with government officials will involve the process of applying for, or the government's denials of, financial or insurance benefits. You and the elder you assist are one case among many. With rare exceptions, the government official has more of a caseload than he or she can readily manage. Because you are one of many, and many others have been unprepared or insulting or abrasive, you will want to stand apart and be better than the crowd. So take care that the agency staff's "first impression" of you should be that you are clear, direct, and calm.

Be businesslike and have all your documents ready to show the workers at the agency, to show eligibility. Be sure to take along a copy of the power of attorney if the elder does not accompany you; this avoids any problem with rules of protection of the elder's privacy that would prevent government employees from discussing the elder's file. Here are some steps to consider:

1. Read about the agency and its program(s) on its Web site, if possible. The public library has excellent research professionals who can help with this basic step toward understanding. The more you know, the less time you will waste, as you go to the right office for the right benefit.

2. Call in the morning for an appointment if possible. Later in the day, phones are answered less quickly and with a tired, less helpful response.

government presents you a bill for $10,000 of reimbursement to the state Medicaid fund, months after you cashed and spent the $10,000 check for settlement of claims against the nursing home. Be cautious in working with your attorney to file a written notice with the state "Medicaid recovery" offices.

## CASE STUDY 1

Mr. Blue, an Alzheimer's patient who was unsupervised when he walked away from the "secure unit" of the Rivers Nursing Home, drowned in a nearby swamp, and his body was found by searchers two days later. Blue's care had been paid for by Medicaid for two years. A settlement was reached in the subsequent negligence suit against Rivers after 18 months of discussions, and Blue's daughter received $125,000 after legal fees and expenses on March 1. On July 1, Ms. Blue received a letter demanding repayment to the state Medicaid fund of $95,000. After further negotiations, she paid the state $77,000 to resolve the demand without going through the extra costs of a lawsuit.

## CASE STUDY 2

Some studies have shown a correlation between strokes and nutritional and hydration deficits in very old nursing-home patients. Expert witness testimony for the plaintiff, asserting that nursing-home negligence caused a stroke in Ms. Golden, will be presented by a national expert. The claim is disputed by the insurance company, using three local expert physicians. In the second year of the suit, after motions and depositions, the defense offers $20,000. The plaintiff's lawyer declines, seeking $150,000. He then hires a jury consultant who sets up an experiment, presenting both sides of the abbreviated case to a panel of the same type and background as the people who would be on the actual trial jury. The mock jury votes 6–3 for the defense. The plaintiff's attorney persuades the guardian for Ms. Golden to voluntarily dismiss the suit; including his time, the plaintiff's attorney has lost $30,000.

defendant use the defendant's medical device within the proper directions approved by FDA?

9. Can you afford the expert witness whose services and opinions are needed to prove the cause of the injury or illness, rebutting the defense's predictable expert testimony?

10. Is there a strong contract defense that could be asserted, because of a waiver or restriction to which the elder or caregiver had agreed?

## MONEY NOW, OR MORE LATER?

Economists talk about the "time value of money" in lawsuit settlements. Is the benefit of receiving $10,000 today better than the uncertain potential of winning a jury award for $20,000 and actually collecting it in three to four years? Probably. Is there a family need for that money today that justifies taking less money in order to have the funds sooner? Perhaps. Many automobile and playground cases involving very young victims settle for a structured annuity of $x$ dollars a month. In elder cases, the long-term payout of a structured settlement is not really attractive, as it might be with a child's accident that settles with a monthly annuity for future medical expenses. Remember that rushing to settlement might induce the defendant's insurance company to "low-ball" the payment and disdain the merit of your claims.

## ACTUAL TERMS OF SETTLEMENT

If you take the option to litigate, and if you have an excellent factual case and a skilled attorney, then receiving money in settlement is probably all that you can reasonably expect, since so few such cases actually go to verdicts. If you have gone through the lawsuit option in hopes of "sending a message" or "exposing and deterring wrongdoing," then the settlement terms attached to the defendant's payment are likely to be a nasty surprise. That is because virtually all defendants demand a secrecy clause, preventing disclosure of the details of settlement. There may be a negotiated public statement, but the nursing home or equipment maker will not wish to sustain both the costs of paying your elder and the negative effects of bad publicity. So such a statement is almost certain to be nonpublic and not a deterrent to others.

## MEDICARE-MEDICAID REIMBURSEMENT

Note that there may be a Medicare-Medicaid recovery from the amount of damages actually paid, if the elder had been receiving these federal and state funds for his or her care. You may be surprised to find that the

in the range of acceptable outcomes. You will need to decide whether or not to accept. Several factors are to be considered.

The hardest part of settlement of an injury or death lawsuit, for the person who brought the suit, is "letting go" of a process that has drawn an emotional investment by the persons involved. This is a real concern for the lawyer, who sometimes sees clients take unrealistic postures. Be more open to the reality of the situation, even if it seems to be less than full vindication of the rights of the elder.

Another difficulty is the appreciation of vulnerabilities that suggest the prudence of a settlement when the other side offers a certain amount less than the lawsuit's demand. You might lose. Most settlements are better than losses. Was there a conscious assumption of risk? Was this a suicide attempt that went bad? Understanding the weakness of your case from your lawyer's experienced judgment is like watching a math whiz handling a Rubik's Cube—a complex design of multiple pieces that somehow all fit together. The puzzle of when to accept a settlement and when to hang in for the next phase is the central theme of your dialogue with your counsel, as you consider whether settling at a particular dollar figure would make sense.

A word about ethics: The client, not the lawyer, decides when to settle The lawyer sometimes is given authority to reach agreement, but when this is not expressed, the lawyer must ask for your consent to settle your case (or for that of the noncompetent elder for whom you have the power of attorney).

## FACTORS TO CONSIDER

1. Did your elder survive the misconduct or accident?

2. Is there photographic evidence of how the incident occurred?

3. Is the elder available and competent to testify?

4. Will the defense delay the case long enough for the elder to lose competence, or even to die?

5. Is the nursing-home defendant just a shell company with few assets to pay a damage award?

6. Is the jury likely to be as sympathetic to your case, if the elder is dead and cannot be available to testify?

7. Is your key witness an ex-employee of (and so not intimidated by) the defendant company, and will he or she be available to testify?

8. Has a key fact been uncovered in depositions or discovery that hurts your view of the causation linkage, e.g., did employees of the

# CHAPTER 13:
# WHEN SHOULD WE SETTLE?

Some elders or their representatives have opted for litigation as a means to compensate the elder (or the estate) and to deter future misconduct. For them, a natural question is, when should we settle our lawsuit? Experience with both sides of litigation teaches that this is a very fact-specific answer, but there are some common principles involved:

1. Listen to what *reasons* your lawyer offers for agreeing to or rejecting the settlement.

2. Listen to the assessment of the *vulnerabilities* that make a full trial risky for your side.

3. Consider the insurance company's claims department's role of wanting *earlier resolution* of the case as a factor inducing some payment of a claim.

4. Consider the long-term desire of the elder's family for "closure."

5. Consider the *costs* to you of pretrial and trial expenses, and the "time value of money" involved.

**CONTIGENCY FEES MAKE "PARTNERS"**

You and your attorney are on a journey together, in which there must be mutual trust. The contingency-fee system means that your attorney doesn't get paid unless and until you receive the check from the defendant (or the defendant's insurance company). He or she has a built-in incentive to make your recovery swift and as large in dollar amount as practicable.

One day, your attorney may call with word that there is an offer to settle your litigation for $x$ dollars. He or she will describe why this is or is not

## WHEN TO CHOOSE WHICH TACTIC TO RESPOND?

court upheld the contract term and sent the case to arbitration. Because the earning capacity of John Green was zero and his existing medical problems suggested a short life expectation, and because the electrical installer was no longer in business, the arbitrator awarded only $30,000 against Egan. After legal fees and $3,000 in expenses, the family received $15,000.

## CASE STUDY 2

Nursing-home patient Ms. Violet received the wrong medication from a new aide who had no supervision during the morning round of distribution of medication. She was severely affected for a week, but survived. The family called a lawyer and also called the state. The insurance carrier paid a small settlement, and the case was closed. But the state's long-term care agency imposed a $12,000 fine on the owner of the nursing home, and suspended its admission of new Medicare-Medicaid patients for sixty days, since the resident of the nursing home had been in "imminent jeopardy" and could have been killed by negligence and the failure to train and supervise newer staff.

## ARBITRATION

Arbitration of disputes means that a neutral person will hear both sides in an informal setting, with no outsiders present, then will judge the merits of the case and announce a dollar amount as the final decision, which is final because both sides have agreed in advance to accept it. Courts, lawsuits, and punitive damages are not involved. Arbitration is often one of the terms and conditions that are required to be accepted in contracts of nursing-home admission. Trial lawyers have strongly criticized these clauses, and some courts have declined to follow their restrictions.

The result of enforcing this term is that faster, less formal decisions are reached, but these decisions lack the punitive force of a "big win" in a liability case. Variables make it hard to generalize. Who selects the arbitrator, what remedies he or she can award, whether the award comes with a written decision, and other uncertainties abound in the process of arbitration. As with the psychological issues discussed above, "closure" and "vindication" are not possible through this channel. Lawsuits are "hot" but erratic in outcomes; arbitration is deliberately "cool" and nonpassionate.

## MEDIATION

Mediation and settlement of litigated disputes is optimal. Relatively quick and private meetings with an experienced mediator tend to be sobering for both sides, and show each side its weaknesses. Drama is minimal; either working out a payment or withdrawing the claim will be the likely outcome. For elders, an outcome that gives a cash award is optimal, since a multiyear structured settlement is unattractive to a person with a shorter life expectancy. Unlike in arbitration, either side could reject a proposed mediated decision and walk away, but most well-planned mediations result in a dollar amount that each side can tolerate.

## CASE STUDY 1

Poorly maintained electrical switches at the Egan Assisted Living Center resulted in a short circuit while resident John Green, eighty-three, was touching the switch. Green was killed and the Green family went to a lawyer. The lawyer estimated that liability for negligence was clear and that the center's insurance carrier would fight to hold down the amount. The family agreed to a contingency-fee contract with the lawyer. Suit was filed; the local court dismissed because Egan Center admission forms had required disputes go to arbitration. Though the Greens protested, the

agency is probably the most viable actor for those in nursing homes; a state consumer-protection agency or the consumer-affairs bureau of a state attorney general's office is optimal for cases of fraud on homeowners; advertising scams are best challenged through the Federal Trade Commission.

Lower your expectations. Regulatory solutions are unexciting compared with the television and movie viewer's expectation of a jury award of massive damages. The downside of awaiting a government decision is psychological: no media hype, no clear triumph or vindication of the elder or caregiver, no television coverage on the courthouse steps reporting on a massive jury verdict against a bad defendant. Penalties or license issues are routine. Government does routine things well, with little drama.

**LITIGATION OPTIONS**

Litigation is the most combative of the alternative remedies for harm. Triumphant winners vanquish losers, in the fantasy world of television drama. But in the real world, almost all cases are settled. The downside of a lawsuit is at the very start, the first meeting with a lawyer who might take on this suit. Consider the cost of a lawsuit; you are hopefully convincing a lawyer to "bet" on your case by taking a contingency fee, paid only upon success. If the case is settled or won, the lawyer typically will take 40 percent of the first $100,000 and 33 percent over that figure: so if the death of an elder results in a $200,000 settlement of a negligence lawsuit, the family will receive around $125,000, minus the expenses of preparing the case.

Defendant corporations with deep pockets and savvy lawyers have a great advantage. You have read the corporate advertisements and press statements that "greedy trial lawyers" are forcing cutbacks in quality and taking money away from caring for sick elders. A reality check shows the insurance companies and the shareholder indifference that lies behind this facade; there is no level playing field for the low-income family whose grandparent has been injured or killed. Many injured people and their families simply cannot afford to sue, unless a lawyer advances the costs and defers payment until the case is closed. More often than not, money and time have been in short supply; when the elder has been seriously injured, the adult son or daughter cannot afford to spend his or her savings on the per-hour cost of a lawyer's efforts. It seems unfair.

Apart from the conventional litigation choice, there are two more moderate alternative options, mediation and arbitration.

# CHAPTER 12:
# WHEN TO CHOOSE WHICH TACTIC TO RESPOND TO THE HARM

Up to this point, the reader has encountered several risks of harm to the elderly person. We have discussed the overlapping systems of regulation and of civil liability, as alternate means to reduce the risks. This chapter deals with tactics to oppose the occurrence of that harm. This discussion assumes that the reader wishes to help an elder avoid one or more harmful situations, through the use of regulatory complaints or lawsuits. When should you choose which alternative way of responding to harm that is being caused or has been caused to the elder?

**REGULATORY-AGENCY ACTIONS**

The remedy of regulatory-agency action is the one option that does not require extensive investment of personal effort and time by the elder or by his or her guardians. Government pays all the costs for the investigation and prosecution of the violators. Its charges make the local news, publicity affects the defendant, and trade associations and periodicals report the regulatory conflicts with corporate defendants. Hopefully, the decision by the government imposing a penalty provides a deterrent to others, or the agency changes the rules prospectively to enhance compliance by other firms. All of us, as taxpayers, pay for this remedy that protects groups or individual elders. Ultimately, the law comes to adapt itself to meet the problem once a significant number of regulatory actions have been taken against individual violators.

How will this government regulatory challenge to a bad actor be accomplished? Several regulatory agencies have some role protecting elders. Select the agency and the level of government that is most likely to take action for the protection of your elder person. A state long-term care

self-neglect. The effects of the suicide are felt by the family and friends; the loss of the individual's will to go on living may be the result of severe alienation, terminal diagnosis, death of a longtime spouse, or other causes.

**CASE STUDY 1**

Ms. Black, eighty-seven, was resistant every day that a nursing-home aide attempted to bathe her. On Monday, she pushed the aide off balance and the aide fell; the aide slapped her, and her head hit the bathroom's tile wall. She died on Wednesday as a result of the fractured skull. The aide was terminated, the nursing home settled the family's assault lawsuit for a small amount, and the prosecutor decided not to prosecute the manslaughter case for lack of external proof of the cause.

**CASE STUDY 2**

The immobile Mr. White's home aide took White's prescribed pain medication to sell to a drug dealer. White suffered greatly from pain for days until he slipped into a coma. When hospital officials analyzed his condition, they reported surprise that the medication did not appear in his bloodstream. Adult Protective Services was called by the patient's prescribing doctor, and determined that the medication had been stolen. Police were then called, and the aide was prosecuted. The home healthcare service was sued for negligent hiring, and settled the claim.

**CASE STUDY 3**

Happy Valley Care Center was inspected by state long-term care officials for a "complaint survey" in response to five complaints from family members about severe weight loss in elders. The survey team applied federal guidelines and state rules, each of which was applicable, and found the wrong food had been delivered to diabetic patients and to a patient with severe digestive problems, each error resulting in a hospital stay. The state then proposed a $4,000 fine against HVCC; after a lengthy process the hearing officer recommended a $1,000 fine, which was appealed. The appeal resulted in a $500 penalty, twenty-two months after the survey occurred.

report the abusive person, out of fear that they might be expelled from the current nursing home and required to live less well at a new location.

## CRIMINAL REMEDIES

The person who commits abuse of an elder may be charged criminally. This charge will only be filed if the elderly victim is competent to testify; or if there is visual evidence such as a videotape of the assault; or if there is physical evidence such as semen after a rape or bruises after a punching incident. Physical evidence plus a police confrontation for questioning of the alleged attacker may produce an admission of liability by the person who committed the act. If an elder-abuse case goes to trial, serious prison time will be requested; if the abuser was a nursing-home caregiver, then the terminated worker may be placed on a state list of persons who have been barred from future work in nursing homes in that state. Police will investigate the capacity of the elder as a witness. Unless there is some proof of the physical abuse, it is unlikely that the criminal charge would be sustained.

## ASSAULTS BY DEMENTIA PATIENTS

In some cases, the assault or abuse is committed by a demented resident of a nursing home or similar facility. That assailant could not be charged with a crime because of the lack of mental capacity to intentionally perform the criminal act. After the attack, any legal liability would fall on the institution, for failing to keep separate a known predator and the person who became his or her victim. Abuse should be reported immediately to the facility manager, and the facility management should isolate this attacker so that the problem does not recur.

Violent action by a dementia patient may induce caregivers to send the person to a secure institution, such as an Alzheimer's unit of a skilled-nursing facility. There are sometimes sudden and severe aggression problems with an elder whose brain is deteriorating. These episodes of aggression have psychological and physical roots, best known to gerontology researchers. Once a case of aggression arises, the duty of the nursing-home management is to educate the staff members to anticipate potential assaults, and to move the aggressor to a more secure area from which escape is less likely.

## SELF-INFLICTED INJURY AND SUICIDE

One aspect of harm is self-inflicted injury. Elders with dementia sometimes cause physical harm to themselves. In the worst cases, depressed and anxious elders may commit suicide by pills, weapons, or intentional

its elderly patient or resident. These institutions have a special status under state and federal laws that deal with elder protection. That status gives rise to special responsibilities of care.

Abuse cases involving elders in a nursing home are usually brought by relatives of the patient, and are often investigated by the individual who has been designated by the state as its ombudsman for that nursing facility. Some abuse claims are mistaken; some are misunderstandings; some are overlooked; and some that are valid are concealed or implausibly denied by the management of the facility. Typically, as a result of the investigation, the complaint is dismissed or specific corrective actions are taken by the nursing-home managers.

## THE REGULATORY RESPONSE

Although state forms and procedures vary, complaints about nursing homes are handled in a comparable manner. An inspection called the nursing-home "complaint survey" is generally assigned by the state when an apparently valid complaint about abuse has been received by state officials. The surveyor representing the state agency comes to the facility, examines the records, speaks with the staff and (where possible) the frailty of the elderly person, and makes a determination of the apparent facts. The state agency responsible for long-term care supervision may impose a very large cash penalty, subject to a later administrative hearing. Some nursing-home chains have been able to compromise the amount of the fine; others have taken appeals to the review board and had their fines reduced.

## CIVIL LAWSUITS

Apart from the complaint-based process for determining the facility's regulatory compliance with protective regulations, there may also be civil-liability lawsuits. These begin with a formal complaint filed in court, then settlement negotiations and motions to dismiss, leading up to a trial in those few cases that cannot be settled. A nursing home does not want the press to report on its abuse cases. A civil case asserting that an institution allowed assault or abuse of an elder would draw substantial negative publicity against the institution. The complainant family could withdraw the elder resident, and inform the media. That reality acts as a restraint on how institutions deal with assertions the abuse of elderly patients. Likewise a family does not want news media reports of their poor care or physical deprivation of an elder.

There is also an incentive for a nursing home not to make reports of abuse to the state. Elderly victims may feel shame or guilt and refuse to

you about how your state's laws and rules apply. Not everything that looks like abuse would be classified as abuse by regulatory enforcers.

In general, two types of caregivers have different sets of legal responsibilities. After an elderly person is declared legally incompetent to manage his or her own affairs, a petition for guardianship can be filed in court. Then a person appointed by a court to be the "guardian" has a legal duty to protect the elderly person, who is designated as the "ward" of the guardian. If the guardian fails to take protective action for the necessary protection of the elderly ward, then the guardian may be held liable in court for elder neglect. A complaint to the court may be successful in removing and replacing that guardian, with an order to repay funds taken from the ward. These become bitter conflicts, and often involve expensive lawyer time, so it may be prudent to seek ways to mediate rather than litigate over the conditions of elder care.

If the issue of the competence of the elder has not been decided by a court, normal interpersonal responsibility among adults is presumed. Neighbors have no legal duty to assist, though of course moral imperatives and community sharing induce cooperation. Personal privacy prevails. The law does not interfere until a report of neglect or abuse is made. If the individual adult who is the informal caregiver in a nonguardian relationship fails to act to protect the elder, then state or local bodies such as an Adult Protective Services office may be called in to assist. The omission of needed care, exposing the elder to risks of harm, may be enough to trigger an elder-abuse claim under state laws. This could be a viable charge if there is some medical proof of deterioration or marks from physical abuse. Omission of necessary care of an elder by a designated caregiver may justify the intervention of probate court or a social service agency, even though the abuse is by nonaction rather than by action. In these neglect cases, the wording of the state law is critical to determining what is likely to be the appropriate remedy. Thus, the experience of an elder-law specialist is essential.

## NURSING-HOME ABUSE CLAIMS

What is abuse within a nursing home? The classic abuse cases would be a worker punching or sexually assaulting a resident who is elderly, impaired, and/or incompetent.

More elder-abuse instances occur as nonphysical mistreatment, neglect, malnutrition, mistakes in handling medication or medical devices, or failure to take protective measures when they are obviously warranted.

The obligation to take protective action on behalf of the elder arises from the special relationship between the nursing home or hospital and

## ASSAILANT'S CONDITION MAY BAR RECOVERY

What happens if the assault is committed by an incompetent person, such as another patient within the dementia unit of a nursing home? The criminal law will not apply, because the person who acted could not have known the consequences of his or her actions owing to the mental illness. Civil damage claims may be asserted against the nursing home if it had knowledge of the dangerous propensity of the assailant and did not act to secure the victim from exposure to a foreseeable attack. Juries tend to give facility managers the benefit of the doubt, so there is no certainty that a plaintiff's lawyer would accept such a lawsuit on a contingency fee.

If it occurs at home, within the extended family, public knowledge of an assault will be infrequent unless hospitalization is required. It is probable that local police will treat the matter as just another domestic-violence call. Family members often decline to cooperate with police against a relative.

Abuse is a significant safety issue affecting many elderly persons who are vulnerable to the angry pushes or slaps of frustrated relatives or caregivers. If the abuse becomes known outside the home, the police determination of whether to make an arrest or seek to prosecute the elderly person for domestic violence will be arrived at on very specific facts, so no general statement can be made about the likelihood of a remedy for the person who is assaulted.

## NEGLECT

Neglect means depriving a person (or oneself) of necessary water, food, shelter, or other essential protections. In some cases, neglect can be a crime as well. Neglect of the physical needs of a person for whom the individual has legal responsibility is a matter of substantial concern. Because this kind of neglect, and the results of this neglect, have serious consequences for an elderly person, the legal system could impose criminal penalties against a caregiver, but only if (1) the obligation to help the elder avoid injury was clear at the time the person decided not to act; (2) the failure to act caused the injury; and (3) the law recognizes this person as accountable for the injury to the elderly person.

## ABUSE OF THE ELDER

*Abuse* is a broader term than *assault*. Cases of abuse of elders have been discussed in the legal literature for many years. State laws vary, so an attorney who has a specialty in elder law, such as a member of the National Association of Elder Law Attorneys (naela.org) can best advise

# CHAPTER 11:
# ABUSE AND ASSAULT

This chapter will deal with the unfortunate effects of physical abuse on the elderly. Our discussion relates to physical and psychological abuse against the elder by a caregiver, a family member, a stranger or intruder, or a person entrusted with medical or nursing-home service for that elderly person.

## DEFINING ASSAULT

Assault is a crime, as well as the basis for an award of damages in an individual injury case. Physical touching of another person without his or her consent is technically an assault, but the law excuses persons who have a specific role, such as a nurse or caregiver for a reluctant incompetent elder who requires a bath. In the nursing-home or hospital context, physicians, nurses, and aides have the responsibility for caring for patients, even those who are reluctant or incompetent, and this responsibility requires them to touch the patients and in some cases to restrain patients who are aggressive or potentially violent. This is what the law calls a "privileged" action, and thus it is not a crime or a source of civil liability.

## RESPONSES TO ELDER ABUSE

What can be done? Confront the aggressor through legal means. Document bruises or other wounds with photographs. Consider filing papers in your local court for a protective guardianship. If the assault occurred within a nursing facility, contact the ombudsman and the state long-term care hotline to ask for an investigation. Demand to see the resulting reports, after a month or two has passed.

## CASE STUDY 5

A North Carolina nursing home had an automated patient trust-fund account. The administrator manipulated the system and created false credit postings to residents' accounts, and then took for herself checks totaling over $70,000. She pleaded guilty to two felonies.

## CASE STUDY 2

Aid to poor children has long been an area of great interest to Ms. White, now aged eighty-one and living on Social Security benefits and her small savings. She sent $25 to a legitimate childrens' charity whose employee was also being paid by scammers to glean names of probable elder donors. First by phone and then in person, a thief gained her confidence and convinced her to take a mortgage on the home she has owned for fifty years, so that she can "live better and donate more to charity." The thief took the money from the loan transaction, telling her it was a donation, and by the time her adult children learned of this, Ms. White was forced to sell her home because the payment due on the mortgage exceeded her income.

## CASE STUDY 3

The author served as legal-aid attorney for an elderly man with a low income, who responded to a knock at his door, was told that his home's roof and gutters needed work, and agreed that the visitor could do the repairs for a small initial amount and future payments. The homeowner signed, without reading it, a paper that gave a "mechanic's lien" to the roofer for $6,000 for work that was worth less, if actually completed. The roofer failed to do the work properly but demanded payment and threatened to sue to enforce the lien. The homeowner came to the legal-aid office for help. In small-claims court, the judge ruled against the roofer and ordered repayment, but the roofer failed to pay. The legal-aid attorney took the judgment to the county sheriff and had the roofer's truck impounded as security for repayment. Within a day, the homeowner had his money back and the Better Business Bureau was advised of the fraudulent activities.

## CASE STUDY 4

An employee of an Oregon home health service was assigned to help with light chores for an elderly woman. Gaining the woman's trust, the aide then ordered excessive quantities of prescription drugs and sold some to friends for cash; she took the woman's ATM card and withdrew enough money over several months to buy a new truck. She went to prison for three years, had three years extra in probation, was ordered to make restitution of $22,760, and was permanently barred from work as a caregiver.

and less protective than had been promised. Demands for immediate payment on the day of the "work" confronts the elder with pressure. Some homeowners are gullible, some unwary, some too "believing" of what is told to them. A state consumer-protection agency or attorney general's office is the best ally to have in the fight against such a rip-off contract.

## IDENTITY THEFT

Stealing the identity of an elder in order to fraudulently use credit cards is a matter of serious concern to law enforcement because of the frequency with which this scam occurs. Newly admitted nursing-home residents are a juicy target. If an elderly person maintains credit cards in force after entering an institutional environment such as a nursing home, the risk exists that a criminally inclined worker might steal the card and run up major bills before the theft is detected months later by an adult caregiver who supervises the patient's finances. Experts advise that credit cards should remain in possession of an elder's guardian or the person with a power of attorney; there is nothing to be bought that cannot be directed by phone or in person to the guardian or other caretaker of financial matters. There is no practical reason why an institutionalized elder's credit card should be left unsecured in a facility with many low-paid service workers.

## THEFT OF POSSESSIONS

A final subset of financial misconduct is the taking of an elder's valuable possessions by a family member or friend. Some may rationalize this taking as simply accelerating their inheritance, but it is an unauthorized taking by deception of another person's property, so it meets the definition of theft.

## CASE STUDY 1

Mr. Black, seventy-eight, suffers from severe arthritis. He receives an e-mail purporting to come from a prominent health facility in his state, encouraging him to order a new vitamin supplement that will relieve the arthritis. He orders the pills from the facility without realizing that the address that looks like that of a nearby facility is actually being used in a scam. His credit-card information is stolen, no pills arrive, and thieves use the card information to obtain cash advances of more than $4,000 before disappearing. Postal inspectors and a state consumer-protection office help him to unwind the scheme, but he loses the $4,000.

### REVERSE MORTGAGES

A conventional mortgage is a lump-sum loan secured by the value of the home, with future monthly payments to the lender. A "reverse mortgage" gives money to the homeowner in monthly payments, with the obligation to repay when the house is transferred, sold, or left in a deceased borrower's estate. The programs offer a benefit to elders, or to the families of elders, whose homes appreciate greatly in value These reverse-mortgage programs can be quite responsible and quite legitimate. Some effective consumer-education efforts regarding them have reached many elders.

But the reverse-mortgage process carries some risk; its real fees and terms should be thoroughly considered with a professional advisor before the elder agrees to such a program. The process may be a surprise for adult children and other heirs, because they may stand to lose their inheritance on what they expected to be the value of their family home. Well-publicized risks related to home mortgages are now alarming some elders, at a time when the market shakeout of 2008–2009 has exposed flaws in the residential-realty lending field.

Reverse-mortgage programs can be a source of high fees for the intermediary, apart from any benefit to the homeowner. Alternative programs may have lower fees. To avoid harm, legal advice from an attorney familiar with protecting consumers in real-estate transactions is recommended.

### HOME-REPAIR ISSUES

Fraudulent home-repair scams have been used by thieves for years. The targets are older homes that have visible deficits in their exterior maintenance; such deficits seem to invite fraudulent repair scams. Quickly signing a large-dollar repair or remodeling contract that the homeowner (or a knowledgeable adult child or friend) has not first read can be a trap for the unwary. Excessive claims and inadequate performance will produce unreasonable payment demands, possible "mechanic's liens" filed against the home's value as a means of coercing payment, and sometimes shoddy work that makes the home less safe or secure. The contract form employed by a fraudulent contractor usually has unreadable tiny print, with payment conditions that are very one-sided, against the homeowner.

Shoddy workmanship by repair-scam operators will pose a problem, sometimes leaving important work undone with an assurance that it has been done, sometimes substituting hidden materials that are less costly

exists in the home, an elder may be seen as a ripe target by the players of "confidence games."

Home-equity frauds and thefts have grown in recent years. Collapse of the residential real-estate market in the 2008–2009 period was in part a result of manipulative and fraudulent practices that became relatively common in mortgage brokerage in prior years. No statistics reveal the ages of borrowers whose loans have dragged them into foreclosure and loss of the home. The wrongful taking of equity dollars out of an elder's residence may be a result of the elder's own error in investment, or it may be the result of fraud or theft. These crimes may go unreported, but they exist nonetheless.

Several schemes aimed at homeowners have stolen money outright; the pot of cash represented by a home-equity loan is the prize. Some others have induced a property transfer that left the homeowner at a severe disadvantage. One of the latter frauds is "deed stripping," in which the elder is offered "help" in resisting a bank foreclosure, in return for signing over the deed for the home. By the time the elder realizes what has occurred, the house has been sold or mortgaged away.

Another scam is an inducement to refinance the equity available in the home, asserting to lenders that the elderly person's income is far above what it actually will be. Sometimes the criminal collects a hefty fee for the transaction and disappears; sometimes the loan is made and the elderly homeowner gets the money minus that fee, but will lose the home to foreclosure as soon as the reality of repayment at an upward "adjustable rate" collides with a shortage of actual monthly income. Thus, adult caretakers should carefully examine the paperwork around the use of elders' homes as collateral for loans.

Some elders despair about stock-market price drops and are vulnerable to an acquaintance's offer of "guaranteed" returns. Disappointment over bad investment choices is widespread in the current market. SEC rules violations abound. The proper licensed brokerage should have qualified the investor to make certain transactions, such as loans based on margins; some of these margin loans are especially ill advised and are influenced by the greed of the sales representative. Actual prosecution of the criminal promoters of bogus investments is occurring slowly, but not with sufficient frequency to deter similar future scams. Various schemes for stock-purchase fraud exist, and are chronicled in numerous books and Web sites. The local library will have plenty of books on investment-fraud avoidance; in a way, the spurt of books on that topic is a symptom of how widely fraud has been recognized in securities transactions.

public protectors of their financial interests. These protectors include the probate courts, consumer-protection offices, adult-protective services, police fraud units, and the like.

**INSURANCE-RELATED MISCONDUCT**

Insurance sellers are generally quite ethical, but some are exploitative. The false promises made by some marketers of long-term care policies and Medicare Advantage policies have been criticized in the media and by government. The performance that the insurance purchaser has been promised does not always match the reality. Medicare officials have criticized the reward system for the sellers of Medicare Advantage group policies; the financial reward of selling the policy is sizable, inducing some promises that are dubious, according to press reports.

Insurance-policy "fine print" may contain exclusions and conditions that actually allow denial of the coverage that had been orally promised to the elder consumer. Or coverage may be priced artificially low, without revelation in the sales pitch that an annual renewal will be due at a much higher rate. A sudden shock might arise for an elder who has faithfully paid long-term care insurance, and then (after retiring on a fixed income) faces losing the policy when premiums are drastically increased. Experts in the long-term care insurance field have warned that conscious underpricing draws in elders who later cannot afford to keep up their policies when sharp rate increases are demanded. There are likely to be extensive problems for elders who are unprepared for later "rate shocks." One solution may be state takeover or liquidation trusts; lawsuits are inevitableto attack prior sales practices and expensive promises.

Usually, the state insurance department's consumer-protection office is most capable of dealing with the misleading performance of an insurance seller. While it does not solve the problem of noncoverage of events that were supposed to be covered, the company could be punished. Unless an insurance company settles, the complaint process may lead to revocation of the state license of the seller, and a misleading agent may lose his or her license and be civilly liable for the effect of the deceptive practice.

**HOME-RELATED MISCONDUCT**

The elder's home is likely to be his or her largest asset. Separating an elderly person from the long-term investment made in a home can be a very lucrative form of theft by deception. Assuming that some equity

# CHAPTER 10: PROTECTING ELDERS FROM FINANCIAL HARMS AND THEFTS

**WHAT IS FINANCIAL HARM?**

Harm to elders takes many forms. The nonphysical injury an elderly person suffers from a financial fraud or theft may cause depression, diminish health, or shorten life. The shock of losing a life's savings may be traumatic, with physical consequences. Fraudulent selling of long-term care insurance may leave a vulnerable elder stranded, unable to pay for suddenly increased premiums. Theft by caregivers is particularly reprehensible, but sadly is commonly unreported or charges readily dismissed on promise of repayment.

Saving up for one's "golden years" is an ideal. That "gold" attracts greedy people; the low pay and long hours of caregivers for the elderly sometimes develops a sense of justification or rationalization for fraud and theft of elders' funds. Avarice within families is legendary. Adult children or adult friends of the elder can be important guards of assets.

Mishandling of money should be carefully avoided by simple bookkeeping measures like reconciling checkbooks each month, or later remedied if a shortfall is found. Some losses are simple errors or movements in the stock market; others are thefts.

Inadvertence, inattention, and confusion make it more difficult for many "older elders" above the age of eighty to monitor their financial affairs without outside help. To the extent that one can generalize, the mental acuity to supervise financial matters is likely to deteriorate with advanced age. With some exceptions, of course, the correlation of elders' ages with the likelihood of victimization is a significant concern among

## CASE STUDY 2

Mechanical maintenance workers at the Willow Rest Haven nursing home are shorthanded, and low wages make it difficult to hire skilled workers. When a new trainee is assigned to repair a leaky junction of medical-gas pipes, he erroneously connects the nitrogen pipe with the oxygen pipe. Within minutes, seven patients with oxygen masks are dead from inhaling pure nitrogen. The nursing home is closed by health authorities until the systems are completely validated. After the nursing home declares bankruptcy, lawyers for the estates of the dead patients seek to collect from the gas supplier, which denies that it caused the problem, and from the designer of the building, who wins dismissal because of the state "statute of repose" that forbids lawsuits about a building installation after ten years have passed.

## CASE STUDY 3

Home health-care patient Mary Blue receives warfarin, a blood thinner, each day to deal with a long-standing medical problem. Because of cost reductions, the visiting nurse who has qualified for prescribing privileges has been allowed fifteen minutes per home visit; she checks Ms. Blue, finds a problem, and calls in a prescription for a painkiller before leaving for her next appointment. The dose of the other medication is excessive for Ms. Blue, but its liver effects are masked by the effect of the warfarin. The nurse's next scheduled visit is canceled, and by the time she again sees Ms. Blue, the patient is severely ill. Ms. Blue is taken to the hospital, but her liver has degraded over the period, and the effects are not reversible. Blue's representative sues the visiting nurse and her company for negligence, and Blue's expert would testify at trial that the failure to adequately consider doses and other medications was malpractice. Ms. Blue dies two months after the suit is filed. State procedures regarding medical malpractice are invoked by the defense the insurance carrier for the home health service negotiates for several more months and the case is settled before trial.

to induce manufacturers to be much more careful in their manufacturing and processing operations. But there is no assurance that a manufacturer will be able to deliver 100 percent of the doses of 100 percent of the drugs it produces, and this is a special concern for generic-drug makers with variable imported sources of complex chemicals for the creation of less expensive "therapeutic equivalent" drugs. So there is some risk that the pharmaceutical may not provide the benefit that is expected.

## UPHILL BATTLES AGAINST DRUG MAKERS

Lawsuits against drug makers for failure to adequately warn doctors about risks are very controversial. Injured patients are more likely to win damages against a distant multinational drug maker than against their own local doctor and clinic. Because the physician and hospital relied upon information from the drug manufacturer, there is usually no liability for either of those defendants, in the event that the drug has an unexpected deficiency that harms the patient. But if the use of the medication was contrary to its directions or exceeded the dose, or was given to the patient for a therapeutic purpose for which the FDA had not approved its use, courts might find the doctor liable for malpractice. If the delivery of the dose by injection or by tablets was badly handled, then the error may be attributed to the staff of the hospital or nursing home, and the drug maker and the prescribing physician will disclaim any responsibility. Nothing about this is simple; the advice of an experienced personal-injury lawyer is a prerequisite to making an informed decision about remedies.

## CASE STUDY 1

Newly admitted nursing-home patient Ms. Grey received a prescription for a heart medication from the nursing home's doctor. The doctor apparently was unaware that the same patient was on a different and incompatible medicine that had been prescribed while she was in the hospital before being discharged into the nursing home. The incompatible medicines clashed in her diminished, weakened liver, and she suffered a substantial medical problem as a result. The Grey family sued the doctor and the nursing home. The minimum standard of care in a nursing-home case is the action set by the federal guidelines applicable to prescribing of drugs for Medicare-Medicaid patients. The two entities, with the same insurer, settled the case before trial after establishing that the staff of the nursing home failed to give their medical director the information from Ms. Grey's hospital chart.

nature of an adverse event that causes concern. Every pharmaceutical ingredient has some adverse effect at some dose; the challenge is to get the right dose, to the correct patient, and to deliver it on the prescribed schedule. The more serious the effect, of course, the more likely that an adverse effect will be warned about in the labeling of the medication.

Prescribing is a vital skill, not an automatic routine. It is the doctor's judgment about the dose and about the selection of the drug that makes the most difference in determining whether the product will be ultimately successful in addressing the patient's medical problem. Courts rarely hold doctors liable for trying a medication that might possibly work; the 1997 standards in the book *Restatement of Products Liability* allow the drug maker to escape liability if there is any reasonable connection between this drug and one of the symptoms the doctor seeks to cure.

**DEFECTIVE DRUGS**

A third problem in medications is that the drug itself might have a problem. The law recognizes there are trade-offs of risks and benefits. Federal approval does not mean a drug has no risks. Since 1938 the U.S. Food and Drug Administration has had extensive power to regulate new drug products, and the FDA has used that authority to require premarketing submission of very detailed scientific proof that the drug will safely deliver the intended benefit to the patient. Some drugs never reach the market, because clinical studies fail to show a real benefit that could justify the risks patients take with them.

When the actual dose of the drug itself is deficient, because of a manufacturing error or a dispensing or substitution error, the consequence can be fatal. FDA uses inspections and requires reports that allow the agency to determine whether the product is performing as expected, or whether there is a significant problem with it, as it has been marketed. For example, when a drug is given to hospitals or physicians in a powder form, to be mixed with water or other materials, it is especially important sterility be maintained so that contaminated water does not affect the beneficial drug mixture.

The FDA's control of medications is not absolute, of course, and sometimes when corners are cut in the manufacturing process the consequences can be very harmful to the patient; this can occur long before the FDA learns of the problems. The FDA prosecutes criminal actions by companies, and occasionally prosecutes individuals who are held accountable when drug-manufacturing processes deteriorate to the point that injury to a patient could result. To a certain extent, this deterrent effect works

medication will vary considerably, affected by factors such as age, blood circulation, compliance with the directions for taking the drug, etc., it is not easy to win compensation through a malpractice lawsuit.

### DEFECTS IN THE DRUG ITSELF

The third risk is that the medication itself has a problem, in that the drug is deficient in how it was formulated or defective as a finished product, for instance, mixed improperly or excessive in the amount of active ingredient ("superpotent"). Or there may be a contaminant in a liquid medication, which could result in adverse effects to the patient taking the medication. These are not intended or desired by anyone, but they sometimes happen.

### PROBLEMS WITH DRUG DELIVERY

Mistakes in the delivery of medication to a patient occur with alarming frequency in the nursing-home setting. Federal guidelines cover issues like the review of the adequacy of delivery of the right medication to the right patient at the right frequency; the guidelines are applied by a team of inspectors, called surveyors, who visit the nursing home and examine its records and its performance.

The nursing home does its best with pharmaceutical-delivery documentation, but sometimes the actual delivery of a pill is mishandled, or sometimes the patient is reluctant to take a drug. Or there may be discomfort for the patient or fear of side effects, and therefore "compliance" is a problem; the staff member must observe the actual ingestion of the pill by the patient.

### MEDICATION ERRORS

When medication errors arise, it may be that the physician placed an order that was misinterpreted by the pharmacist, either because of a writing error or through inadequate listening to an oral order from the physician. There are numerous "soundalike" drug names for pharmaceuticals that could be harmful if administered in lieu of another drug. The physician's medication order should be confirmed in writing or in electronic form, to satisfy state pharmacy laws and regulations.

### ADVERSE EVENTS

The physician may determine that the patient should receive a particular dose of a particular medication. Then, adverse effects begin to appear as the patient suffers an unexpected negative impact. It is the unexpected

# CHAPTER 9:
# MEDICATION ISSUES FOR ELDERS

In this chapter we will address problems arising out of harm to an elderly patient who has received a medication, when it is later found that the medication caused or contributed to the patient's death or serious physical injury. These are cases in which the illness worsened or the patient died as a result of taking the prescribed medication. Many of these issues arise in nursing homes, where government estimates say the average resident takes nine or more medications daily. Picture a small cart with a lower-paid aide delivering drugs that the consulting pharmacist at a local drugstore has provided; errors in delivery, like physician errors in selection, can have fatal effects.

**TYPES OF DRUG ERRORS**

The medication errors that are likely to occur and cause harm are three types. First, the wrong medication is administered because of a mistake by the pharmacist, the supervisory nurse, the nursing aide, or other staff members. This is especially a problem in nursing homes, with large volumes of medication being administered to large numbers of persons. Sometimes the name sounds like the name of another drug; sometimes the label reader lacks skills in English; sometimes an inadvertent switch is made between adjacent patient rooms.

**UNEXPECTED ADVERSE EFFECTS**

The second risk is that the medication may be properly prescribed by a physician or under a nursing-home medical director's "standing orders," but that taking that drug would be seriously adverse to the health of this patient. Unexpected adverse reaction to a medication occurs frequently, and sometimes with slow follow-up to the patient's condition. Because medicine is not an exact science, and the ability of individuals to tolerate

If probate or surrogate courts have been involved, the guardian or court-appointed conservator will have an obligation for periodic, at least annual, reports to the court.

Veterans' benefits for home and board may be available as well. These may be paid to third parties for care; as with Medicaid-funded programs, these payments come with reporting obligations.

## CASE STUDY 1

Out-of-town adult relatives come to visit an eighty-two-year-old aunt, Ms. Silver, who lives in a small home in the inner city. Leaks, broken windows, junk, and piles of litter signal that the aunt should be in a safer area. She refuses and sounds quite confused and agitated. The relatives contact Adult Protective Services for that area, which interviews the family and the aunt. APS petitions for and obtains a guardianship from probate court. The guardian moves Ms. Silver into an assisted-living facility, sells the home, and uses the proceeds to fund her stay in the new residence.

## CASE STUDY 2

World War II veteran Harry Brown has remained independent at home but is losing his eyesight. A small kitchen fire, quickly extinguished, arose from his inability to see. His doctor believes that he needs to have assistance from a home health aide, but he is not poor enough to qualify for Medicaid. With the help of a veterans' organization, Brown receives VA benefits for home assistance and is able to remain home.

## CASE STUDY 3

Lois Green lived independently, drawing income from a trust established by her late father, until last year, when a caregiver was needed to help her remain at home. Lois always used the same accounting service for her trust paperwork and taxes. This year the accounting firm received several copies of notices of financial problems from the trust company, and called Lois. The caregiver told the accountant that Lois would no longer need their service. The accountant called Lois's daughter, who lived in another city. The daughter visited and found that the caregiver had siphoned off $17,000 in checks forged with Lois's signature. At the daughter's request, police arrested the caregiver. It turned out that she had been convicted in previous elder-care scams and had served time in prison. But none of this had been asked about or checked when the neat, kindly caregiver was hired. The daughter convinced Lois to move into a respected local assisted-living community.

facilities. Waiver of the right to sue is a common requirement. Contracts signed upon admission to a facility may force a dissatisfied resident or family to use arbitration that tends to favor the owner of the facility.

Step 3 is for the family to visit the assisted-living facility and check the actual conditions of support for residents with moderate but not severe health problems. The probability is that all will look wonderful and shiny on the day of the tour; calls to relatives of other residents may be a good way to check the actual quality of services.

Step 4 is for the elderly person to be moved from home into the assisted-living facility, preferably with the aid of a transition-moving service that specializes in comfortable "downsizing" of an older person. Getting settled, the new resident should be shown around the facility and the area, and any known risks that should be avoided will be explained.

Step 5 is for the family to visit at least monthly, and stay in touch by phone, to respond carefully to any suspicions of a caregiver's physical abuse of the elder. There will inevitably be some accidents with impaired or immobilized residents. Was this bruise the result of use of excessive force to compel the resident to bathe or to eat? Has the elder had rapid weight loss? Was there an apparent act of negligence in handling (or dropping) a bed-to-floor transfer of the impaired resident?

Step 6 is for the family to monitor financial records as an additional recipient of bank or broker statements. This enables the family to watch for potential signs of fraud. An adult child or family friend should review the bank and the residential facility's financial records periodically, at least quarterly, to check the financial record for the resident with the operator of the facility. Fraud on Medicare is a potential problem if the person is billed for help not actually provided, and excessive billing for work that should have been included in the basic rate is a red flag of possible financial fraud. Exploitation of funds on deposit by the caregiver is a financial risk. The risk of financial withdrawals by the durable-power holder can be a problem; the power of attorney might be for health care but not include control over funds.

Step 7 is to keep up with government supervision requirements. For residents in licensed nursing homes and licensed assisted-living facilities, state supervision on individual-care conditions is specific and detailed. Join the family council of residents' families; check the Medicare.gov Web site for nursing-home quality reports on the facility. Some low-income elders are not in licensed facilities, but have been in contact with social-services entities. There may be adult-protective services requirements for periodic reports of a caseworker contact.

staff members, as well as by adequate hiring evaluations and checks of the references and criminal histories of persons hired. These protections, though, do not apply if the caregiver was hired by the family rather than through a more structured service.

**MAKING THE COMPLAINT**

What should you do if the elder for whom you provide assistance is injured by the active misconduct or grave mistake of a person to whom you have entrusted his or her care? You could call the state long-term care agency for help, or file a lawsuit.

Why should there be any basis for a lawsuit? The obligation to take care of an elder arises when the individual is acknowledged to be in a vulnerable condition. There is not a general obligation to intervene, to take care of adult persons who are otherwise capable of caring for themselves; the distinction drawn in the law looks at the vulnerability, and a defendant's knowledge of the vulnerability, of a person who is in a health-care facility. For the most part, obligations to protect will be evident from the status of the individual in a protective setting, such as in the nursing home. The law is a fallback, and not a primary source of protection of the elder. This is because regulatory agencies have in place a system of control over nursing homes, and nursing staffs generally protect a vulnerable person more efficiently and effectively than will an award of damages after the death of the patient.

**CAREGIVER PROBLEMS**

We next consider the choices to be made: Step 1 is the choice of an appropriate living arrangement for the elder. The family and the elder together will discuss this sensitive topic, often for months or years, before a change is made. The risk to an elderly person of remaining at home is different from the risk of residing in a specially designed elder facility. In a new setting with adaptive bars, floors, and wall handles, the elder still has some potential issues of accidental injury or wandering off, but is more likely protected from accidental harm. Remaining at home with assistance from health-care aides is better for morale and better for recovery from surgery, with a few risks to be avoided. Hiring the right person with the right set of skills is a basic need; checking the references and police record of the applicant is an important protective measure.

Step 2 is reading carefully each of the documents presented when the elder moves into a new facility. The family or other advisor should be aware of financial commitments a resident makes in different types of

## RISK AVOIDANCE

The better home health-care agencies follow the same infection-control methods in homes as in clinics. The simplest of these requirements are the use of gloves and other "universal precautions." Legal remedies are rarely available since causation is rarely found. It is not likely that the infection and the costs of dealing with the infection can be conclusively attributed to the negligent handling of the patient in the home. But this is an area in which hospitals, nursing homes, clinics, and assisted-living facilities should be paying close attention to the avoidance of harm through careful compliance with state regulatory controls. Depending on state law, there may be an opportunity for an injured or ill person to obtain tort damages for the inadequate protection accorded by health-care workers.

What would happen if a facility caring for an adult patient were swept by a bacterial infection or virus, which caused disease? When that occurs, the typical case will involve death or serious impairment of the health prospects for the ailing elderly person. Individualized proof of damages from specific negligent acts will be hard to discern.

## PHYSICAL RISKS

Beyond infection, there are many physical injuries that can result from negligent caretaking by individuals working at an older person's home or an assisted-living facility. The liability risk of dropping a patient, or not supervising a patient who is no longer capable of steady walking, is a substantial concern for the risk manager of a facility caring for the elders.

A way in which the defense in a home or assisted-living injury suit may respond will be to tie the remedy to a contract limit like arbitration. For example, the injury may occur in the hallway of an assisted-living facility when the elder trips over a box left there by a janitor. But because of an arbitration clause placed in the enrollment documents as a precondition to entering the assisted-living facility, there may be no jury trial and no serious financial recovery. The family of the elder may have waived some of their rights to sue for damages after an accident occurs, if the agreement was signed and is upheld in court.

In some health-care settings, the injured person may be so weak that he or she is very vulnerable to physical or sexual abuse. In those circumstances, the basis for a lawsuit arises after a caregiver assault, because a duty of care existed, owed by the entity that should have protected the plaintiff from such sexual exploitation or physical abuse. Assaults should be preventable through adequate supervision of the activities of

# CHAPTER 8:
# REMEDIES FOR HOME AND ASSISTED-LIVING HEALTH-CARE RISKS

Another area in which a civil-liability lawsuit is potentially available is that of patient abuse, neglect, or avoidable infection caused by home health-care service providers and those servicing assisted-living facilities. Regulation in these circumstances is minimal, if the state regulates them at all. Lawsuits are few; proof is difficult to gather; and where the care is provided by an individual rather than by a service company, the likelihood of a collectible jury award against an individual home-care provider is minimal. This makes the home-care setting a matter of "risk without remedy."

A later chapter on fraud and financial issues deals with the problem of theft by caregivers. This chapter deals with physical risks at home or in an independent-living apartment setting.

**UNCERTAINTIES**

In contrast with reports readily disclosed on nursing homes, data on home health–related injuries are hard to find. Reporting of injury and illness incidents by nursing homes gives a tentative backdrop for the general estimation of illness or injury that may occur in home health care, but no estimate of incidents related to home health-care situations could be completely accurate. There are protocols for the use of medical products in nursing homes, for example, that require "universal precaution" measures to be taken, such as using gloves and antibacterial cleaners to avoid transmitting disease. A large home health-care service provider is likely to follow that set of precautions; others may not do so.

supervising nurse; she told the person who notified her to "let him finish" before taking action against the rapist. The supervising nurse's license was revoked, and the 1993 *Yaw* case upheld the revocation.

## CASE STUDY 2

At the request of a hospital's discharge planner, a nearby nursing home had accepted as an incoming patient a person with dementia and a past history of crimes and of "acting out" violently. The admissions manager did not immediately advise the staff, who put the newcomer into an activity room full of residents. The new patient assaulted and beat another male patient before the staff could separate them. The family of the victim sued and the nursing home's insurer settled rather than fight the claim.

## CASE STUDY 3

Ms. Brown, seventy-four, came to a ten-story downtown nursing home with heart problems, mild dementia, and an extreme depression for which the staff had flagged her file for "special observation." Twice she had attempted to exit from floor to floor of the nursing home and had been stopped. The administrator had arranged a transfer to a more secure facility in the suburbs for Monday; on Sunday afternoon, the roof door was found open and Ms. Brown was found dead in the alley, having apparently jumped from the roof. Her estate sued for negligence, and the court found that the nursing home had failed in its duty to secure Ms. Brown once it recognized her potential wandering risk.

facility, as the elder's health needs expand. It is well recognized that home or apartment independent living is most desirable when the resident can be mobile, can obtain food and cook it, and can maintain a reasonable dietary intake that enhances health. The many "meals on wheels" programs are an intermediate step in the progression.

Lack of adequate nutrition has direct adverse consequences, such as skin conditions, dental problems, tiredness, and even reduced walking mobility of the elder. Food service is thus an important benefit of institutions that wish to serve an elderly population.

In the nursing-home setting, dietary plans must be created for each individual within a brief time after his or her arrival. The plan will take into account the allergies, preferences, and medical condition of the resident. An improper diet might counteract the benefit of drugs, cause stomach problems, or spark an allergic response.

The legal system cannot force a reluctant elder to eat, unless a doctor has prescribed a liquid diet as medically necessary for the person's health. The system can use state enforcement powers to penalize a nursing facility that fails to meet federal or state requirements as to patient nutrition for government-funded residents.

## INFECTION

Nursing homes train their workers to protect against infection by applying "universal precautions against bloodborne pathogens," as directed by federal workplace-safety standards. The harm of spreading infections to elderly residents is very visible; cleaning fecal matter from an incontinent elder is a necessary part of the aide's job, but it also risks spreading disease germs. Plastic disposable gloves and frequent hand washing and disinfecting are the primary protections against the spread of infections. Regulatory surveyors will observe the adequacy of cleaning steps and may cite a nursing home for violations.

There are few legal remedies available if an infection is spread in the nursing-home setting. Any lawsuits against the nursing home would probably be dismissed, unless there were absolutely effective testimony based on DNA or similar proof that the disease could only have been transmitted as a result of the negligence of staff.

## CASE STUDY 1

The Connecticut nursing-license board heard testimony in the case against a nursing-home supervisory nurse. When an aide was discovered in a patient's bed raping the helpless resident, other aides alerted the

otherwise would have to watch over elders' movements. Experts in the residential elder-care field have long urged that a facility should not use these restraints, but should instead train and equip staff members to handle residents' needs with more constant supervision. Part of the problem of restraints is that the elderly person loses mobility, loses the incentive to walk or move, and is more prone to infection and pneumonia from lack of physical activity. Another safety issue is the long history of strangulations that occur when a frustrated and confused older person tries to remove or escape the restraint and is accidentally entangled, so that he or she is found dead in a "noose" formed by the strap and the side of the bed or chair.

## ASSAULT

This chapter and the longer Chapter 11 address aspects of elder abuse and the subcategory of assault. Rape and sexual assault of nursing-home patients by staff members, intruders, visitors, or other residents should never happen. Sadly, they do occur in some cases. Some facilities disguise assault or deny the fact that it occurred, in some cases denying that a rape could possibly have occurred (after terminating the accused employee). Disgust and shock are common feelings experienced by families of the victim, with guilt and shame felt by some victims who are traumatized by forced sexual activity. The public does not know the problem exists, but the shortage of aides has led nursing homes to reduce their prescreening; it is possible that some sexual offenders are working in the local nursing home, without families' awareness.

Several steps are recommended to reduce assaults:

- Cameras can be used to record activity in corridors and public places.
- Background criminal-record checks are now routinely required.
- Standard procedures for reporting possible abuse are tighter than ever.
- Prosecutors are more willing to seek heavy sentences against assailants.

## NUTRITION

Nursing-home admissions often occur when elderly persons "can no longer care for themselves," and that often refers to providing oneself with nutrition. Harm to homebound elders from malnutrition is a real concern, one that induces some families to move their relative or friend to an assisted-living facility that provides meal plans, and later to a skilled-nursing

## RISKS FROM ELDER WANDERING

Death of a slow-moving pedestrian or a demented elderly person in a vehicle-pedestrian collision is a very avoidable tragedy. Drowning of a wandering elder in a pond near a nursing home is a very avoidable tragedy. Searches of wooded areas for the body of a lost elderly resident are the worst kind of publicity for a facility. Each of these is connected to the duty to protect residents from harming themselves.

As brain function deteriorates, a person with dementia or Alzheimer's disease may become a "wanderer," a person who seeks to leave the shelter of the nursing home or who escapes his or her own home to walk away in search of some unknown attraction elsewhere. Articles and studies tell stories of elderly persons who walked for miles to reach a once-familiar neighborhood or the home from which they had departed years before. Memory losses and confusion are one source of wandering; another is discomfort or unhappiness at a residential facility and a resulting desire to walk away to reach some better place. Longtime urban residents can recognize the patterns of this type of wandering, as they sometimes encounter confused elders in city parks or at bus stops.

The best means to avoiding harm to the elder is early diagnosis. Awareness by caregivers may lead to moving a patient with dementia or early Alzheimer's disease to a more secure residential facility. He or she should wear an identity bracelet giving the facility's phone number and address in the event a wanderer is found by "normal" persons outside. Living quarters may need to be secured in an area that is not easy for demented patients to leave without some knowledge of exit-door codes or other safeguards that require sophisticated awareness. The facility's outdoor garden or recreation area should be fenced and gated. Local police should be advised of the protocol the facility will use when one of its residents is missing and is presumed to be "wandering." A well-planned search of the area should be executed when the door alarm indicates an unauthorized departure by an elderly resident. Maintaining door alarms and egress codes is an important priority for the facility's management.

## PATIENT-RESTRAINT DEVICES

Although federal requirements prohibit the routine use of bed restraints except for special medically indicated instances, the problem of overuse of straps, belts, cuffs, and other physical-restraint devices persists in some nursing homes. Restraints save the time of overworked aides who

bedding, causing irritation of the skin surface and eventual breakdown of its protective layers.

Once skin breakdown is observed, the nursing-home patient should have a plan of care including more frequent cleansing of the affected area, application of creams, drug therapy, frequent scheduled turning of the body of an immobile patient, and movement of a mobile patient in a walker or otherwise out of the sitting or lying position.

**RESIDENT FALL INJURIES**

Falls occur among the great majority of elders in nursing homes, and lead to a greater or lesser degree of injury. Death can come quickly to elders after falls. For some it is immediate, as the concussion of forcefully hitting a hard surface causes brain death. For some it comes slowly from fractures caused by falls, as their condition deteriorates after a broken hip or leg fracture immobilizes a once-active person. For others the fall is not reported to medical intervenors, so hidden traumatic injuries are not perceived until it is too late to counteract their negative effects. Studies and books on elder health all emphasize the avoidance of any preventable falls as a critical objective.

Prevention of falls by elderly persons begins with recognition of an elder's risk factors by a medical or nursing expert:

- Does the person have the physical ability to walk steadily ahead?
- Is the person moving around a flat, secure environment, or moving on stairs and around corners and curves with others passing by?
- Does the person have an unsteady gait?
- Does the person have a need to hold on for support while walking?
- Is there a vision problem that impairs the use of stairs?
- Is there a hearing problem that makes a collision with bicycles or pedestrians more likely?
- Is there an observed side effect of medications that includes unsteady gait or lessened feeling in the legs or arms?

Once a fall occurs, injury can follow. Compensation through lawsuits and claims does not bring back the hip or arm that is fractured, or the rain that is destroyed. Since legal liability is tied to "foreseeable" effects of "known" risks, the remedy may be too uncertain and may come too late to help this elder. Thus, advocacy work is done for the future deterrence of bad conduct.

through the Center for Medicare and Medicaid Services (CMS), whose guidelines for inspectors ("surveyors") are a detailed catalog of all the ways in which harm to elders should be avoided in the daily operation of a nursing home.

There are three aspects of nursing-home funding that have the greatest impact: federal funds; state implementation of standards; and private long-term care insurance for the benefit of some nursing-home residents. These three sources of nursing-home oversight may have distinct criteria. In addition, an indirect deterrent force comes from liability litigation. Lawsuits against negligent or willful acts by nursing-home staff and regulatory penalties for violations of standards are two means for inducing more safe and more healthful practices.

The law relating to injury compensation for nursing-home patients has become much more sophisticated in recent years. The interplay of CMS standards with the tort system's "reasonable care" standard has become a source of serious liability. Defenders of the for-profit industry chains assert that civil damage liability of a nursing home is unnecessary, because regulatory controls are robust. Challengers against nursing homes point to continuing abuses, wide variations in actual state oversight, and other factors. Many have insisted on restoration of an activist leadership for CMS.

## SKIN PROBLEMS

The most common harm to elders in the institutional setting is the breakdown of skin integrity, beginning with excessive pressure on a bone causing small red pressure sores, later manifested by ulceration and infection of larger sores, with possible amputation of the arm or leg necessary if gangrene sets in. The proper care of elderly patients' skin is well understood in the nursing and medical-gerontology fields. But actually taking the steps to avoid these problems requires hours of personal attention from dedicated staff members. A well-documented program of examining skin, caring for skin, and treating early signs of sore formation should be in place. Whether the elder is mobile or not, the pressure-sore problem should be handled through careful evaluation and scheduled assistance to the elder in turning, moving, and exercising the limbs.

Skin breakdown results from several factors. Lack of motion leaves the weight of a bone on top of the skin to compress the skin, causing disruption of skin's natural processes. Dietary problems and hydration problems add to difficulties that would not be seen with the normal skin of active adults. Urine and fecal incontinence soaks clothing and

The vulnerability of the type of patient who enrolls in a nursing home is a constraint on what could be achieved through therapy or recreation. It is inevitable that a portion of the facility's residents will die each year and be replaced by others.

Some of the best facilities are those that consistently receive high ratings from state long-term care facility surveys, and that consistently are ranked well by the families of residents. Most nursing homes will pass inspection easily, yet virtually all will have areas for correction noted in their listing. A history of past abuses in the nursing home will be evident from a Web site listing that allows scrutiny of the facility's past violations of state requirements. If the state has found "imminent jeopardy" to patients at the facility, then it cannot receive any more publicly funded patients until corrections are made to the state's satisfaction. The conundrum is that nursing-home safety and health problems tend to correlate with lack of staff; lack of staff comes from lack of money; lack of safety leads to withdrawal of Medicare-Medicaid approval; loss of even more money when further Medicare or Medicaid patient placements are foreclosed may cause the facility to close.

Comparisons like "Nursing Home Compare" at the site Medicare.gov help provide consumers with a baseline on what violations have been caught in past inspections. Other sites offer different perspectives, and individuals are encouraged to ask additional questions before selecting a facility. The process of meeting the federal norms may not be flattering to all facilities, but the best homes are often rated highest in state surveys. Internet databases make this search easier than ever before. The Internet has truly changed the availability of data to "consumers," especially families of potential long-term care patients.

Decisions to have an elderly relative or friend enter or move out of a nursing home should be made on all the available data, not merely on the elements compared in the state reports. These are data points that should answer the questions family and friends ask when interviewing the nursing-home admissions office.

### EFFECTS OF POLITICS AND MONEY

Regulatory control to protect the weakest and most vulnerable has been in place for decades, but there are countervailing forces pushing back against the regulators. Political power and the importance of the nursing-home lobby in recent years have made it more difficult to enact tighter regulatory controls on what happens inside the homes. Federal funds to support patients in long-term care facilities come

# CHAPTER 7:
# NURSING-HOME RISKS OF HARM

Any study of harm to elderly persons must include consideration of risks that arise inside nursing homes. These are the institutions into which tens of thousands of elders are being relocated, at a point in their lives when medical or psychological reasons make it impossible for them to remain in their own homes. Regulatory control has followed past abuses. Protecting elders from harm is the underlying motive for many federal and state requirements. Historically, the use of liability lawsuits, together with regulatory controls, has actually altered (for the better) the awareness of resident safety among many of the operators of these long-term care facilities.

Special relationships lead to special obligations. The facility that calls itself a skilled-nursing facility must have both "skills" and "nurses" among its caregivers. Care quality appears to correlate strongly with the personnel practices and retention rates of the nursing home's managers. For purposes of protecting the elderly resident from harm, each relative or friend who is engaged in the process of selecting a nursing home shares responsibility for making an informed choice. They should read the descriptive information in the Medicare.gov "nursing home compare" Web site. A home that rates poorly and has extensive violations noted in the most recent survey should be avoided; that eliminates harm that could befall the potential resident.

**WHAT TO EXPECT**

Nursing homes do not cure residents of the problems that aging imposes. Vulnerable people concentrated in one site will be vulnerable to a variety of harms. There may be an ideal of what the perfect nursing-home setting might be, but the average facility is reasonably safe for its residents.

## CASE STUDY 1

A clinic whose mammography machine was not functioning properly knew that its diagnostic efforts were being affected. But it continued to use the deficient machine for several hundred breast examinations, after being notified of the problem. The federal Food and Drug Administration imposed, and the courts upheld, a multimillion-dollar penalty against the clinic. On appeal to the courts, the huge penalty was upheld.

## CASE STUDY 2

The hospital admission of Mr. Black from the Lakeside Alzheimers Nursing Home seemed routine, as he was experiencing shortness of breath, but the transmission of his nursing-home records was delayed. The emergency-room physician called for the records and was given a brief statement by an LPN from the nursing home; the phone report did not advise about his frequent wandering tendencies and several escapes. Black was admitted and moved to a sixth-floor room; soon after the floor nurse left him, he wandered out of the room into an unlocked stairwell, and died when he fell thirty feet onto a concrete landing. The Black estate sued both the hospital and the nursing home for negligence. The motions to dismiss were denied. The jury found the nursing home liable but cleared the hospital of negligence.

from a particular failing is much more difficult, because the science of virus and bacteria transmission is not sufficiently certain and the defendant in a lawsuit or regulatory action will always argue that this infection occurred without any involvement by a particular defendant.

## OMISSIONS

Perhaps the most difficult harm to demonstrate in a regulatory hearing or trial is the omission of care, which the plaintiff or the person representing the estate of a deceased patient shows to have been a matter of a duty for the nursing home, hospital, or other health-care institution. This is quite difficult to demonstrate, because the institution can always find someone to testify that the standard of care was reasonably met by its actions or those of the individual physician. Because this health-related harm is a form of neglect, no damages or regulatory penalty would apply unless it could be shown that there was direct proof of an obligation to take a particular safety- or health-related action. Thus, if the family of the deceased patient sues the nursing home for not protecting the elder from falling out of bed, the nursing home will usually win the case, because it is so difficult to demonstrate foreseeable knowledge of the likelihood of fall and injury.

## BARRIERS

We must also discuss the barriers that the jury system and the legal system in general place against remedies for injuries to the elderly. First, the patient may be dead, and the records may be inadequate. Second, memories and recollections about what precisely happened are notoriously fragile. Sometimes the only witnesses are employees of the defendant. Third, expert-witness testimony has become more difficult and expensive to obtain, and more difficult to sustain in the face of challenges. Fourth, legislation limiting malpractice cases has deterred many lawyers from taking medical-liability lawsuits, which are difficult and expensive cases to conduct, compared with other trials with greater likelihood of success in recovering damages. Fifth, the defense in a medical case virtually always argues that the jury's sympathies should be with the institutional defendant because the costs of health care will go up if the plaintiff wins large damages that have to be passed along to other patients who pay the same hospital for their services.

Because of these factors, the defense is in a very good position to prevail in many medical-malpractice claims, despite the media hype about the great importance of these cases in raising medical-insurance rates broadly.

waiting periods, or arbitration or mediation mandates, all of which are intended to reduce the likelihood that a jury would award a large damage judgment against a hospital or physician.

## NURSE LIABILITY

The second category of legal protections from harm is the available claim that an institution's nurse has committed malpractice, such as by failure to observe the patient and to act accordingly, or failure to properly administer a prescribed pharmaceutical drug, causing injury to the patient. Claims of failure to supervise lower-skilled staff, such as a "certified nursing assistant" employed for patient care at a nursing home, go against the institution that entrusted care supervision to that nurse. Nurse malpractice through omission or neglect of the patient is a challenging case to prove, more so than that by a specific physician treating one specific patient's needs.

## INADEQUATE PROTECTION

The third category of remedies for health-care harm is a claim against the institution for hospital or nursing-home malpractice through inadequate care or insufficient protection given to an elder. The handling of the elder by a health-care aide may produce a physical injury such as burns or excess force. Another hospital patient or a visitor might assault the bedridden patient.

## DOES REGULATION WORK?

For all three categories, there has been debate about the effectiveness of regulation, and especially about the effectiveness of lawsuits, as means to ensure protection of the patient. Professionals in the medical-care field often respond to criticism with the answer that they face sufficient oversight. Doctors are particularly offended: they do not need to be second-guessed by a jury, years after their decision was made about a particular patient's care.

Some of the areas in which harm to elders would be quite difficult to prove include infection of the patient, resulting from hospital or nursing-home exposures. The presence of universal precautions to avoid spreading infections has reduced patient-exposure problems and has cut the rates of transmission of infection. Expanded use of antibiotics has helped to reduce the severity of infection and resulting diseases.

Infection control is highly desirable, but proving to a regulatory agency, or to a trial court in a damages case, that a particular infection came

These are not simple cases for the plaintiff to win; sometimes a "marker" protein exists that allows experts to testify that a virus found in the operating room at the time of the plaintiff's surgery has also been found in the blood of the patient, lending credence to the claim that hospital failures of sanitation and sterilization have caused this harm. Was it negligence, and was the hospital worse than its peers in infection control?

## MEDICATING PATIENTS PROPERLY

Delivery of the correct medication to a specific patient is an area of potential risk, especially where the patient is not capable of self-protection. Dosing and medicine-interaction risks should be mitigated by the presence of an experienced clinical pharmacist, who could warn the prescribing doctor about the additional risk that a particular medication could cause for a patient who already receives numerous other drugs. "Polypharmacy," giving the patient multiple drugs that do not work well together, is a foreseeable problem that the consulting pharmacist may be able to avert.

## MEDICAL ERRORS

The most visible harm to health is the medical-treatment error. When the care of the patient becomes the responsibility of a health professional, that person (or his or her institutional employer) is held accountable if the service does not meet the standards of care of similar professionals in that area. Accountability could mean a loss of license or other professional discipline; most often, though, it means a medical-malpractice lawsuit.

Medical malpractice is the best known and most controversial of the health-related harms to elderly persons. Decisions about the treatment of an elderly patient by a treating physician, or by a physician who works in the nursing-home setting, have an inevitably important role in the future health of the patient. The standard of care in medical-malpractice lawsuits is whether the physician acted as a reasonable physician would have acted, in that same community, with that same set of information about the situation. The person who considers suing a physician needs to understand that medical decisions about dosing of drugs, potential interactions among drugs, and the FDA status of particular drugs for particular indications are very specific sets of facts which may not favor the plaintiff in that case. There is no automatic yes or no, in or out, of practical risks. Some state legislators have listened to the lobbyists for physicians, and have created caps on recovery, have closed their emergency departments, so elders from nursing homes may not be able to be treated at certain formerly preferred venues.

Medical malpractice and nurse malpractice are common complaints when a serious injury has occurred in the hospital setting. Standards of good medical practice within that community are applied to measure the competence and reasonableness of the treatment provided by the health professional.

## EQUIPMENT DEFECTS

Hospitals provide services that are increasingly software driven or equipment specific. The proper operation of machinery and the proper calibration of validation of devices is the responsibility of the hospital or clinic where the equipment is being used. The training of these staff operators is usually part of the installation costs to be charged by the seller of the machine or device.

Sometimes the civil tort-liability system applies; sometimes the government uses its power to impose penalties on the user of deficient equipment. A defect in a piece of medical equipment should be immediately reported to the FDA if the failure rate exceeds the rate shown in the brochures and training materials delivered with the machine. If the failure hurt a patient or seriously compromised his or her care, risk managers from the hospital will check on the possible causes of the failure. Plaintiffs in liability suits love to have the power of electronic discovery of internal e-mails in these kinds of cases.

If the injury was affected by lack of warnings with the equipment, there may be a court case asserting the failure to properly inform and educate operators. If it occurred because the device was being used for a purpose that FDA had not approved, and if the device's maker encouraged that use, then this off-label promotion might cause FDA to challenge the maker's marketing plans. Remedies could include a fine by FDA.

## INFECTION ISSUES

Infection control is an important aspect of liability avoidance for the hospital. Accreditation standards of the Joint Commission and disease-transmission cautionary recommendations by the Centers for Disease Control, endorse the use of "universal precautions" for preventing the spread of disease. Failure to follow precautions can cause harm. That harm might be traceable back to a procedure done by the hospital; an infection's causation might be confirmed by expert testimony.

Proving liability or a regulatory claim against a hospital is likely to be a complex challenge. When an elderly patient dies after what appeared to be a routine surgical procedure and routine postsurgical recovery, the potential exists that the nursing staff, anesthetist, or surgeon (or a combination of these) had erred in handling this patient. Of course, it is natural that their interests will quickly diverge, once their separate insurance carriers are notified.

Plaintiffs in the liability system or regulators in the government system have an interest in discovering documents about the patient and may interview staff members, surgeons, and nurses to discern what caused the death. The logs, recordings, and standard operating procedures will be important. The potential defendants have an incentive to blame the problem on a preexisting condition or on some nonhospital actor, such as the maker of a device or drug.

When a problem or death is reported to government officials, the typical government reporting form (FD-3500) contains a box to check: was the injury a user error or a product problem? The form probably will be completed in a way that downplays any error or omission by the hospital or its staff. No one likes to admit that a patient's death was caused by their mistakes, although all recognize that some errors are inevitable when humans conduct the surgery, prescribing, or other care.

**LEGAL DUTIES**

The hospital's duty to the patient is to provide a reasonably safe environment, with reasonably competent staff members, facilitating the surgeon's or treating physician's care of that person. State hospital-liability laws describe and sometimes limit these obligations toward the patient. The typical cases are slip and fall, acute injuries from accidents such as dropping the patient from a gurney or a bad catheter placement, or a technical error such as misfiring X-rays without shielding the patient so as to cause burns.

Elders do not have a legal right to be treated at any hospital they choose; the marketplace and particularly employer health-care contractors are selective among the competing venues. Federal laws protect the rights of the emergency patient to be treated by hospitals that have functioning emergency-room services. Yet sometimes the patterns of federal and state funding reductions have discouraged hospitals from offering emergency care because the public-funding or reimbursement climate causes financial loss to the hospital operator. Some hospitals

# CHAPTER 6:
# HOSPITAL-RELATED HARMS

The American medical system is one of the most technologically advanced health systems in the world. But the system has considerable problems with the safe and consistent delivery of efficient care to our most vulnerable elder patients. Harm that occurs to an elderly person in a hospital might be compensable in damages, but damage awards are fewer and smaller because lobbyists for hospital and medical groups have worked hard to place caps and controls on malpractice litigation today. These defense actions have driven lawyers for many of the injured persons to bring multiple suits against multiple players.

**UNEXPECTED FATALITIES DRAW INQUIRIES**

Why cover hospitals in a discussion of elders at risk? Because a certain percentage of deaths of elders are caused by conditions inside the walls of a hospital. Let's examine the steps that influence your decision as the survivor or executor for an elder who died unexpectedly.

After a generally healthy inpatient dies unexpectedly while at a hospital, there will be questions about causes, and at least an informal investigation by the risk-management office of the hospital. The coroner or police may also inquire, but the inside inquiry seeks to protect the hospital by defining what the condition of the patient had been upon admission to the hospital, and then if possible linking death to the cause that had been the original reason for hospitalization. Infections carried inside the body and into the hospital room are examples of circumstances leading to death that are not likely to cause liability or regulatory concerns. But a healthy woman who goes to the hospital for gallstones is not expected to die there. The hospital's infection-control procedures, the handling of the patient before surgery, the actions of the surgeons, etc. will be part of the internal investigation.

## CASE STUDY 3

A sudden collision at an intersection caused a rollover of the Ford SUV in which Mr. Green, age seventy-eight, was riding as a rear-seat passenger, on a trip out of his nursing home to a family dinner. His head hit the heavy chrome roof light inside the SUV, and its edge caused a contusion and heavy bleeding. While Mr. Green was hanging upside down awaiting rescue, the effects of the sharp blow to his head and the bleeding caused him to go into shock. Extensive hospitalization and related expenses followed. His claim was for damages against the other car's owner. By May 15th the personal-injury claim had been settled. The other driver's insurance carrier was able to settle quickly with Green, but in a follow-up CAT scan in July, bleeding on the brain was detected. Green's lawyer sought to reopen the closed case against that driver, but the signed release was upheld as binding by the court. Green then sued Ford, asserting lack of "crashworthy" design in the use of a heavy ceiling light in close proximity to passengers. The case went on through motions and countermotions, and ultimately the court held that the design had met minimum federal auto-safety standards, which preempted state tort laws as to design features. Ford escaped any liability.

It may be necessary for the family to remove the elder from access to his or her car, either directly by taking the keys, or through inventing reasons why the car is suddenly not available. The family of an elder person may need to hide the car or take away the keys, or even mechanically disable the car. This difficult decision is made so that the elderly relative does not become a casualty of his or her own inattention, as perception and reaction times begin to deteriorate.

The family in a smaller community may be ready to seek the assistance of local police to stop the dangerous elder driver. The police in such a place are more likely to recognize the struggle by the family to keep him or her from driving, in a situation where injury to others is a serious concern. So police officers may take the elder driver out of the car and return him or her home, calling the caregiver for a "rescue" at the roadside. Of course, this does not apply in a larger city or other impersonal setting, where the police will treat the elderly impaired driver as they would any other impaired driver.

**CASE STUDY 1**

Some elder drivers have experienced a deterioration in peripheral vision that inhibits their night driving. The driver's-side mirror placement on the Citroen sedan created a large "blind spot" that made it difficult to see a car that was passing. After a side-to-side accident with a car heading in the same direction had injured several passengers, the elderly driver was sued; his lawyer brought a suit against Citroen, arguing that its mirror design was deficient and had contributed to the crash. The court granted dismissal on summary judgment because the car was within acceptable standards for "normal" drivers and Citroen did not have a legal duty to accommodate elder drivers.

**CASE STUDY 2**

Mary Grey walked with a walker inside her assisted-living community. She was in a group of residents who took an outing to a downtown museum. After exiting the group van, she stepped off a curb and fell forward, into the path of a car driven by an uninsured immigrant. She was killed on impact. Her estate sued the community owner, asserting that a failure to adequately supervise the group outing was negligent in light of their knowledge of her unsteady gait. The state had not adopted any assisted-living community legislation that would create a special legal obligation. Just before trial was to commence, the judge directed a verdict dismissing the case on a finding that the community had no legal duty to protect adult residents outside of its grounds.

a person with vision deficits and memory lapses has been permitted to continue driving.

## PEDESTRIAN RISKS

Unlike the situation involving driver-related injuries, the elder pedestrian who is struck and injured is more likely to obtain a substantial recovery. This assumes that he or she had been within a marked or lighted crosswalk when struck by the moving vehicle. Crossing signs, blinkers, and pavement marking generally give rise to the presumption that the designated crossing point may be used with reasonable care by pedestrians of all levels of physical strength.

Some injured plaintiffs have better cases than others who were arguably contributing to their own harm, in retrospect. If the patient released from the hospital goes to a rehabilitation facility, for example, then a walk outside of the facility may be a beneficial form of exercise. The driver of the automobile or truck that hit the pedestrian in the crosswalk is likely to be held liable in a lawsuit, even though the older person had not specifically asked about the risk or specifically prepared for the contingency of a collision. The lighting, warning signs, and visible marking at the crossing will often be the difference for jury regarding how much it would award to an insured elderly pedestrian. The pedestrian is likely to be able to claim that the driver exceeded the speed limit, drove without paying close attention, or otherwise failed in his or her duty as the driver of the vehicle.

If all other grounds for winning damages fail, the defendant could still be held accountable through some form of official action instigated by the plaintiff's counsel. Prosecution for negligent homicide might follow a fatal pedestrian wreck. Results could include damages against the corporate owner of the vehicle, if any, and punitive damages because of the recklessness involved, to the extent that the state allows punitive-damage claims in writing.

## TRANSPORTATION

In theory, the availability of public transportation in a community reduces the need for an individual elder to continue to drive a personal car. But the freedom of having a personal vehicle is viewed as an important part of normal social life, which the elder is reluctant to surrender. An older person who forgets his or her location and the route home is less able to maneuver through traffic and will be a risk to others. After an accident harms someone, their suit may allege that the adult children of the elder had acted negligently in not stopping his or her driving.

TRAFFIC-RELATED RISKS OF HARM

**ROADWAY PROBLEMS**

Second, after an accident there may be assertions that the elder was not at fault, or less at fault, because of the condition of the road, or of the lighting on the roadway. Usually there is immunity for the government entity such as the state highway department, unless there were unusual or exceptional circumstances. In general, all drivers are required to use ordinary care in driving. So the elder driver's vision challenges in night driving are not an excuse; the failure to use ordinary care is not excused by normal deficiencies in the condition of the road.

**VEHICLE DEFICIENCIES**

The third possible legal complication for the elder driver is a deficiency in the vehicle. Though some defects are found that would harm any driver, such as a wheel not securely bolted onto an axle, this discussion usually arises when the elderly person needs to avoid a hazard that he or she sees in time to avoid an accident. Courts tend to be unsympathetic to claims that the design of a commonly used product should have been protective of the interests of a person who had an impairment, such as an elderly person with limited vision who had slower reaction times. In some cases, courts dismiss the claim of a defect on the basis that federal auto-safety standards preempt the state and can thus block juries from awarding damages on the basis that the design was negligent or defective.

Crashworthiness is a legal doctrine about the carmaker's duty to anticipate how, at the time of the accident, occupants of the car will be hitting the dashboard, side walls, air bag, etc. The crashworthiness of a passenger car will be measured by the ordinary driver's condition. Airbag explosions are very forceful, as they should be, but they may injure the frail elder passenger. After the accident occurs, the frailty of the vehicle occupant will be one factor in deciding how much the car's intended design features can be held to be a cause of the injury.

As result of these three factors, the elder should not expect that the courts will reward the victim of an accident in a vehicle case. Damage awards are unlikely unless the ordinary reasonable person would have been able to recover damages in a comparable case. The law does not favor special treatment of older drivers, and in some respects disfavors older drivers by making testing for the renewal of licenses more difficult in some states. This is a policy choice; legislators can hear from elder advocates on this and other issues, but they recognize this is a safety trade-off and will be approached delicately. No license official wants to answer, after a child pedestrian is killed, the question why

# CHAPTER 5:
# TRAFFIC-RELATED RISKS OF HARM

This chapter addresses accidents involving vehicles, drivers, and pedestrians. Avoidable deaths in traffic accidents and pedestrian-related injuries are a national problem. Accidents involving elderly drivers and those involving elderly pedestrians are too significant a subgroup of these problems, and remedial action is needed.

Legal systems and civil-engineering skills need to be used to reduce this problem of elders injured in traffic situations. The avoidance of accidental harms to elders will require better training, better pavement marking, stronger driver's-license competence requirements, and other measures. The legal system provides for the protection of drivers through standards for driver performance; signs and barriers to protect against accidents; and safety standards for vehicle design, like air-bag rules and readable information in warnings.

**DRIVER LICENSING**

The first issue is the competence of the driver to react quickly to road hazards and to actions by other drivers. Legally, driving licenses are considered a "privilege" rather than a constitutional right. The elder driver is usually given the same eye test and skills test as other drivers, but in some states there is a retest of all drivers who renew licenses over a certain age. The retest of skills recognizes that driving safely may be more difficult with older drivers, as vision and physical response time diminishes. If state law prevents the elder person from renewing his or her license without reestablishing competence, some older drivers will be unable to drive. Suing the state licensing agency is fruitless; courts are not likely to side with the motorist, since the license is a privilege that requires the person to demonstrate capacity to perform regularly with the same capability as other younger drivers.

dying in the hospital two weeks later. The daughter sues the alarm company, which demonstrated the product in her living room at the time of sale. The company defends on the basis that the product would function normally in her home, but thick Montana stone in the basement blocked all radio signals. Experts disagree on whether the signal could have been made stronger in light of the condition of the basement walls. The judge grants judgment for the company before trial.

## CASE STUDY 1

Ms. Burns lives alone in a small city house built in 1905, with electrical work dating from 1956. She buys a small refrigerator and plugs it into an extension cord suitable for a lamp; the cord overheats and the rug ignites, causing thick black smoke. While attempting to flee the flames and smoke, she slips and hits her head, but is still alive when fire fighters arrive. But the smoke has overcome her and she dies. The cord maker, refrigerator maker, and rug importer are sued by the estate of Burns. The cord maker shows that its cord had warning tags that placed a wattage limit on its uses, which she has exceeded. The refrigerator maker shows that it has warnings about strengths of extension cords in its owner's manual. The rug was imported many years ago and no manufacturer can be traced. After depositions and motions, the refrigerator maker makes a small settlement payment and the other cases are dropped before trial.

## CASE STUDY 2

Mr. Green, age eighty-two, uses a walker and a specially equipped van to get around his small Rhode Island community. His apartment is near the bay, and quite windy. The landlord ordinarily removes snow and ice as soon as a storm passes, but the landlord goes to Florida for a week in February. On Sunday evening, Feb. 16, as Green leaves the apartment building, a driveway patch of "black ice" causes him to fall; he has a serious concussion and dies. His estate sues the landlord; it argues that the pattern of good removal led Green to expect the ice would have been removed. But the defense argues that no statute or ordinance requires removal of ice from private property, and state case-law precedents hold rental tenants responsible for using due care in snowy conditions. The landlord's insurance carrier declines to settle, and the jury declines to hold the landlord liable for negligence.

## CASE STUDY 3

Ms. Pink, age seventy-six, lives alone in Montana. Her daughter from Texas has bought a necklace-mounted emergency signal device for her mother, to connect her with a national alarm-monitoring company. Ms. Pink has arthritis, leg problems, and great difficulty in rising from a sitting position. She insists on keeping a clean house, and as she washes the basement floor she slips, fracturing her hip. She tries to use the signal device, but it is not strong enough to transmit out of the basement. By the time neighbors call police to search for her two days later, her condition has worsened and she is very weak, ultimately

chance of compensation. Lawyers will not take on these cases; insurance claims are not likely to generate large compensation. Jurors in a civil lawsuit involving a fall or burn injury will be hesitant to accept a claim of product or landlord fault. The jury may conclude that the in-home risk was one that was recognized and assumed by the individual. The exception might be a product-liability lawsuit if the actual injury came from a defect in a familiar household product, like a collapsing chair that had been purchased new from a retail store within a short time before the accident.

Suing the landlord likewise offers like probability of success. When the elder rented that apartment or the room at the residential facility, such as a "board and care" residence, was he or she aware that the risky conditions were present? If open and obvious conditions could have been seen by a healthy adult, a rental property's visible risk will not result in a successful claim against the landlord after an accident occurs. Facilities that simply provide living space, and not also health-related assistance, are not held to the same standard as long-term care facilities.

## ELECTRICAL RISKS

The electrical-safety concerns for elderly persons who live at home are twofold: fire danger from overloaded extension cords or frayed electrical cords and shock trauma from voltage passed through the body from an electrical appliance or other equipment.

Fire danger from appliances is a product of misuse, old or obsolete units, overloading of extension cords, mistakes in installation, or carelessness. The post-fire investigative report may fault the extension cord, but it is also likely to observe that the homeowner overloaded the cord. Makers of home electrical equipment have been careful in recent years to provide cautionary statements on packages and to disclaim responsibility for excessive overloading.

Shocks that cause death or serious injury should be rare in the modern home, but some elders live with older appliances or with poorly repaired connections to their lamps and wall switches. Older aluminum wire and older appliances pose a risk that circuitry may malfunction and cause harm. Regulatory controls and voluntary standards apply to current designs and currently manufactured products, but no regulation applies to preexisting products and residential conditions. Civil tort-damage cases are very expensive to prove, and unless large damages are possible after a fatal fire has occurred, few experienced lawyers will accept such a case under the typical contingency-fee arrangement.

Indoor, clear pathways for walking, clearly marked stairs, and effective lighting will reduce the risk of serious or fatal falls. Night lights, light switches that glow in the dark, and other means of aiding walking around the home after dark will reduce the risk of falls.

## DOOR SECURITY

Elders want to be protected from crime. Safety can sometimes include safety door locks to keep the mentally impaired person from an unauthorized departure. When the elder is a person with dementia, care at home requires changing door security; to avoid wandering into hazards, there should be a means of securing the person in an area of the home while the caregiver can perform necessary tasks like laundry and dish washing.

Access for first responders in the event of an accident is an important consideration; clear paths to an easy exit will save lives, if a smoker sets fire to the living-room couch. A good question to ask is, "What would the ambulance team need, in the event of a sudden emergency?" There is a sort of built-in tension: an elder whose judgment is impaired should not be able to wander out into the busy or snowy street, yet access should be clear and functional for rescuers if there were a sudden emergency.

Another aspect of home-based risk issues involves the landlord's obligation to protect residents who rent property. It may be obvious that the apartment is being rented without certain desirable physical safeguards, such as lighting and rails on steps, and with potential areas of physical harm. The landlord has obligations under state law to provide a reasonable amount of safety, but the tenant is responsible for cleanliness and maintenance of the paths and walkways he or she controls. For example, northern American climates feature months of ice and snow, which can cause fatal falls. Snow removal typically would be the responsibility of the tenant in a single-family rental home, who has day-to-day possession of the property. Shifting the obligation from the tenant to a greater imposition on the landlord would depend upon the amount of advance notice and negotiation or communication. An elderly retirement community designed by architects to be used by persons with limited capabilities will be held to a higher standard.

## LEGAL CONSEQUENCES

Ultimately, risks that elders encounter in their own homes are likely to be treated by the legal system as "your own fault." The typical injured elder who is harmed in a home accident will be left without much lobbying. So a bed fire will result in a mattress company or clothing company being sued, while the cigarette maker escapes liability.

In addition to cigarette risks, the igniting of loose sleeves while cooking over open flames poses a substantial risk. Most adults realize that clothing or nearby towels may catch fire in a kitchen accident. The flammability regulations of the Consumer Product Safety Commission have been in place for decades, and will need further updating to enhance safety. For now, the burning of clothing, linens, grease on a stove, and kitchen accessories pose the most likely threat of fire to the elderly person.

Related to this issue is the matter of egress or ability to exit. Plans for fire evacuation are an essential aspect of nursing-home design and operation. Can the person in a wheelchair escape this fire hazard? If he or she dies, was there any legal duty in local or state laws that required this landlord to act differently? When a nursing home burns, its contingency plan for evacuation should be executed; if no plan exists, federal guidelines and state laws can probably be invoked as a basis for a lawsuit against the management of that facility.

## BUILDING-RELATED RISKS

Thousands of elders are injured in their own homes by preventable accidents each year. Protecting them usually requires attention to the total environment of the home, especially those areas in which upward and downward walking is intended to occur. Books on home design to protect elders offer great suggestions.

Steps are a potential killer, because falls fracturing hips can have the effect of shortening the life of the elder. Wheelchair access requires ramps; small lifts and adjustable ramps, along with grab bars and other stability-enhancing designs, will reduce the risks of falls. The floor surface should be uncluttered carpeting or clean, textured tile in hard-surface areas, and not slippery. Area rugs can cause tripping and should be avoided, as experts warn that elders are more likely to fall by catching a shoe on the edge of uneven flooring.

Lighting improvements and contrasting colors will improve visibility and help to avoid accidents for the more mobile elderly. The use of color contrasts to enhance the safety of those with weak vision is highly recommended by safety experts and designers. The home can be attractive and functional and yet have the enhanced lighting that facilitates safe movement by the elder.

Dangers of fractures from falls on dark, steep steps are the enemy of the elder resident. Exterior stair lighting and handrails will be essential.

caused similar harm to multiple users are a real concern that prudent manufacturers want to avoid. Thus, design decisions on products to be used by the elderly will take into account the manufacturer's desire to avoid legal vulnerability for injuries that should be foreseeable among a large class of users of those products.

For example, the maker of a bathrobe has a strong incentive to comply with government requirements for flammability testing of that bathrobe; the jury would hear the standard and see videos reproducing conditions of the product's failure. The bathrobe marketer would be vulnerable to a large damage award in a lawsuit if the robe were to be substantially more flammable than the consumer had expected, and if it was the defect in the robe, rather than user error, that caused severe injuries to occur. The same can be said about other consumer-product standards.

Liability lawsuits have a real deterrent effect on companies' conduct. Their reminder to designers to protect the product user builds upon the other reasons for risk avoidance, such as regulatory-agency controls. Damage- or death-related lawsuits draw publicity about product risks that is a negative form of consumer-risk education ("I didn't know that kind of accident could happen."). Sometimes the result of a lawsuit is a recall along withother forms of remedial action, which is publicized. Sometimes a letter to users or a specialized product mailer cautions against a particular risk, for example warning the bathrobe consumer against contact between clothing and flame.

The cumulative effect is that education, regulation, and liability work together to protect the elderly person. When education works, no liability suits arise; when regulation works, fewer injuries occur; when others in the same industry face very large punitive damages, all industry participants take notice. So the cumulative effect of products liability is implicit protection through safer designs, achieved through multiple means.

**FLAMMABILITY RISKS**

Fire is an especially frightening aspect of the elderly person's environment. At home or in institutional settings, the risk of this kind of harm comes from two principal sources: cigarettes and stove tops.

Cigarette smoking, of course, is dangerous in many immediate and long-term ways. Some elders lack sufficient motor control to securely hold a lit cigarette, or may fall asleep while smoking; either may drop a lighted cigarette onto bedcovers, newspapers, or other flammable items. Fires from cigarettes are a substantial safety problem. The legal obligation of the cigarette makers is virtually nil, because of their success over the years in avoiding both liability and regulation through skillful

Should elders' needs and abilities to handle products be accommodated better by product designers? Yes; and specialized markets do exist for elder-friendly products. Should product manufacturers and designers be required by civil tort-case juries to pay damages to injured elders, who misunderstand or fail to properly operate the "normal adult" product? No, say manufacturers; yes, say elder-law advocates. Trends in design practices in recent years appear to favor more marketing of products that are designed to benefit elderly users, such as easier-to-open packages or easier-to-grasp handles. The trend is toward greater safety, but for those persons injured by "old-style" products, this does not make those products legally vulnerable to suits alleging they pose a greater-than-expected risk. In general, the law does not consider that the appearance of a safer model renders earlier models unsafe.

Government design standards for home products are increasingly taking into account the aging of the population, which is more vulnerable when using products like flammable garments. The obligation to avoid risks in the construction of housing manifests itself through state building codes and the actual building inspection before occupancy. Elder-protective designs are becoming more readily available, and other architectural practices are being adopted which tailor the design to its use—the assisted-living community or elder-retirement communities with design features that are very protective of elders' vision, hand coordination, stability in walking, and so on. It's not a basis for a lawsuit to assert that the consequences of an accidental injury could have been avoided if the existing, older residential property had been retrofitted; the person who chose to rent or buy is presumed to have known of its condition. The law does not generally force an upgrading when new building-code requirements are adopted, and does not award damages for an older building not being "better than normal" in its design or equipment. But when new federal funds are used, HUD standards of accessibility will be incorporated into the building and its interior spaces.

## LEGAL REMEDIES FOR AN ELDER'S ACCIDENTAL INJURY

A third method of giving business some greater incentives for protection of elders is the threat of juries awarding punitive damages in negligence-liability cases. Insurance companies have made their clients well aware of this threat. Business managers recognize that civil juries will impose damages and liability upon companies that negligently market products with serious and substantial risks. This operates as an implicit deterrent.

Losing a lawsuit about unsafe design of a product is an experience prudent companies wish to avoid. Class actions asserting the same product

older electrical systems, stairs, badly maintained heating and electrical units, and a myriad of other injury-threatening risks can make the elder person's home the most likely site of falls, burns, or other accidents. There are three possible means of protection of the elderly person against accidents inside the home.

The first and simplest is education, training and (in cases of dementia) retraining the elder to avoid risks. Education in this context means "coaching," making the competent and attentive guardian or caregiver aware of how to assess the risks to their elder from darkly lit spaces, uneven surfaces, stairs without sufficient rails, and other very common items. Ideally, the education would extend to the elder person as well. If the elder is no longer able to understand and process the information, then educational efforts should be directed to the caregiver.

**SAFETY STANDARDS TO PROTECT ELDERS**

The second means of protection is an organization in federal, state, or local government to establish a standard for safety, which enhances protection of the elder. For example, a federal standard on flammability of drapes and furniture attempts to reduce in-home fire dangers. It would establish a specific rule that the makers of all home products would have to satisfy, requiring them to avoid potential risks to elders, in the furniture or drapes or other fabric products they design and sell.

Standards should be understandable and realistic to implement, and should not assume an error-free environment for the use of the product. For home products, errors by an adult user are to be expected. Any lawsuit claiming a product was unsafe as designed is usually rebutted with a response that the consumer had misused it. The law treats elders among the adult users of a product, and does not generally protect against the consequences of a confused or agitated dementia patient using a product inappropriately and being harmed. It is up to caregivers to make the home more user friendly when late-night wandering and confusion begin to appear.

Consider an analogy to child-oriented products like toys, which protect the younger user who makes a foreseeable error. Parents are aware that the design of children's products tends to be very protective against user error. These design decisions recognize the need for caution—children will be careless at play, and may be at risk if the toys or other child products are not safely used. As with this designer caution, a similar awareness of diminished capacity among elders should induce marketers to bring out elder-"friendly" versions of adult home products, where risks from a conventional product might harm the unwary elder.

# CHAPTER 4:
# REMEDIES FOR INJURY AT HOME

What can and what will the legal system do to protect against risks inside an elder individual's home? This chapter will cover four potential sources of harm to the elder in his or her personal residence:

- accidents at home;
- assaults at home;
- neglect by in-home caregivers; and
- financial harms.

"I've fallen and I can't get up!" The television commercial used fear to sell a signaling device for elders. Accidents at home can cause fractures, burns, hospitalization, loss of lifestyle, and in some cases, death. Sometimes these are the elder's own fault; quite often, the elder did not appreciate the risk before it hit him or her, and by then the consequences were painful.

Assaults injure the victim physically and increase fear and detachment from a sense of security. Assaults and abuse are addressed in Chapter 11 of this book. Neglect jeopardizes the safety of a person who is vulnerable by reason of mental or physical incapacity; Chapter 11 also covers these risks, under the umbrella term "abuse." And financial harms result in serious negative consequences for the lifestyle—medical and other attributes of life—for the elderly person. Financial harms are addressed in Chapter 10.

## EDUCATION TO AVOID HOME ACCIDENTS

Accidents in the homeare a substantial venue for injury. Though no statistics are definitive, we can assume that hospitals and nursing homes are relatively safer locations than the individual's home. Clutter,

members on the relevant legislative committee were met by a delegation of elders from their districts, and the change was made.

## CASE STUDY 2

Repeated efforts to improve the support staff at the Diamond Jubilee Nursing Home had failed, and many residents were inadequately fed and bathed; numerous serious medication errors were made as well. After one periodic scheduled visit found deficiencies, three surprise inspections were done over a three-month period, upon complaints. The most recent incident was classified as putting residents in "imminent jeopardy," so new patient Medicare-Medicaid enrollment was suspended. After a hearing at the state long-term care agency, the nursing-home operator was barred from new Medicare-Medicaid payments. Later the state held a second hearing and denied an application for a renewed license. The firm closed the nursing home and ultimately lost its state licenses for other homes as well.

## CASE STUDY 3

The federal Center for Medicare and Medicaid Services (CMS) usually works through insurance carriers as the state financial contractor for reimbursement programs. A carrier in one state decided not to pay for a particular medical device that reduces pain, considering its use not to be necessary as an adjunct to surgical recovery. Elder-advocacy groups and surgeons' groups protested to the carrier but it would not revisit the issue. The device maker appealed to CMS's central decisional body, and that office deliberated for months without response. After a delegation of elders from a certain state visited one of that state's senators, who is chairman of the Senate committee on elder issues, CMS managers received a call from the Senate staff inquiring about the decision and suggesting that a hearing might be held. Within a week, Medicare reversed the decision and allowed reimbursement for the pain device.

The Postal Inspection Service investigates marketers who promise a false product benefit in rteurn for payment by mail. These are the experts in mass mail-fraud detection and prosecution. Their extensive information about frauds and related Web information can be reached through the Postal Service Web site, postalinspectors.uspis.gov.

The Office of the Inspector General of the Department of Health and Human Services (OIG) have become seasoned veterans of fraud in nursing-home, hospital, and doctor billing frauds against Medicare. If the abuse or fraud occurred in a Medicare recipient hospital, nursing home, or clinic, or if the patient received federal health-insurance funding, the OIG has the funding, the expertise, and the ability to punish fraudulent actions and other law violations.

State and federal securities agencies are actively seeking to protect elders from stock fraud. Claims of the "greatest investment ever!!!" or the "stock buyer's opportunity of the year!" may sound too good to be true, especially if the breathless excitement comes across an internet message line. Before sending—and losing—this money, a trusted investment advisor in the elder's local area should be consulted. Legitimate brokers are licensed by the Securities and Exchange Commission after completion of training and testing. In the event that the stock seller vanishes or the stock turns out to be worthless (apart from ordinary market losses, which occur inevitably), complaints to the SEC and to state securities commissions should be made, to help with arrest of the thief and to possibly get back a portion of the losses if the criminal had any assets to be seized and forfeited. To be clear, normal losses in marketplace investments are not covered; frauds in sale of stock should be reported to the Securities and Exchange Commission at sec.gov.

**CASE STUDY 1**

Building codes for apartment construction in one state were older and did not provide for wheelchair-accessible bathrooms and fixtures. Elders who lived independently and who had wheelchairs needed a change in the code, but the building owners objected to the additional design and construction costs. The elders studied the percentages of the rental market at which tenants of different ages were moving into apartments. Working with disabled-veterans groups and senior-advocacy organizations, the proponents of the change met with the state commerce secretary, and asked a representative of the governor to attend the meeting "in preparation for our request to meet with the governor soon." A factual and statistical case was made favoring the change;

has held back from doing a more careful evaluation of vitamin claims in most advertising. The regulatory control of false claims has been mostly left to the Federal Trade Commission. But for the most part, "Buyer Beware" is the right attitude.

### Injury and Side-Effects Reporting

Adverse-event reports about injuries to elders that are associated with drugs or medical devices are tracked by FDA's Medwatch database. A patient takes a generic form of the cholesterol drug Lipitor®, for example, and has a sudden weakness in the arms and legs. The science of epidemiology studies patterns of illness. This science has enabled FDA to look for patterns of problems in patients' experience with marketed drugs. Computerized tracking has developed with increased communication and data-compilation tools. FDA uses advanced computerized-analysis tools to evaluate how the recently marketed drugs are performing across age categories of patients. If the drug appears to be causing increased risks to consumers, FDA may order a change in label warnings. Because some of the risks are not seen in conventional limited clinical studies, adverse events that happen while newer drugs are out on the market are essential clues to the risks of a new pharmaceutical.

### Bone-Fracture Prevention

Bone-health products, designed to prevent fractures among elderly patients, are a huge sales market for drug companies. The avoidance of broken hips saves hundreds of millions of dollars in lost mobility and subsequent harms. The FDA drug-approval process has therefore been used to clear for marketing a number of drugs that build stronger bones or that prevent the deterioration that some elders will experience.

### Other Economic Protections from Fraud

There are other federal agencies that specialize in combating the fraudulent deception of elders, schemes to steal money from the more gullible or vulnerable consumers. Several books about scams and rip-offs that are available in libraries and bookstores exhaustively describe the means by which thieves have stolen from elderly victims. Our purpose is to catalog the types of government action you may seek in response to a fraud or theft case.

Local police and prosecutors often lack the resources for detection of the perpetrators of multistate fraud; your case may cross state lines, may involve the internet, and may be a deception that took advantage of the elderly person's pleasant and trusting demeanor. You may wish to notify both the local police and the federal and state protective agencies described below.

doctors to prescribe generic drugs for elderly patients, ending their use of the name-brand drugs, as early as possible after FDA has approved the sale of generic-equivalent medications. The majority of large-scale pharmaceutical products now have a generic equivalent, or several generic versions. These deliver approximately the same amount of the active ingredient, plus or minus 25 percent, the variation permitted in most cases. The trade-off for receiving the generic is strictly a price advantage. The research-driven development of beneficial drugs is repaid through the initial high price of those few drug compounds that reach the market, after dozens or hundreds of others have failed to clear safety and effectiveness testing. Those high prices compensate for the high costs of a pioneering a new compound. After the patent expires and any special period for exclusive marketing expires, the generic product can be launched; the first sale of the generic version tends to reduce the price of the "pioneer" innovative product slightly; prices drop by perhaps 70 percent when there are multiple alternative generic versions that will compete on the basis of their lower prices.

**Imported or Internet Drug Purchasing**

Tied in to the rise of generic drugs is the sharp increase in sales of non-U.S. drugs to U.S. patients from internet sources, from Mexican or Canadian pharmacies, and from nontraditional suppliers who are beyond the reach of state pharmacy-licensing boards. Some but not all are valuable and valid; too many are deficient or fraudulent. FDA has proven by random sampling of incoming drug shipments that a significant portion of these drugs are not what they claim to be; some deliver less active ingredient than the claimed amount, some are much more potent than expected, and others do not contain any of the active drug that is claimed. FDA is concerned that so many of the imported drugs have no traceable sources, coming from unidentified factories somewhere in the Third World. FDA or other nations' health officials will never know the quality of the conditions under which the pills were packed.

The FDA has begun several programs to deal with this increased spread of diverted drugs. Congress has allowed drug imports from Canada, once the FDA certifies that they are equivalent in safety to the U.S. products, but FDA cannot issue a certification because the "pedigree" of so many of these drugs is dubious.

**Vitamins and Supplements**

Fraudulent claims of benefit to elders from certain dietary supplements have been challenged in some FDA proceedings. Congress rewrote the law governing vitamin products in 1994, to restrict FDA enforcement powers. Thus a wider variety of claims have been tolerated, and FDA

### Getting the Right Drug

FDA recognizes that seniors take multiple medications, and that as patients age doctors prescribe more long-term maintenance drugs to be taken on a daily basis. The potential for a fatal mix-up among doctor, pharmacist, caregiver, and patient is severe. As the agency that approves applications to market new drug products, the Food and Drug Administration has used its authority over new drug names to help avoid confusion when two names sound alike but the drugs have very different uses. Readable labels on consumer nonprescription drugs were an innovation when the "Drug Facts" uniform panel was adopted in recent years.

Getting drug containers "right" for easy and safe opening involves a balance between allowing arthritic fingers to open a container, and necessary avoidance of toddler and child access to potentially poisonous drugs inside the home. Packaging for drugs that are sold over the counter must be childproof, except for one size that is permitted to be in more easily openable packaging with clear markings on the retail box.

### Safer Implantable Parts

Can we rely on the safety of surgically implanted body parts? Generally, yes. Surgeons and hospitals will depend on well-established networks and FDA will oversee the quality standards used by these networks. Metal and plastic designs must be manufactured precisely and sterilized for implantation; the delicate nature of these products will require a very precise devotion to accurate measurement.

It is not easy to inspect all of the parts made here or overseas, or to supervise the safe handling of transplantable human body parts "harvested" from donors or from cadavers. Implants and replacement body parts such as artificial hips are regulated by two separate parts of the FDA. The artificial hips, knees, and other body parts manufactured for medical uses are regulated by FDA's medical-device center. Actual human parts that can be transplanted from living persons or from cadavers are regulated as biological substances. With the rise of imported transplantable parts, such as corneas for eye surgery, the FDA has had some difficulties in keeping up with the increasing volume.

### Generic Drug Controls

Generic drug substitution is a remarkable cost-savings opportunity. If the FDA controls work as planned, the patient gets a comparable health benefit at a great saving. Medicare and Medicaid have shifted to emphasize more use of generic drugs. Likewise, private insurance companies and the recently evolved "pharmacy benefit managers" have pushed

## WHAT FEDERAL AGENCIES CAN HELP ME?

### Federal Trade Commission

The first protector aims at economic harm from consumer fraud. The five-member Federal Trade Commission and its nationwide staff specialize in marketing and advertising fraud prevention. Protection of elders from fraud is a high priority for the Bureau of Consumer Protection at the FTC. Examples of its focus are nutrition-supplement "infomercial" promotions for health preservation, magazine ads for "antiaging" creams, and television pitches for insurance products that claim to meet special needs of elders.

### Consumer Product Safety

The second federal protector is a small but important agency, the Consumer Product Safety Commission (CPSC), founded in 1972 and dramatically overhauled in 2008 legislation. Relatively few products have mandatory standards relevant to elders, though the glass used in showers and bathroom enclosures is subject to a safety standard. Although the commission cannot usually force a company to make a safer design, it can force recalls and impose penalties. Makers of products study the problems that others are having, so indirectly there could be standards for performance that make it necessary to alter an unsafe aspect of the product's features.

On its Web site, CPSC posts special information on elder-home safety, reducing risks of grandparents' medications being accessible to children, improved lighting and vision risks, and flammable fabrics, as well a self-test for elders. The safety of imported products is also a matter for increased concern. The CPSC law was changed in 2008 to require more checking of imports. The CPSC was also given new enforcement powers, backed by penalties, to force companies to send more rapid reports to the commission when consumer products fail to meet safety standards after testing.

### Food and Drug Administration

The largest agency on this list of federal protectors is the Food and Drug Administration (FDA). The most significant FDA program themes impacting elders can be summarized as:

1. medicine mistakes—names, packaging;
2. generic-drug substitution;
3. internet and imported drugs;
4. adverse-event reports; and
5. bone-health products.

Opponents of a final regulation will fall back on their ability to influence the interpretation manuals, which explain the regulation. If they can "explain away" the kind of protection you thought was guaranteed in the law or rule, their efforts to forge links to the bureaucrats who write the guidance documents will pay great dividends. An experienced lobbyist will fight what soldiers call a "rearguard action," with the objective of snatching victory from the jaws of defeat; you celebrated the words in the legislation, but while you weren't looking they have undone your efforts by influencing the interpretations and guidance documents on this specific issue.

**HOW TO MAKE GOVERNMENT A TRUE HELPER**

Harms to the elderly should not be tolerated. Intentional, calculated cost-saving decisions that harm the elderly should be publicly condemned as soon as they are made, preferably during reelection-campaign season. In many years of his local political involvement, your author has seen hundreds of instances of elected officials seeking elder citizens' support in photos, videos, and in-person efforts. But you will never see published photos of elected officials embracing a group of the owners of local nursing homes, or of makers of infomercials who hustle miracle youth pills to elders.

Be aware that their desire for reelection may be your best leverage for convincing officials to act in favor of the elders for whom you seek protection or remedial action. A group representing the county's senior center or AARP or an elder-action coalition will always be able to get a visit on the governor's calendar, so why not ask?

To be most effective, act with the help of an advocacy group and an attorney. There are bar association volunteer programs where you can get recommendations on lawyers willing to help. Explain to the head of the government agency that you have a specific proposed action for them to consider, and that you have the data to support that action. Enlist his or her commitment to "doing the right thing" for your group of elder citizens. Volunteer to testify at legislative budget hearings and to organize writing campaigns to persuade reluctant legislators to honor their past promises of support for the area's elder residents. Make visits to fence-sitting and doubtful legislators. Attend legislative-committee hearings. Follow up on what is actually being done and ask what else your group needs to do to have it done. Remember to be flexible and principled; stay focused on your goal when the opposition offers a compromise that has several attractive aspects but does not meet your objective.

• Fifth, determine which person(s) holds the key to change—the state senator who chairs the key committee, the cabinet secretary or governor or another—and ask intermediaries about his or her preferences or experience on related issues: is there a large pattern of contributions from nursing-home owners, a history of consumer advocacy, or a past vote favoring elder rights, for instance?

• Finally, determine what approach is most likely to succeed with that key official, based on his or her political philosophy, past news interviews, past campaign speeches, etc. This research is much more readily done with the advent of internet search engines that make no past statement "out of sight, out of mind" for elected officials.

**SNATCHING AWAY YOUR SUCCESS**

Your comments and input may succeed at a high level, but lose the war at the operational level. Nursing-home chains are particularly adept at making this happen. Look at your state's Web sites of registered lobbyists and clients; the corporate owners of long-term care facilities have long since hired the best advocates in your state capital to advocate their side of any issue.

Reducing harm to elders requires a combination of effective legislation, effective policies, and effective day-to-day implementation of policies by the actual staffers of the government entity that is tasked to work in favor of elders. A law that goes unenforced or a policy that has no funding for real work does not protect real people. A cynical commentator has said that "The law in its wisdom and majesty permits both the rich and the poor to sleep under bridges." It's not just what the law *says*—it's what the law *does* that matters for advocates of elders' rights.

If you succeed in winning legislation, look next at the regulations that implement the law. Skilled opponents may slip in an exception, a clause that excuses performance, or a cross-reference to another statute that would undercut the mission you seek to accomplish. Courts are bound by these exemptions and exceptions, so pay close attention.

If the regulation tracks closely with what you wish, look next at the "guidance documents." For example, the performance of nursing homes is evaluated under terms of a "Guidance for Surveyors," a large updated loose-leaf book of federal directives to be applied when actual inspections occur at a nursing home. This massive text is the Bible for institutional managers and operational staff, so guidance that is less than a final rule still has plenty of impact.

the problem very soon. For example, Medicare officials may require an offending hospital to establish a timetable and a specific program for the protection of elderly patients from harm caused by their confused wandering off the grounds. FDA has forced some medical-device companies to send notifications that new surgery may be needed to remove an implanted joint or heart device that has the potential to fail. The states can place a long-term care facility licensee on probation.

**CHANGING BAD CONDITIONS**

What can be done to improve conditions for elders? Apart from lawsuits and potential damage awards, improving conditions through government rules is a viable option. This requires elderly persons and their advocates to persuade government bodies to do the work, serving all elders alike. Patience, flexibility, and clear thinking are all needed.

Effectively using petitions and advocacy groups to impact on government is a specialized skill. Advice from an experienced administrative lawyer is optimal. Your author has done this work for three decades, and has written a textbook on the administrative rule-making process. The learnings boil down to these steps, for persons planning to give input:

- First, focus on facts. Have as much data as possible in support. Tie in with expert researchers and experts in professional societies who may have the additional data you need to overcome opposition.

- Second, understand what today's state and federal laws and final regulations, as well as any federal guidance documents, say about this topic. Advocacy is easier if the law already provides for this approach, and if you seek implementation of that existing law by the bureaucracy.

- Third, understand the budget implications of what you seek, both immediately and in subsequent years, for the implementing agency. A common argument of opponents will be, "this will cost too much in 2020"; include in comments a rationale for your expectations and assumptions of future trends.

- Fourth, explain how the benefit of making this change is worth the cost to the government agency's other priorities. For example, if the state health department would have to transfer twelve professional staff members to implement your proposal, explain why this will have greater public impact than the existing alternative uses of that group of skilled employees.

There are hundreds of Washington specialists in enabling a company to win Medicare-Medicaid coverage.

*Prohibitions* and barriers are used to "police" some of the functions that affect elders. The law requires these prohibitions to be published, as a part of a state code, an administrative-regulations code, or the federal statutory system, the United States Code (only public laws adopted by Congress are in this code). An example of a prohibition would be a law defining impaired driving as the driving of a vehicle while the driver has a blood alcohol level greater than a certain percentage. Barriers to otherwise permissible actions would be typified by crosswalk flashing signs and speed humps. These laws and rules are protective of elders because they induce avoidance of harmful behaviors: no speeding through the crosswalk in front of the Senior Center, and so on. In the case of elder safety, prohibitions against mistreatment of elders by nursing homes are the most visible, with literally hundreds of pages of command-and-control steps that a nursing home must obey if it receives federal funding.

## REMEDIAL STEPS

After harm or injury occurs, government has a vital role in taking remedial steps. It can use such actions as direct punishments, financial consequences, or administrative corrective actions.

*Direct punishments* include prison time for elder abuse, withdrawal of an operating license for a deficient nursing home, civil fines for a company that falsely billed the government for care not actually provided, and others. Rape or sexual assault inside a nursing home is a felony that draws long prison sentences. Harm to elders by malnutrition in a poorly managed nursing home is less likely if the repeat violator loses its license to accept Medicaid patients. The infliction of harm on an elder by a certified nursing assistant can result in jail time, revocation of the worker's state license, and listing on a state long-term care agency "do not hire" list.

*Financial consequences* include cash penalties as punitive fines, imposed after opportunity for a hearing; costs imposed after an official order to remediate a bad situation in a hospital's elder-care unit; and income lost where license revocation closes down a nursing home or eliminates an important group of users of the deficient company's services.

*Administrative corrective actions* include a requirement that the regulated organization that has a deficient facility must invest money to fix

- Government then considers *standards* of care or standards for products.

- Sometimes government provides a direct *benefit* in cash or free products or services.

- Finally, government sets into place bans, *prohibitions,* or controls that operate prospectively, after the date of the rule, to limit future accidental or intentional harms to elders.

*Education* is the least costly method of reducing risks. An example would be a Federal Trade Commission brochure on avoiding fraudulent sales pitches for unnecessary supplemental insurance. Most of us are well attuned to this role of the government agencies, disseminating self-help information in readable form: "Only You Can Prevent Forest Fires" was the classic Smokey the Bear message from the Forest Service. Mass media, Web sites, e-mails, mailing lists, publications are all in this category. Effectiveness of educational materials is limited by the ability and willingness of elders to read, digest, comprehend, and act upon what government is telling them to do or not do. Numerous books and other resources discuss "risk communication" and its limitations.

*Standards* require much up-front planning, careful evaluation of technical data, and clear expression in binding rules or nonbinding "guidance" documents. Government takes several years to create and finally adopt a binding standard. By that time, compromises have reduced the "rough edges" of the requirements, tests of a rule's actual application have been made, and the resulting final rule has induced preparations and accommodations among the persons likely to be affected. For example, child-resistant medicine-bottle caps have been required to be accessible to elders, with instructions on how to open them. Standards are set and remain in place for years, because of the lengthy effort needed to make changes.

Governments also spend money on protection by giving direct cash *benefits* to elders or to persons who do certain beneficial things for elders. For example, the federal Center for Medicare and Medicaid Services (CMS) administers federal health programs that impact on millions of elders. A decision by CMS to pay a certain amount for a service done by a physician or a nursing home has major consequences for the ready availability of that product or service nationwide. For example, payments for the "scooter chairs" that allow disabled persons to ride instead of walk are an authorized federal Medicare reimbursement for certain diagnosed problems for elders, and that potential money in turn induces many other decisions, as by investors in chair-building companies and retailers of other high-ticket assistive items for the elderly.

# CHAPTER 3:
# HOW DOES GOVERNMENT PROTECT ELDERS AGAINST RISK?

This book focuses on protection of elderly persons from harm and on the remedies that can be used to limit or respond to that harm. Physical harm can be avoided with one set of protections, and financial harm can be avoided with another. The categories of harms to be covered include:

- dangers of falls or fires at home;
- risks in traffic situations;
- risks within nursing homes or hospitals, including the use of medications;
- physical abuse and neglect; and
- financial fraud.

Remedies include lawsuits, other adversary claims, and regulatory controls by government. This chapter addresses the ways in which government can be used to protect elders against risk. Two types of government action are discussed: *preventive* actions that are taken before harm occurs, and *remedial* actions that occur after an elder has been harmed.

### PREVENTIVE ACTIONS

Preventive actions by government include the work of federal agencies, state agencies, and local governments aimed at protectingelders from harm. These can be considered in four categories:

- Government first uses *education* to enhance self-help by more knowledgeable consumers of services or products.

bank, where she told the teller that she wished to close her account and give all $88,000 in cash to her friend, who was going to buy a house with it. The bank manager called the police and her daughter. The police did not have sufficient evidence to charge the driver with attempted theft by deception, but the daughter changed her accounts to make cosigning mandatory for future withdrawals. Shortly thereafter, the old woman fell and broke her hip. Hospital evaluation led to a probate conservatorship and to placement in an Alzheimer's residence center.

the elder gets 60 percent of the first $100,000 and 66 percent of the amount over that number. If the case is dismissed or lost, the elder pays only for the expenses (under most contingency-fee contracts).

What proportion of elder injuries result in lawsuits? Very few fractures lead to a suit. Deaths are more likely to draw lawsuits, as state wrongful-death statutes allow more ready access to compensation than would a product-liability or nursing-negligence case.

What proportion of lawsuits for injury to an elder result in compensation? No sound statistical base exists to answer this question. Compensation occurs in some cases; whatever is paid from insurance claims is certainly more than compensation received after a civil jury trial.

### CASE STUDY 1

Nursing-home resident Mr. Green had a tendency to wander, a symptom of his dementia. On overnight shift, aide Ms. Brown was tired of chasing the wandering Green, so she attached a restraint strap to hold him in bed. Federal and state guidelines prohibit the use of restraints, unless there has been a physician's order for their use, in limited circumstances. When the morning-shift nurse entered his room, Green was found dead on the floor next to his bed, with the strap around his neck. Brown was not charged by the prosecutor, but the nursing home terminated her immediately and settled the subsequent lawsuit by Green's family. It also paid a $20,000 penalty to the state for the violation of nursing-home safety requirements.

### CASE STUDY 2

Ms. Redd was very independent and reclusive in her deteriorating older home in a city neighborhood. The deterioration was becoming obvious and a nuisance. A neighbor called Adult Protective Services, which reported that Redd was "self-neglected," confused and extremely thin, with a house full of cats and garbage. On petition of the state APS attorney, the probate-court magistrate had the police bring Redd to court, and adjudicated her to be in need of a guardian. The appointed guardian placed Redd in a nursing home and sold the house, creating a trust fund for her further care. Redd was better cared for and gained weight in her first month in the nursing home.

### CASE STUDY 3

The author's mother-in-law refused help with her affairs in her older home, and was becoming more affected by growing dementia. One day she called her "friend," a taxi driver, and the driver took her to the local

also sets standards for some of the services or products used by elders, and violation of those standards can be used against the defendant.

What role does government have in aiding elders—as protector of vulnerable elders or as regulator of businesses impacting them? This is one of the basic philosophical questions community leaders must decide. Protecting elders from harm requires that laws be written, rules drafted, enforcement staff be in place, and then inspections and follow-up actions be taken. Is all this worth doing? Or must any remedy require a lawsuit? Societies that value their elders' wisdom also value their peaceful retirement from daily workplace conflicts. Government should do what it can to reduce harms and to alleviate their consequences.

Does regulatory protection really serve elders' needs? Yes. Government does what the market won't do; vulnerable elderly people are not going to be protected by the free market with its deregulated and diminished "safety nets." The very aged person— over eighty—is likely to be vulnerable, as his or her ability to self-protect has diminished with age and physical infirmity. Government regulation exists to protect the least powerful in society, and thus addresses services and products affecting the elderly.

If we can complain to government, then why is civil litigation necessary? Complaints that trigger positive changes, with or without regulatory-agency intervention, are the ideal. But sometimes it will be necessary to go beyond corrective actions, to gain compensation for harm or to ask a court to intervene in a bad situation to prevent further harm. In general, litigation makes sense when a company or person cannot be persuaded to change behavior and the government has failed to act in support of an elder's needs.

Who can sue? An injured elder could retain an attorney and bring suit. A guardian appointed by a court, or a person with a durable power of attorney, can sue on behalf of the interests of an elder. If the elder dies while the case is still going on, the executor of the estate takes over and seeks damages to be paid to the estate.

What will a lawsuit cost, and how can we pay for it? Sad but true, litigation costs thousands of dollars and months of time, so the person who makes a claim or initiates a lawsuit must have some funds to pay attorney fees, expert-witness fees, evidence costs, filing costs, court-reporter charges, etc. If the elder is indigent, local legal-aid offices and some elder-advocacy or elder-rights groups may wish to assist. More likely, the lawsuit will be handled on a contract that rewards the lawyer only if the case is settled or won; then, of the amount actually received,

Will anyone act on my complaint? Yes. If you act in a calm and businesslike manner, your complaint will receive respect and attention. The more specific you are, the more likely it is that an investigation will begin. Persistence matters, but keep your actions polite and firm.

When must the responding person act on your complaint? The response can vary depending on the person contacted; unfortunately, that person may choose to ignore your complaint entirely. Bureaucrats "must act" when the law requires a response. Ombudsmen for nursing-home patients must act in accordance with their government office's standards for investigation. Private companies and persons may ignore the complaint, if they choose, but doing so is usually bad for public relations and may induce the person complaining to bring a lawsuit.

How should I best assert my complaint? Visit or call, and be specific; in some cases, be ready to write if the ombudsman or government office requires a particular letter or standard form to be submitted.

Should complaints be initiated locally, and made to the officials of the government agency or of the company affected? Yes. The first step is the nursing-home administrator, the seniors-housing director, or the human-services agency director. Physical-abuse cases should go to the local office of Adult Protective Services or its equivalent. If the offending entity is a provider of services receiving funds from the government, like a nursing-home chain, then consider a complaint letter to the headquarters of that entity, with a copy shown and sent to the federal Office of the Inspector General (oig.hhs.gov) or the state agency (listed in Appendix 1, below).

Has this type of harm happened before, or does my case show the necessity of new regulatory protections? Sad but true, the patterns of elder abuse are very well known. If abuse of your elderly friend or others in this nursing home looks very bad, the chances are that other situations have looked worse. Usually the shortcoming is not that the protections are missing from the rules or manuals or procedures—it's that they are not actually being implemented. It takes time to discern what's occurring behind the facade of dignity and caring.

What role does government have as the entity arranging or paying for services to elders? The benefit of government involvement is that its extensive paperwork requirements will create a record that specifies what happened, through what means, with what persons involved.

In practice, this means the possible civil case can be more readily proven. In some cases, the violation of the federal standard or state law will be negligence "per se," so the injured person will win. Government

# CHAPTER 2:
# WILL ANYONE HELP MY PARENTS?

It is a natural human feeling to want to safeguard our parents and elderly friends from harm. This book is about consequences and about remedies that will be available when adults seek to aid elders. This chapter will address some of the common questions that arise when people try to protect an elder from harm. Your personal efforts will be important for the elder you're helping, and for society in general as we try to assist those who need support and protection. You are not alone in this struggle for the right legal remedies; others have had the same experiences.

The natural first question is: Should I complain about what I see happening with this elderly person? If you are concerned about safety or risk, or about financial fraud against an elder, yes: express your concerns. The recipients of the complaint will vary according to the situation. If a person is living alone at home, and you believe is in some danger or difficulty after speaking with him or her, consider contacting the local office of your state "Adult Protective Services." To make it more likely that action will occur, call them with facts, names, or any other details that may facilitate their decision to investigate.

How will I know that the elder needs help? If an elderly neighbor comes to the door covered with bruises when you check in with her, this may be a signal of caregiver abuse. If you are a branch-bank manager and a confused elder comes in to withdraw cash, call the adult son or daughter responsible for this person, if you have that information from bank records. If you visit a nursing home and see deplorable treatment of one or more patients, request a meeting with the administrator. If this does not satisfy your concerns, then contact your health department or state long-term care officials; if you can find the ombudsman for nursing homes, that local person should be contacted.

when the governmental agency uses the proceeds from your lawsuit to pay back the federal or state funds from which care had been given to that elder. You need to recognize the peculiarities of this field; this book will give you sufficient knowledge to assess your situation before you arrive at the office of the attorney who can handle your specific situation under your state's laws.

What portion of injuries is the result of fault or misconduct by others? Falls by elders are often caused by internal problems in balance, gait, etc. Many fire cases are attributable to negligent failure to protect oneself or to avoid contact between stoves and sleeves of garments. Death by the wandering of a dementia patient outside of the zone of safety is a high risk, but it is not really a matter of "fault," except where a legal duty to protect from risk arose from the status of the patient and the caregivers.

What legal remedies are available for protection of the elder or for compensation to his or her estate? This book's chapters describe each of the major risk factors and then the remedy for them, as well as barriers that the defense will use against any challenge.

How are harms from financial fraud on elders considered? When a fraud or rip-off occurs, the first priority of government should be to stop others from a similar theft by deception. The second priority should be to force repayment, or to liquidate any assets of the fraudulent seller and to distribute the funds to the victims of the fraud.

Can we rely on government to prevent frauds on elders? No. There are not enough federal or state investigators to conduct all the inquiries needed to respond to complaints. Outnumbered by fraudulent operators and harassed by their lawyers into lengthy procedural fights, government is wary of taking on all the violators who could be targeted. Thus, a government investigation is rarely done without nagging from some individual or group complainant, who is persistent in seeking remedies. That's why so many criminals get away with a series of small frauds. Often, these criminals end up reaching too far, into a large scam, which results in prosecution. The answer then is that government cannot be relied upon to prevent fraud being done to elders.

So how can I use this book? If you have a concern about the way harm has been experienced by an elder, read the relevant chapter and decide if your situation warrants government action and/or a lawsuit brought against an entity that caused the harm. You will not need an attorney to file a governmental complaint, though that can improve the chances of a successful response and successful action by the government. But you will need a local attorney to file a lawsuit; you should consider lawyers specializing in elder cases, such as members of the National Association of Elder Law Attorneys (naela.org), who have probably encountered your situation before, as they worked with others. There are thousands of civil-litigation lawyers available; the reason for using a specialist is that Medicaid-Medicare liens for recovery of public-assistance benefits might take away much of the value of your efforts

of nursing-home and home health-care services are predominantly persons over seventy years old.

What physical harms pose particular risks to elders? Many, but especially falls, fractures, abuse, neglect, assault, infections, and death by accident after wandering as a result of dementia.

What financial harms pose particular risks to elders? Thefts and deceptive sales tactics, including schemes to steal property or equity from homeowners, are the most serious. Greed motivates the less ethical sales representatives to target the savings of elders; in part this reflects a belief among criminals that elder victims are less likely to confront and prosecute when they have been victimized.

How do elders' injuries and illness occur? Multiple ways exist, just as for any adult population; but with our book's focus on preventing harm, we will focus on a few risk events: negligent acts by family and caregivers; errors and accidents by the elder himself or herself; malpractice by professionals; omissions of protective duties; or abuse or assault by a caregiver.

What are the principal medical responses to these problems? Acute injuries bring doctor intervention with medical devices and pharmaceuticals, sometimes with hospitalization, and always with attention to the preexisting physical condition of the elder. Medication for brain stability in depressed elders; physical protection through facility security for confused dementia patients who could wander; and assistive devices for mobility, for those unable to maintain a steady gait, are examples of the responses to harms.

Can an elder rely on government for protection from physical harms? No: most of the scenarios in which an elder is hurt do not have a particular harm that was planned for in advance. Government can write rules or guidelines that aspire to prevent physical harm, but elders should never rely on the rules to be "out in front of" the situations that cause harm. Government's decision-making process is so slow that injury risks are well known before they are stopped (or attempts are made to lessen them) by government regulations.

What portion of injury or illness cases is avoidable? It's difficult to generalize. No definite statistics exist, beyond anecdotes. Projections from small samples are notoriously inaccurate. Many illnesses like influenza are not going to be remedied by laws or lawsuits; many accidents like suffocation from restraint straps in a nursing home are going to be deterred by regulations that prevent the use of straps and by lawsuits that have won large verdicts against strap-employing nursing homes.

# CHAPTER 1:
# UNDERSTANDING THE RISKS TO THE SAFETY OF ELDERS

All of us will be elders someday—at least we can hope for long lives. It is sad, frustrating, and sometimes infuriating to see the harm that occurs to some elders. It is doubly frustrating when we don't know what we can do to stop that harm, deter future harm, or compensate them for past harm. That's why you have opened this book: to get the benefit of reasoned and succinct observations from experienced advisors.

Our purpose in this book is to discuss the harm that can occur to elderly persons and the ways in which you can use the legal system to avoid some harms, shield some elders from harm, and compensate other elders or their surviving family members. We write it because of the experiences we have had protecting elders, and the lessons we have learned from years of research, lecturing, and writing in the field of elder safety.

Though there are many books that deal with specific risks and numerous detailed lawyers' textbooks on specific types of lawsuits, our objective is to clarify for you the ways in which you can use the remedies provided by law to protect an elderly friend or relative.

For purposes of this book, we will use the term *elder* to describe a person over seventy years of age who has certain infirmities. Euphemisms like *senior citizen, older American*, and the rest are widely known, but for simplicity we select the respectful title *elder*. The selection of seventy reflects the age at which a substantial number of impairments become manifest in a substantial number of people. Of course, we could choose age groups like those sixty and sixty-five years old, but on the whole they are still quite active and involved. Populations of users

## INTRODUCTION

perhaps an experienced elder-law counselor near you can help chart your course. Remember at every stage that the victory you win acts as an incentive for some and a deterrent for others. Do not give up on your elderly friend or relative, and your persistence and prudence will achieve your goal of success.

The author appreciates the assistance of Ms. Holly McEntyre, University of Cincinnati Class of 2009, for her gathering of bibliographic materials. The author especially thanks his family, Carol, Jessie and C.B., for their enthusiastic and loving encouragement of this project.

Prof. James T. O'Reilly

Cincinnati, Ohio

# INTRODUCTION

This book aims to help the reader who has a relative or friend over the age of seventy—or younger but with an impairment like dementia—who faces the risk of harm from one of several risks. Remedies for harm are available in the American legal system, but they are not easily obtained. For the average layperson, the legal system is a daunting wall to climb, a barrier to overcome, without a skilled elder-care attorney to provide advice. The author, as a member of the National Association of Elder Law Attorneys and as a scholar, researcher, and veteran legal-aid advocate, has seen the complexities grow so great that the typical layperson feels overwhelmed. While this book is not endorsed officially by any organization, years of experience and our law textbooks on nursing homes and on elder accidents and injuries have shaped its advice to the reader.

This book helps you to understand the twin legal systems—regulation and litigation—that are used to respond to elders' safety and harm issues. Each system has utility, and this book explains each so that you can maximize its responsiveness. Each has problems, and we lay out some of the issues to facilitate your overcoming them. Please consider carefully whether to engage the services of an experienced elder-law attorney at the outset of your efforts; their expertise and the collective wisdom of their national association will be very helpful and will save you considerable difficulties.

Lastly, there's a special place in heaven for those who honor and support their elders. Whether that kind of folk wisdom appeals to you, the honorable and noble quest for justice on behalf of elders exposed to harm is laudable. Your effort to gain compensation, or to prevent others from experiencing the same harms, is to be applauded.

Along the way to the remedy, you will face inertia in some offices, hostility from negligent or willful violators, and complexities at every turn. This book gives you an overview. From here you can discern a path, and

# ABOUT THE AUTHOR

Professor James T. O'Reilly teaches at the University of Cincinnati College of Law, and has published thirty-eight textbooks on legal issues. He is a member of the National Association of Elder Law Attorneys and is a former chair of the 16,000-member Section of Administrative Law and Regulatory Practice of the American Bar Association. The ABA Press published his earlier textbooks on nursing-home legal issues and on injuries and accidents affecting the elderly. His previous work has been followed by federal and state courts, and the U.S. Supreme Court quoted one of his earlier books as the "expert" on medical issues, in a 2000 FDA decision. In addition to assistance to family members and friends affected by the subject matter of this book, Prof. O'Reilly has aided elders through the Volunteer Lawyers for the Poor program in Cincinnati and the National Veterans Legal Services program in Washington, D.C. He is a graduate of Boston College and of the University of Virginia School of Law.

ASSAILANT'S CONDITION MAY BAR RECOVERY. . . . . . . . . . . . . . . . . . . . . 76
NEGLECT . . . . . . . . . . . . . . . . . . . . . . . . . . . . . . . . . . . . . . . . . . . . . . . 76
ABUSE OF THE ELDER . . . . . . . . . . . . . . . . . . . . . . . . . . . . . . . . . . . . . 76
NURSING-HOME ABUSE CLAIMS . . . . . . . . . . . . . . . . . . . . . . . . . . . . . . 77
THE REGULATORY RESPONSE. . . . . . . . . . . . . . . . . . . . . . . . . . . . . . . . 78
CIVIL LAWSUITS . . . . . . . . . . . . . . . . . . . . . . . . . . . . . . . . . . . . . . . . . 78
CRIMINAL REMEDIES. . . . . . . . . . . . . . . . . . . . . . . . . . . . . . . . . . . . . . 79
ASSAULTS BY DEMENTIA PATIENTS. . . . . . . . . . . . . . . . . . . . . . . . . . . . 79
SELF-INFLICTED INJURY AND SUICIDE. . . . . . . . . . . . . . . . . . . . . . . . . . 79
CASE STUDIES . . . . . . . . . . . . . . . . . . . . . . . . . . . . . . . . . . . . . . . . . . 80

## CHAPTER 12:
## WHEN TO CHOOSE WHICH TACTIC TO RESPOND TO THE HARM
REGULATORY-AGENCY ACTIONS . . . . . . . . . . . . . . . . . . . . . . . . . . . . . . 81
LITIGATION OPTIONS. . . . . . . . . . . . . . . . . . . . . . . . . . . . . . . . . . . . . . 82
ARBITRATION. . . . . . . . . . . . . . . . . . . . . . . . . . . . . . . . . . . . . . . . . . . 83
MEDIATION . . . . . . . . . . . . . . . . . . . . . . . . . . . . . . . . . . . . . . . . . . . . 83
CASE STUDIES . . . . . . . . . . . . . . . . . . . . . . . . . . . . . . . . . . . . . . . . . . 83

## CHAPTER 13:
## WHEN SHOULD WE SETTLE?
CONTINGENCY FEE MAKES "PARTNERS". . . . . . . . . . . . . . . . . . . . . . . . . 85
FACTORS TO CONSIDER . . . . . . . . . . . . . . . . . . . . . . . . . . . . . . . . . . . 86
MONEY NOW, OR MORE LATER? . . . . . . . . . . . . . . . . . . . . . . . . . . . . . . 87
ACTUAL TERMS OF SETTLEMENT . . . . . . . . . . . . . . . . . . . . . . . . . . . . . 87
MEDICARE-MEDICAID REIMBURSEMENT. . . . . . . . . . . . . . . . . . . . . . . . . 87
CASE STUDIES . . . . . . . . . . . . . . . . . . . . . . . . . . . . . . . . . . . . . . . . . . 88

## CHAPTER 14:
## MANAGING THE INTERACTION WITH GOVERNMENT OFFICIALS

## APPENDICES
1: STATE ELDER-CARE OR LONG-TERM CARE
   CONTACTS FOR PROBLEMS . . . . . . . . . . . . . . . . . . . . . . . . . . . . . . 91
2: EVALUATION OF POSSIBLE ABUSE CLAIMS. . . . . . . . . . . . . . . . . . . . 95
3: ELDER SELF-NEGLECT: ADULT PROTECTIVE SERVICES CHECKLIST . . . 97
4: HOME FRAUDS PROTECTION CHECKLIST . . . . . . . . . . . . . . . . . . . . 99

GLOSSARY . . . . . . . . . . . . . . . . . . . . . . . . . . . . . . . . . . . . . . . . . . . . 101
BIBLIOGRAPHY. . . . . . . . . . . . . . . . . . . . . . . . . . . . . . . . . . . . . . . . . 105

RISKS FROM ELDER WANDERING . . . . . . . . . . . . . . . . . . . . . . . . . . . . . . 51
PATIENT-RESTRAINT DEVICES . . . . . . . . . . . . . . . . . . . . . . . . . . . . . . 51
ASSAULT . . . . . . . . . . . . . . . . . . . . . . . . . . . . . . . . . . . . . . . . . . . . . . . . 52
NUTRITION . . . . . . . . . . . . . . . . . . . . . . . . . . . . . . . . . . . . . . . . . . . . . . 52
INFECTION . . . . . . . . . . . . . . . . . . . . . . . . . . . . . . . . . . . . . . . . . . . . . . 53
CASE STUDIES . . . . . . . . . . . . . . . . . . . . . . . . . . . . . . . . . . . . . . . . . . 53

## CHAPTER 8:
### REMEDIES FOR HOME AND ASSISTED-LIVING HEALTH-CARE RISKS
UNCERTAINTIES . . . . . . . . . . . . . . . . . . . . . . . . . . . . . . . . . . . . . . . . . 55
RISK AVOIDANCE . . . . . . . . . . . . . . . . . . . . . . . . . . . . . . . . . . . . . . . 56
PHYSICAL RISKS . . . . . . . . . . . . . . . . . . . . . . . . . . . . . . . . . . . . . . . . 56
MAKING THE COMPLAINT . . . . . . . . . . . . . . . . . . . . . . . . . . . . . . . 57
CAREGIVER PROBLEMS . . . . . . . . . . . . . . . . . . . . . . . . . . . . . . . . . 57
CASE STUDIES . . . . . . . . . . . . . . . . . . . . . . . . . . . . . . . . . . . . . . . . . 59

## CHAPTER 9:
### MEDICATION ISSUES FOR ELDERS
TYPES OF DRUG ERRORS . . . . . . . . . . . . . . . . . . . . . . . . . . . . . . . . 61
UNEXPECTED ADVERSE EFFECTS . . . . . . . . . . . . . . . . . . . . . . . . . 61
DEFECTS IN THE DRUG ITSELF . . . . . . . . . . . . . . . . . . . . . . . . . . . 62
PROBLEMS WITH DRUG DELIVERY . . . . . . . . . . . . . . . . . . . . . . . 62
MEDICATION ERRORS . . . . . . . . . . . . . . . . . . . . . . . . . . . . . . . . . . 62
ADVERSE EVENTS . . . . . . . . . . . . . . . . . . . . . . . . . . . . . . . . . . . . . . 62
DEFECTIVE DRUGS . . . . . . . . . . . . . . . . . . . . . . . . . . . . . . . . . . . . . 63
UPHILL BATTLES AGAINST DRUG MAKERS . . . . . . . . . . . . . . . . 64
CASE STUDIES . . . . . . . . . . . . . . . . . . . . . . . . . . . . . . . . . . . . . . . . . 64

## CHAPTER 10:
### PROTECTING ELDERS FROM FINANCIAL HARMS AND THEFTS
WHAT IS FINANCIAL HARM? . . . . . . . . . . . . . . . . . . . . . . . . . . . . . 67
INSURANCE-RELATED MISCONDUCT . . . . . . . . . . . . . . . . . . . . . . 68
HOME-RELATED MISCONDUCT . . . . . . . . . . . . . . . . . . . . . . . . . . . 68
REVERSE MORTGAGES . . . . . . . . . . . . . . . . . . . . . . . . . . . . . . . . . 70
HOME-REPAIR ISSUES . . . . . . . . . . . . . . . . . . . . . . . . . . . . . . . . . . 70
IDENTITY THEFT . . . . . . . . . . . . . . . . . . . . . . . . . . . . . . . . . . . . . . . 71
THEFT OF POSSESSIONS . . . . . . . . . . . . . . . . . . . . . . . . . . . . . . . . 71
CASE STUDIES . . . . . . . . . . . . . . . . . . . . . . . . . . . . . . . . . . . . . . . . . 71

## CHAPTER 11:
### ABUSE AND ASSAULT
DEFINING ASSAULT . . . . . . . . . . . . . . . . . . . . . . . . . . . . . . . . . . . . 75
RESPONSES TO ELDER ABUSE . . . . . . . . . . . . . . . . . . . . . . . . . . . 75

## CHAPTER 4:
## REMEDIES FOR INJURY AT HOME

**EDUCATION TO AVOID HOME ACCIDENTS** .......................... 23
**SAFETY STANDARDS TO PROTECT ELDERS** ........................ 24
**LEGAL REMEDIES FOR AN ELDER'S ACCIDENTAL INJURY** ............. 25
**FLAMMABILITY RISKS** ......................................... 26
**BUILDING-RELATED RISKS** ..................................... 27
**DOOR SECURITY** .............................................. 28
**LEGAL CONSEQUENCES** ......................................... 28
**ELECTRICAL RISKS** ........................................... 29
**CASE STUDIES** ............................................... 30

## CHAPTER 5:
## TRAFFIC-RELATED RISKS OF HARM

**DRIVER LICENSING** ............................................ 33
**ROADWAY PROBLEMS** ........................................... 34
**VEHICLE DEFICIENCIES** ........................................ 34
**PEDESTRIAN RISKS** ........................................... 35
**TRANSPORTATION** ............................................. 35
**CASE STUDIES** ............................................... 36

## CHAPTER 6:
## HOSPITAL-RELATED HARMS

**UNEXPECTED FATALITIES DRAW INQUIRIES** ........................ 39
**LEGAL DUTIES** ............................................... 40
**EQUIPMENT DEFECTS** .......................................... 41
**INFECTION ISSUES** ........................................... 41
**MEDICATING PATIENTS PROPERLY** ................................ 42
**MEDICAL ERRORS** ............................................. 42
**NURSE LIABILITY** ............................................ 43
**INADEQUATE PROTECTION** ...................................... 43
**DOES REGULATION WORK?** ...................................... 43
**OMISSIONS** .................................................. 44
**BARRIERS** ................................................... 44
**CASE STUDIES** ............................................... 45

## CHAPTER 7:
## NURSING-HOME RISKS OF HARM

**WHAT TO EXPECT** ............................................. 47
**EFFECTS OF POLITICS AND MONEY** .............................. 48
**SKIN PROBLEMS** .............................................. 49
**RESIDENT FALL INJURIES** ..................................... 50

# Table of Contents

ABOUT THE AUTHOR .......................................... ix
INTRODUCTION ............................................... xi

**CHAPTER 1:**
**UNDERSTANDING THE RISKS TO THE SAFETY OF ELDERS**

**CHAPTER 2:**
**WILL ANYONE HELP MY PARENTS?**
CASE STUDIES ............................................... 8

**CHAPTER 3:**
**HOW DOES GOVERNMENT PROTECT ELDERS AGAINST RISK?**
PREVENTIVE ACTIONS ........................................ 11
REMEDIAL STEPS ............................................ 13
CHANGING BAD CONDITIONS ................................... 14
SNATCHING AWAY YOUR SUCCESS ............................... 15
HOW TO MAKE GOVERNMENT A TRUE HELPER ...................... 16
WHAT FEDERAL AGENCIES CAN HELP ME? ........................ 17
   Federal Trade Commission ............................. 17
   Consumer Product Safety .............................. 17
   Food and Drug Administration ......................... 17
      Getting the Right Drug ........................... 18
      Safer Implantable Parts .......................... 18
      Generic Drug Controls ............................ 18
      Imported or Internet Drug Purchasing ............. 19
      Vitamins and Supplements ......................... 19
      Injury and Side-Effects Reporting ................ 20
      Bone-Fracture Prevention ......................... 20
   Other Economic Protections from Fraud ................ 20
CASE STUDIES .............................................. 21

This Book is Dedicated to

Alfred K. White, Jr.

Eminent International Law Counselor,

Tireless Mentor to Young Lawyers, and

Constant Inspiration to Our Community

# OXFORD
UNIVERSITY PRESS

*Oxford University Press, Inc., publishes works that further Oxford University's objective of excellence in research, scholarship, and education.*

Copyright © 2009 by Oxford University Press, Inc.
Published by Oxford University Press, Inc.
198 Madison Avenue, New York, New York 10016

Oxford is a registered trademark of Oxford University Press
Oceana is a registered trademark of Oxford University Press, Inc.

All rights reserved. No part of this publication may be reproduced, stored in a retrieval system, or transmitted, in any form or by any means, electronic, mechanical, photocopying, recording, or otherwise, without the prior permission of Oxford University Press, Inc.

Library of Congress Cataloging-in-Publication Data

O'Reilly, James T., 1947–
 How to protect elders from harm/by James T. O'Reilly.
  p. cm.—(Oceana's legal almanac series. Law for the layperson)
 Includes bibliographical references.
 ISBN 978-0-19-538174-0 ((hardback) : alk. paper)
 1. Personal injuries—United States—Popular works. 2. Older people—Legal status, laws, etc.—United States—Popular works. 3. Remedies (Law)—United States—Popular works. 4. Medical personnel—Malpractice—United States—Popular works. 5. Older people—Care—United States—Popular works. I. Title.
 KF1257.O724 2009
 346.7303'23—dc22
                                                            2009000020

**Note to Readers:**

This publication is designed to provide accurate and authoritative information in regard to the subject matter covered. It is based upon sources believed to be accurate and reliable and is intended to be current as of the time it was written. It is sold with the understanding that the publisher is not engaged in rendering legal, accounting, or other professional services. If legal advice or other expert assistance is required, the services of a competent professional person should be sought. Also, to confirm that the information has not been affected or changed by recent developments, traditional legal research techniques should be used, including checking primary sources where appropriate.

*(Based on the Declaration of Principles jointly adopted by a Committee of the American Bar Association and a Committee of Publishers and Associations.)*

---

You may order this or any other Oxford University Press publication by visiting the Oxford University Press website at www.oup.com

---

# How to Protect Elders from Harm

*by*
**Prof. James T. O'Reilly**
University of Cincinnati

Oceana's Legal Almanac Series:
*Law for the Layperson*

**Oceana®**
NEW YORK